Counsel in the Caucasus: Professionalization and Law in Georgia

Law in Eastern Europe

A series of publications issued by the
Institute of East European Law and Russian Studies
Leiden University Faculty of Law

General Editor
W.B. Simons

No. 54

Counsel in the Caucasus: Professionalization and Law in Georgia

Christopher P.M. Waters

Springer-Science+Business Media, B.V.

A C.I.P. Catalogue record for this book is available from the Library of Congress.

Printed on acid-free paper.

ISBN 978-90-04-13947-3 ISBN 978-94-017-5620-4 (eBook)
DOI 10.1007/978-94-017-5620-4

Originally published by Koninklijke Brill N.V., Leiden, The Netherlands in 2004.
Softcover reprint of the hardcover 1st edition 2004

http://www.brill.nl

This book is dedicated to the memory of my maternal grandfather

Bagrat Badalian

(1914–1999)

Contents

Acknowledgements

Robert Austin, Ferdinand Feldbrugge, Christopher Harland, Richard Janda, Stephen Jones, Tony Rhinelander, Peter Solomon and Christoph Stefes provided advice and assistance at important junctures.

I never anticipated the kindness and hospitality shown to me in the Caucasus by students, friends and complete strangers. Special thanks for assistance with field-work are due to Giorgi Chigogidze, Nino Dzotsenidze, Lena Gvinchidze and Lusine Hovhannisian.

This book has its origins in my doctoral studies at McGill University's Institute of Comparative Law. At McGill I was extremely fortunate to have had the guidance and encouragement of Roderick Macdonald.

Financial and/or logistical support from McGill University, St. Thomas University, the Civic Education Project, the Centre for Russian and East European Studies at the University of Toronto and the Canadian Embassy to Georgia, is gratefully acknowledged.

Many thanks to the editor of this series, William Simons, whose suggestions have resulted in numerous improvements.

Without question, I owe the completion of this project to the assistance and support of my wife Anneke Smit.

Map of Georgian Cities

Political Map of the Caucasus

Common Abbreviations

AAA	Azerbaijani Association of Advocates
ABA	American Bar Association's Central and East European Law Initiative
ABCNY	Association of the Bar of the City of New York
ALA	Association of Lawyers of Azerbaijan
CLE	Continuing Legal Education
GBA	Georgian Bar Association
GCG	Georgia Consulting Group
GYLA	Georgian Young Lawyers' Association
ICRC	International Committee of the Red Cross
LCB	Legal Consultation Bureau
MDP	Multidisciplinary Practice
TSU	Tbilisi State University
UNDP	United Nations Development Programme
UNHCR	United Nations High Commissioner for Refugees
UARA	Union of Advocates of the Republic of Armenia
USAID	United States Agency for International Development
YSU	Yerevan State University

Introduction

Is There a Post-Soviet Legal Profession in Georgia?

Simply stated, the goal of this book is to study Georgia's post-Soviet legal profession. This statement makes two assumptions which require clarification. The first is that the "Soviet" moniker is still normatively significant. The second is that there is a legal profession in Georgia.

The assumption that the term "post-Soviet" has descriptive significance (beyond the historical fact that Georgia was a constituent republic of the USSR) is uncontroversial. Despite the passing of the first post-communist decade, Soviet legacies remain in each of the fifteen successor republics, albeit adapted to different circumstances. The continuity is evident in various problems, from authoritarianism to corruption to Russian imperialism. The legal sphere is no different: attitudes of the ruled and the rulers towards law, legal education and practice all bear characteristics of traditions once common throughout the USSR. And building on this continuity (and in light of the material interests at stake in keeping an academic field alive), Sovietologists have successfully transformed the academic institutions of Soviet studies into a viable field of post-Soviet studies.

In the Soviet period, law was studied as an element of the totalitarian state or as a force of change in the maturation or development of socialism. Scholars were also interested in how law and lawyers worked. One of the gaps in Soviet-era research on law, however, was the focus on Russia to the exclusion of the non-Russian republics. More than that, the focus was on the Centre: Moscow and Leningrad. In part this was a by-product of the limits put on field research by Soviet authorities. There were also few formal legal differences among the republics—to understand Soviet legal thought in Moscow was to understand Soviet legal thought in Tbilisi or Tashkent. Finally, this focus was due to the fact that Sovietologists (and their funders) were interested in power, and power was thought to be at the centre, not the periphery. Consequently, little was written on law or lawyers in the Soviet borderlands of Transcaucasia or Central Asia. This academic legacy has continued into the post-Soviet era and there remains little writing on law in these regions. I aim to partly address the lacunae by examining lawyers in Georgia. Comparison will also be made to the other Transcaucasian Republics, Armenia and Azerbaijan.[1]

1. "Transcaucasus" literally means "across the Caucasus", or, in other words, across the Caucasus Mountains from Russia. These lands at the border of the Empire have held sway over the Russian imagination as the "near-abroad" and a natural place for Russian suzerainty. Not surprisingly, some Transcaucasians bristle at any term for the area which makes Russia the reference point: for Georgians, Armenians and Azerbaijanis, *Russia* is their Transcaucasia. They argue that the more appropriate term for the area is the "South Caucasus" (the North Caucasus belonging to the Russian Federation). Nonetheless, I use the term Transcaucasia in this book as it is less cumbersome than the alternative and remains in widespread use. Furthermore the term has a long pedigree in the region itself and is more evocative of a normative entity—which in my view it is—than the physical descriptor, South Caucasus. Unless otherwise indicated references to the "region" should be read as "Transcaucasia" throughout this book.

The second assumption, the existence of a profession, leads one into a definitional morass. To refer to *a* Soviet legal profession is to admit a lack of understanding of the Soviet system, and comparativists are quick to criticize those who refer to Soviet "lawyers".[2] All those who graduated from legal studies in the Soviet Union could be called jurists, a term familiar to continental Europeans (with their formally divided professions) but one that does not sit easily in English.[3] There were several types of jurists: advocates who represented clients at preliminary inquiries and trials and dispensed legal advice from a semi-autonomous position, *jurisconsults* who worked in (or for) enterprises as legal counsel, members of the judiciary, and prosecutors who had a supervisory role over the administration of justice. Jurists were also recruited into police, party and state organs and into universities or institutes of legal "science". Each of the Soviet legal professions had different requirements for entry, different modes of practice and different levels of power, prestige and autonomy from clients or the state. Although more fluid now, the Russian legal professions continue to be distinct from each other. And observers continue to study Russian *advocates*, for example, rather than *lawyers*. This is not the case in Georgia.

The distinction between advocates and other jurists in Georgia (with the exception of judges, prosecutors and notaries) now has little significance. But this is not because the Georgian bar has unified along North American lines. The Soviet Georgian *advokatura* was de-institutionalized in the early independence period and for several years there were quite literally no required formal qualifications for lawyering. Although in 2001 a law on the bar was passed by Parliament—acting under pressure from the Council of Europe—its ability to govern lawyers is questionable. At the same time as formal state regulation is weak, the numbers of lawyers and law students have multiplied. The modes of legal practice are tremendously diverse, and there is little sense of corporate identity. Indeed it is fair to ask: is there any legal profession at all in Georgia? Given the fact that Georgia remains a partly failed state, the absence of regulation is perhaps not surprising. What is surprising is that lawyers as a whole have not actively sought exclusive license to practice (monopoly), standardization of qualifications or self-governance backed by the state.

For most Western law reformers, the apparent reluctance to professionalize presents an unexpected and frustrating challenge to the axiomatic principle that professionalization is in the interest of lawyers and the public. The seem-

2. See C. Osakwe, Book Review of *Russian Lawyers and the Soviet State: The Origins and Development of the Soviet Bar, 1917-1939* by E. Huskey, 19 *New York University Journal of International. Law & Politics* 1987 No. 3, 739-750, 748-750.
3. Of course, classic statements of the formal divisions in the Continental European professions (such as J.H. Merryman, *The Civil Law Tradition*, Stanford 1969) should be supplemented with the view that there are no *de facto* undivided legal professions in the Anglo-American tradition either, a topic to which I will return.

ing reluctance also poses an unexpected challenge to the prevailing theories about professions. Various theories have been put forward to explain professions—Weberian, Marxist, structural-functionalist—but most of the theoretical contributions to the study of professions assume the presence of a functioning state and regulated market capitalism. In Georgia, with its weak state and distinct business culture, the statist and market-oriented theories provide an insufficient picture. They must be supplemented with the insights of area studies (Soviet and post-Soviet space, Transcaucasia) and a legal pluralist approach, which reveals a complex mixing of legal regimes. The relevant pluralisms are both internal and external to the profession. Internally, for example, traditional reliance on reputation plays an enormous role in informally regulating lawyers, as do voluntary "bar associations" which have established their own admission and disciplinary functions (albeit weak ones). Externally, Georgian non-state law rivals formal law (popular punishments for example) or simply ignores it (extensive reliance on personal networks in conducting business). While this study focuses on issues internal to the profession, it attempts to ground the profession within both state and non-state law.

Ultimately, using a Weberian analysis, I argue that despite the initial fall of the profession in the early 1990s, some segments of the profession are rising. These lawyers are successfully pursuing market control and upward collective mobility (as revealed through the professional "badges" of prestige and collegiality). However, this rise is informed by traditional Georgian preoccupations with reputation and networks and looks very different from the monopoly-focussed Western models on which theories of professionalism were built.

Chapter Outline

Chapter One reviews the relevant area and disciplinary literature on lawyering and establishes the main theoretical questions for this book. Chapter Two looks at Georgia's legal history, paying particular attention to the emergence of lawyering. I argue that in 1991 Georgian lawyers found themselves in a post-Soviet world without an indigenous tradition of lawyering and without any significant "memory" of European law or lawyering. The persistence of non-state law in Georgian history is also highlighted. Chapter Three addresses the contemporary Georgian context. It looks at the challenges to state-building which Georgia has faced, including violent ethno-territorial conflict, incomplete reform of the judiciary, corruption and human rights abuses. These factors shape what lawyers currently do and limit what lawyers can potentially do.

Chapters Four through Six of the book are based on field-work. They provide what is essentially an internal view of the Georgian legal profession revolving around three themes: i) legal education and access to the profession; ii) the politics of regulation, self-regulation and market control; and iii) stratification and collective mobility.

Chapter Seven then compares Georgian lawyers with their Armenian and Azerbaijani counterparts, rounding out this book as a regional study and providing case studies to determine whether the Georgian experience can be generalized. Finally, the Conclusion will review the empirical findings and point out the main implications for studies of legal professions. The Conclusion will also suggest a research agenda for examining links between professionalization and the rule of law.

Field-work

I conducted field-work in Transcaucasia at various times between February 1998 and July 2001.[4] For much of that period, I was a participant-observer in the area of legal education. I taught comparative law, international law and contract law at the International Law and Relations Faculty of Tbilisi State University, the International Business Faculty of Tbilisi State University, the Humanitarian Institute of the Georgian Technical University and the Law Department of the American University of Armenia.[5] The range of courses and sites (the Faculties and Universities differ considerably in terms of student profile and prestige) provided various insights into legal education and the level of "legal culture" of both law and non-law students. These placements also allowed for insights into the academic enterprise through my contacts with faculty and day-to-day observation of university life. It should be noted, however, that my impressions may be skewed by the fact that students who attended my classes spoke English, thus making them non-representative in terms of socio-economic status (they generally had studied English through private lessons). One might also speculate that they had a somewhat more pro-Western outlook. I attempted to compensate for this by guest-lecturing and interviewing law students and professors at other faculties and universities, including the Law Faculty at Tbilisi State University.

In the Spring of 1998 I began interviewing people with a global overview of the Georgian legal system and practice. They tended to be foreigners working in the area of law reform and young Georgian lawyers who had studied in the West. In turn, I asked them to recommend lawyers with whom I should speak in order to gain an understanding of Georgian legal practice. Not surprisingly the group of recommended lawyers had profiles and shared viewpoints similar to those of the "young reformers". To balance this line of interviews I randomly interviewed lawyers in Legal Consultation Bureaus—legal collectives from

4. Fifteen months in total were spent in Georgia, four months in Armenia and two short trips were made to Azerbaijan.
5. The placements in Georgia were made by the Civic Education Project, a non-governmental organization based in Budapest with links to the Central European University. This organization works on higher education reform in the former Soviet Union and Eastern Europe.

the Soviet era—where older advocates were to be found. Their perceptions of the legal system and the profession differed significantly from the first-round interviewees. In the Spring of 1999 I began to interview other actors involved with the legal system, including judges, court officials, prosecutors, clients, business people and human rights activists. The bulk of my interviews were in Tbilisi, although I also conducted some interviews in Georgia's second largest city, Kutaisi, and in the smaller city of Gori.[6]

Based on the experiences of interview projects with Russian lawyers in the Soviet and post-Soviet periods, I initially prepared a standardized list of questions. However, in the absence of a global perspective on Georgian lawyering—which turned out to be markedly different from the Russian experience—these standardized questions were not particularly useful. Accordingly my early interviews were unstandardized (I had to learn the right questions[7]) and gradually became more standardized as time went on. Initially I had intended to survey only advocates. However, it quickly became clear that the term "advocate" in Georgia had little descriptive value following de-institutionalization of the Soviet-era Bar. To understand law and lawyering in Georgia in the absence of previous scholarship, it was necessary to use a purposive sampling to ensure that various types of lawyers were examined (those who had been advocates and jurisconsults as well as younger lawyers who had been neither, Western and Georgian trained lawyers, criminal and civil lawyers). Purposive sampling was also used to observe other actors involved in the legal system including judges, prosecutors, businesspeople, court officials, clients and activists.[8] I trust that there will be increased scope for more standardized interview projects—which target specific groups of lawyers or other actors in the legal system and in specific regions—in light of this study.

Initially the interviews were taped and later transcribed. However I found that while many respondents spoke freely in preliminary informal discussions on sensitive issues like corruption, when I began taping the interviews (with permission) the interviewees were less frank. Accordingly I then began taking notes during interviews which were later transcribed or summarized. There are over 40 of these formal interviews which I believe are fairly representative of the profession in terms of practice (old-style advocates from the Soviet era, young lawyers practicing in firms, company lawyers) as well as age (which also

6. Further work needs to be conducted in the Georgian regions, including those where significant numbers of ethnic minorities are present, as well as in the breakaway areas of Abkhazia and South Ossetia.
7. B.L. Berg, *Qualitative Research Methods for the Social Sciences,* Boston 1989, 15-19.
8. Purposive sampling has been described as follows: "[R]esearchers use their special knowledge or expertise about some groups to select subjects who represent this population. In some instances, purposive samples are selected after field investigations of some group, in order to ensure that certain types of individuals or persons displaying certain attributes are included in the study." *Ibid.*, 110.

reveals exposure to communism) and gender. All of the formal interviewees were informed of the nature of my research and no guarantees of confidentiality were given, except in a handful of cases where requested. Nonetheless to respect the privacy of the interviewees and to avoid possible repercussions for those who spoke frankly on sensitive topics, I use letter codes rather than sources' names or initials. Brief descriptions of each interviewee are contained in Appendix A. None of the interviewees were paid.

In addition to interviews, field-work also consisted of observing court offices, monitoring trials, reviewing the local press and attendance at meetings of the most prominent legal non-governmental organization—the Georgian Young Lawyers' Association—which was considering a law on the bar. Invaluable data was also gained from locally available studies conducted for the World Bank and other international organizations. These studies have allowed me to introduce a quantitative element to this analysis. Finally I engaged in an assistance programme to Article 42, a Georgian legal NGO, which was financed by the Canadian Embassy to Georgia in the Fall of 2000. Part of this project involved a series of seminars on legal ethics given to lawyers and law students who were members of this NGO, providing me with an insight into how at least one segment of Georgian jurists perceive and resolve ethical conflicts.

Language interpretation—with all its potential pitfalls—was used for the formal interviews, which were conducted in the national languages (except where interviewees spoke English). I conducted a number of informal discussions in Russian (supplemented by basic Georgian and Armenian), a language widely spoken in the region and which I speak at an intermediate level. Georgian and Russian-speaking research assistants were also used for media review and to locate and translate a number of key documents and texts.

Every effort has been made to ensure that the information contained here is current to January 2002.[9]

9. As a post-script, it should be noted that as of the end of 2002, amendments to the 2001 Law on the Bar were being actively pursued. One observer hyperbolically suggested that the amendments, if adopted, would "inhibit the formation of a Western-style Bar Association..." (K. Stier, "Proposed Law Amendments Threaten to Stall Judicial Reform Efforts in Georgia", *Eurasia Insight* 12 June 2002). Whether or not these amendments are passed alters the substance of this book very little; either way the "main story" will be unofficial regulation for some time to come.

Chapter 1
Approaching Georgian Lawyers

There are few references to post-Soviet Georgian law or lawyering in Western academic literature. And while there are numerous articles on law and lawyering in the Georgian literature, these tend to be concerned exclusively with the "law on the books". This book is not written in a scholarly vacuum, however, as there are several relevant bodies of literature. The first is the literature on the professions, and the legal profession in particular. The second is the scholarship dealing with law and lawyers in the Soviet Union and post-Soviet Russia. While these bodies of literature do not provide exact parameters for this study—the Georgian legal profession is distinct from both its Western and Russian counterparts—they dictate the nature of some of the questions to be asked. To help account for the diversity of the legal profession within the former Soviet Union, within Transcaucasia and within Georgia, these questions will be supplemented with others suggested by a legal pluralist perspective.

Legal Professions (or the Study of Western Lawyers)

Several definitions of "profession" exist. The first use of the word is the easiest to distinguish for it is the common definition—profession is nearly a synonym of occupation. One can be a professional mover, carpenter, fire-fighter or athlete, provided one adheres to the occupational standards and is not an amateur or unpaid. Two other definitions lead to confusion. One class of occupations is marked by a recognized body of expertise which is received through training. This category has been termed professional through a "historical definition", which traces the growth of "general professions" such as managers and computer programmers and their widespread presence in contemporary developed countries.[1] These professionals may have a relationship to the state through credentialing (exams for stock-brokers and insurance agents). In other cases, such as managers with MBAs or librarians, the expertise is recognized through employment which implicitly recognizes the expertise and grants a certain degree of prestige. There is a class-based, "white collar" component to this definition.

In contrast to the common and historical definitions, the sociological definition is more restrictive. It has generated a great deal of arcane controversy of the line-drawing sort, though this debate seems to have abated.[2] What is clear from the literature is that there are classic or ideal professions, specifically the Anglo-American legal and medical professions. The contours of these ideal professions are fairly clear. Like the general professions, these ideal professions have mastery of a recognized body of expertise received through training. Similarly,

1. H. Kritzer, "The Professions are Dead, Long Live the Professions: Legal Practice in a Post-Professional World", 33 *Law & Society Review* 1999 No. 3, 713-759, 716-717.
2. For a discussion of definitional problems see E. Freidson, "The Theory of Professions: State of the Art" in R. Dingwall & P. Lewis, eds., *The Sociology of the Professions*, New York 1983.

they combine exclusivity (only licensed doctors may practice medicine) with the application of abstract knowledge. Some of the general professions may do this as well, but classic professions have successfully translated the combination of exclusivity and application of abstract knowledge into degrees of autonomy from the state (so-called self-governance) and the client (the professional controls the relationship to a greater degree than in other occupations).[3] Other badges of the classic professions include higher education, notions of altruism and a calling, codes of ethics, socialisation, internal hierarchies and prestige. Although these badges may have little basis in fact—indeed many of the myths of the profession have been debunked[4]—they exist at least as archetypal constructs.

The more interesting questions deal with where professions come from and how they behave. The prevailing approach for many years was structural-functionalism associated with Talcott Parsons,[5] but with deeper roots in Durkheim.[6] Parsons and others focused on professions as necessary elements in the ordering of society. They saw legal professions coming historically at a certain point in societal development, when knowledge-based experts were needed to negotiate and provide order to an increasingly complex and regulated society. As a result, communities of expertise with a genuine role to play in the ordering of society appeared. State grants of autonomy were a part of a bargain between professionals and society for the specialized governance needs of expertise. In the 1970s power or capture theories reacted to the structuralist approach, seeing the latter as too closely reflecting what the professions say about themselves. Of these power arguments, a Marxist approach focused on class (and the uncomfortable fit of professionals in the class structure),[7] and

3. The frequently used definition of self-governance is a misnomer since the professions ultimately rely on the state for legitimacy and power.
4. Notions of an altruistic profession have been challenged beginning with the law school experience: R.V. Stover, *Making It and Breaking It: The Fate of Public Interest Commitment During Law School,* Evanston 1989. For a critique of the idea that the self-represented badges of professionalism ever existed, see M. Galanter, "Lawyers in the Mist: The Golden Age of Legal Nostalgia", 100 *Dickinson Law Review* 1996 No. 3, 549-562. For a work which takes what professionals say about themselves more seriously, see T. Becher, *Professional Practice*, New Brunswick, NJ 1999.
5. T. Parsons, "A Sociologist Looks at the Legal Profession", *Essays in Sociological Theory*, Glencoe 1954.
6. See Durkheim's views on the need for different sets of moral standards (and associations to guard those standards) for different professional groups. In particular see Chapter One of E. Durkheim, *Professional Ethics and Civic Morals*, trans. C. Brookfield, Westport, CT 1983. A return to Durkheim is suggested as an antidote to the fact that "mainstream sociology of the professions today is too often just concerned with the thesis of professional capture of political power". [Perri 6, Book Review of *Émile Durkheim: Law in a Moral Domain* by R. Cotterrell, 27 *Journal of Law and Society* 2000 No. 3, 481-485, 484.]
7. For the view that semi-autonomous workers (presumably including employed lawyers) have "contradictory class interests" see E.O. Wright, *Class, Crisis & the State*, London 1978. For the view that professionals form a new class see C. Derber, W.A. Schwartz & Y. Magrass, *Power in the Highest Degree,* New York 1990.

a Weberian approach focused on how professions manipulate the market to establish and maintain monopoly.

Magali Sarfatti Larson, the leading thinker in the Weberian school, posed the central question as follows: What do "professions actually do in everyday life to negotiate and maintain their special position"?[8] Larson's response was the "professional project". The project has two elements, market control and collective mobility (which while conceptually distinct, serve each other in a reciprocal way and can be "'read' out of the same empirical material").[9] In Larson's view, the project is not inevitably fulfilled, but rather is actively pursued by elites of some occupational groups. Taking the "professional project" as a starting point, Richard Abel and others have analyzed the legal profession. Abel argues that lawyers attempt their market control both through restricting supply and creating demand.[10] Historically supply was restricted directly through quotas on entrants or bars to entry for women and minorities. Current restrictions on supply come in the form of what initially appear to be meritocratic mechanisms for selection: formal education (often bearing little relation to the actual practice of law), professional examinations (with shifting pass levels), and the need to obtain apprenticeships and initial positions (which admit class and other bias). In addition to restricting supply through selection, lawyers strive to define and protect their monopoly (against paralegals for example). Lawyers have also attempted to stimulate demand by, among other things, seeking state subsidies in the form of legal aid.[11]

I find the Weberian approach—as characterized by Abel's scholarship—to be convincing and it provides an important theoretical framework for this study (the approach is expanded upon in Chapters 4, 5 and 6). In the end, however, I suggest that certain aspects of the Weberian approach—notably the fixation on monopoly—do not fit the empirical evidence from Georgia and its neighbours.[12] In this context at least, Abel's conclusions need to be tempered by paying close attention to the peculiarities of culture and the nature of the post-Soviet transi-

8. M.S. Larson, *The Rise of Professionalism*, Berkeley 1977, xii. In turn Larson builds on Friedson and his approach to the question of how professional prestige is asserted (E. Friedson, *The Profession of Medicine,* New York 1970).
9. Larson, *ibid.*, 66.
10. R.L. Abel, "Comparative Sociology of Legal Professions" in R.L. Abel & P.S.C. Lewis, eds., *Lawyers in Society: Comparative Theories* (v. 3), Berkeley 1989, 80 (hereinafter *Lawyers in Society* (v. 3)).
11. These power theories have been criticized in turn by those who argue that in fact lawyers have little control over the market or their clients: A. Paterson, "The Legal Profession in Scotland—An Endangered Species or a Problem Case for Market Theory" in R.L. Abel & P.S.C. Lewis, eds., *Lawyers in Society: The Common Law World* (v. 1), Berkeley 1988, 76 (hereinafter *Lawyers in Society* (v. 1)).
12. While others, notably Terence Halliday (*Beyond Monopoly*, London 1987), have argued that pursuit of monopoly does not dominate professional activities to the extent suggested by Larson and Abel, few have suggested—as I do in the Transcaucasian context—that lawyers are ambivalent about or even opposed to monopoly.

tion. Abel himself suggests that the Weberian theory is not a complete account (although perhaps he does not practice what he preaches):[13]

> Any attempt to understand lawyers must address the Weberian questions of how they constructed their professional commodity (legal services) and sought to control their market and raise their collective status by regulating the production *of* and *by* producers and stimulating demand, the Marxist question of the class location of lawyers as defined by the structures within which legal services are produced, and the structural functional questions about lawyers in the system of stratification, professional autonomy, self-governance and self-regulation.

Other observers have argued that the theoretical debate as to the nature of the archetypal professions is increasingly irrelevant as we enter an age of post-professionalism.[14] For Herbert Kritzer, post-professionalism is marked by tendencies such as a loss of exclusivity (threats to lawyers from accountants and other non-lawyers) and technological pressures (non-lawyers can access legal information on their own).[15] But in this scheme professions do not die—there is no complete deprofessionalization. Rather, the "ideal" professions meld into the "general professions" as monopoly is reduced and multi-disciplinary, globalized practices rise. While partial deprofessionalization has occurred for Soviet trained advocates, this process is not simply a result of inter-professional competition, technology and globalization. The causes for the deprofessionalization are historically traceable and will be examined, as will the interesting paradox that Georgian lawyers most subject to the pressure of globalization are the most professional.

Taking another tack, some have suggested that the theorists' obsession with the structure of the professions has resulted in the neglect of what lawyering actually entails. As Andrew Abbott puts it, the theories of structure tell us "less about what professions do than how they are organized to do it".[16] Some studies present detailed research on how lawyers have translated client needs into legal strategies and recommunicated the strategies to clients, courts, authorities and others.[17] Somewhat belatedly in the three-volume study which focused

13. R. Abel, "American Lawyers" in R. Abel, ed., *Lawyers: A Critical Reader*, New York 1997, 128.
14. Kritzer, *op. cit.* note 1.
15. *Ibid.* For a similar approach focussing on the impact of globalization on Canadian lawyers, see H.W. Arthurs & R. Kreklewich, "Law, Legal Institutions, and the Legal Profession in the New Economy", 34 *Osgoode Hall Law Journal* 1996 No. 1, 1-60 and H.W. Arthurs, "Lawyering in Canada in the 21st Century", 15 *Windsor Yearbook of Access to Justice* 1996, 202-225.
16. A. Abbott, *The System of Professions: An Essay on the Division of Expert Labor*, Chicago 1988, 1.
17. To take an example of this sort of research, one study has detailed how New York lawyers during the insider trading scandals of the 1980s not only handled routine legal transactions for their clients but, through creative lawyering, were able to mediate with regulatory officials to establish greater determinacy for rules regarding trading: J. McCahery & S. Picciotto, "Creative lawyering and the dynamics of business regulation" in Y. Dezalay &

on the comparative structures of legal professions, Abel and Lewis also called for studies to "put the law back into the sociology of law":[18]

> The roots of sociology of law lie in the recognition that formal law never is an adequate account of behavior, even that of legal officials. A vital inquiry thus becomes what lawyers actually do for their clients and employers (public and private), how this is shaped by lawyer-client and employment relationships, and what difference it makes that *lawyers* are doing these things.

This present study does look at what lawyers do. Indeed I attribute the slow rise in prestige of the profession to the fact that lawyers can now do more for clients than they could during Soviet times. There is a good deal more work to be done on this point, however, and I have suggested avenues for future research.

Soviet Lawyers

If Soviet studies began in earnest as a distinct academic field in the early 1940s with an attempt to get to know an ally better, they took off in the 1950s with an attempt to get to know the enemy better.[19] During the 1940s and 1950s, several well-funded multidisciplinary centres were established in the U.S. with governmental and foundational support, such as the Harvard Russian Research Center that opened in 1948. In addition, academic associations were created and a number of journals launched.[20] One of the initial paradigms for studying the USSR was "totalitarianism", although this concept meant different things to different scholars. For some, it was a reference to the total state (a monopoly of power in all spheres of society) while for others it was associated with the despotism of Stalin and the similarities of communism to fascism. This static approach however was challenged by developmentalists who traced the de-Stalinization process and posed questions regarding the transformation or maturation of communism in the modernization process.[21] In the 1960s

D. Sugarman, eds., *Professional Competition and Professional Power,* London 1995. For studies of this sort in the Canadian context, see the collection of essays in C. Wilton, *Beyond the Law: Lawyers and Business in Canada, 1830-1930,* Toronto 1990.

18. Abel & Lewis, "Putting Law Back into the Sociology of Lawyers" in *Lawyers in Society* (v. 3), *op. cit.* note 10, 513-514. The belatedness of this chapter was noticed by McCahery & Picciotto, *ibid.,* 266-267, ft. 1.
19. My discussion of Soviet area studies relies on V. Bonnell & G. Breslauer, "Soviet and Post-Soviet Area Studies", April 1998, a working paper available from the Berkeley Programme in Soviet and Post-Soviet Studies, University of California (Berkeley). Unfortunately the paper ignores legal scholarship.
20. The most notable association being the American Association for the Advancement of Slavic Studies (1948). Journals established during this time including the *Slavic Review* (1945) and *Problems of Communism* (1952).
21. The classic works are C.J. Friedrich, ed., *Totalitarianism*, Cambridge, MA 1954 and C.J. Friedrich & Z.K. Brzezinski, *Totalitarian Dictatorship and Autocracy*, Cambridge, MA 1956.

and 1970s much of the focus of the developmentalists, at least in the field of political science, was on the rise of elite technocrats and the "rationalization" of Soviet society (could Soviet society be reformed?). Social historians also began to document revolutionary and Soviet history "from the ground up" with new studies on peasants and culture.[22] Explorations of the second economy, including Georgia's second economy, were also published.[23] Until the Gorbachev years, however, research on the Soviet Union was data-starved by limited academic exchanges, the lack of access to the regions outside of Moscow and St. Petersburg and limited archival access. The problems were mitigated somewhat through interviews with refugees or exiled dissidents, but obviously this was not an ideal solution. Gorbachev's reforms vastly improved access to data, although the theoretical concerns of Sovietologists from the Brezhnev era (interest in the reformability of Soviet communism) and the one-republic focus continued through the *Perestroika* era. Active consideration of the possible transition from communism to a democratic, capitalist state remained limited.

Like their counterparts in the social sciences, the sustained focus of legal scholars on the Soviet Union came only in the wake of World War Two. Some of the initial studies of Soviet law looked at their subject with the stated aim of theorizing about law. One of the pioneers of Soviet legal studies wrote in the preface to his 1965 work that "[i]t is the purpose of this volume to test with Soviet data the thesis that modern man can settle his disputes with simplicity, without elaborately organized tribunals, without legal representation, without complicated laws, and without a labyrinth of rules of procedure and evidence."[24] Those who studied Soviet law from law faculties tended to take a comparativist approach which saw socialist law as one of the three major systems of law in the Occidental world, the other two being civil and common law. In this view, socialist law was another legal family—Romano-Germanic with a revolutionary twist—whose principles could be known and systematized.[25] Socialist law should be taken seriously and studied not only for academic interest (including the interest in generalizing about law) but for practical purposes as well (to facilitate transnational business transactions with the Soviet Union for example).[26] This was accompanied by a great deal of translation of Soviet

22. A pioneering study in this field is L. Haimson, "The Problem of Social Stability in Urban Russia, 1905-1917", 23 *Slavic Review* (Part I) 1964 No. 4, 619-642 and 24 *Slavic Review* (Part II) 1965 No. 4, 1-22.
23. See for example, G. Mars & Y. Altman, "The Cultural Basis of Soviet Georgia's Second Economy", XXXV *Soviet Studies* 1983 No. 4, 546-560.
24. J. Hazard, *Settling Disputes in Soviet Society: The Formative Years of Soviet Legal Institutions*, New York 1960, vii.
25. R. David & J. Brierley, *Major Legal Systems in the World Today*, London 1985. Though others, notably Harold Berman (*Justice in the U.S.S.R.*, New York 1963), stressed similarities between Russian and Soviet law (as distinct from the "Western legal tradition" of common and civil law).

Constitutional and legislative documents, as well as case law. Attempts were also made at encyclopedic systematizing.[27] The comparativists did not neglect lawyers, and a good understanding of the formal development and structure of the bar was achieved early on.[28]

Most of the legal literature during this period was distinctly in the developmental rather than totalitarian frame, watching socialist law develop and gain in complexity and even humanism.[29] Gradually legal scholars and social scientists added a sociological view of the law and legal institutions to the comparativist scholarship which had concentrated on "the law on the books". Peter Solomon, for example, has traced the decline of acquittals in the post-war Soviet criminal justice period to the point where they practically "vanished" by the 1970s and 1980s.[30] He argues that this phenomenon cannot be explained through legislative developments, but rather through an examination of the bureaucratic measures to which judges and prosecutors were subject, such as work performance appraisals. This growing concern with how law actually worked encompassed Soviet lawyers as well. Solomon reported that faced with the near impossibility of obtaining acquittals, advocates would sometimes informally negotiate with prosecutors (essentially plea-bargaining) to gain more lenient sentences for their clients.[31] Successful negotiations were regarded as victories. Obviously a look at the formal law alone would not detect these out-of-court activities.

Several studies from the 1980s focussing specifically on Soviet lawyers should be noted. Eugene Huskey's seminal analysis of the transformation of the Soviet Bar between the October Revolution and 1939 drew not only on legislative artifacts but also examined institutional phenomena such as communist party penetration of the *advokatura*.[32] Similarly, his institutional analysis of the *advokatura* in the late communist period showed how lawyers did retain relative autonomy despite absorption into the Soviet system.[33] For her study, Louise Shelley interviewed émigré Jewish jurisconsults and was able to portray

26. See the introduction in W.E. Butler, *Soviet Law*, London 1988.
27. F.J.M. Feldbrugge, ed., *Encyclopedia of Soviet Law*, Dobbs Ferry, NY 1973.
28. See the pioneering work of Hazard, *op. cit.* note 24.
29. Although the legal aspects of totalitarianism continues to be of scholarly interest: A. Podgorecki and V. Olgiatti, *Totalitarian and Post-Totalitarian Law*, Aldershot, UK 1996.
30. P.H. Solomon, Jr., "The Case of the Vanishing Acquittal: Informal Norms and the Practice of Soviet Criminal Justice", 39 *Soviet Studies* 1987 No. 4, 531-555.
31. *Ibid.*, 546-548.
32. E. Huskey, *Russian Lawyers and the Soviet State*, Princeton, NJ 1986 (hereinafter *Russian Lawyers*).
33. See E. Huskey, "The Limits to Institutional Autonomy in the Soviet Union: The Case of the *Advokatura*", XXXIV *Soviet Studies* 1982 No. 2, 200-227. On advocates in the Gorbachev era see E. Huskey, "Between Citizen and State: The Soviet Bar (Advokatura) Under Gorbachev", 28 *Columbia Journal of Transnational Law* 1990 No. 1, 95-116 (hereinafter "Between Citizen and State").

in some detail what these lawyers did in everyday Soviet work life.[34] Although journalistically styled, Robert Rand's detailed observations of how *Perestroika*-era Soviet advocates actually worked in the legal consultation bureaus and courts is also useful.[35] These Western accounts were supplemented by the writings of some émigré jurists.[36]

Generally the Western writings on Soviet lawyers from the Soviet era borrow little from the theoretical principles drawn from studies of Western lawyers. In fact, there is little theorizing at all about the nature of professions *per se* in the Soviet era studies, although many have considered the nature of Soviet elites.[37] When Sovietologists have looked to the Western professional models it has been to discuss the uniqueness of the Soviet experience. Louise Shelley for example has concluded:[38]

> The history and the nature of the Soviet state has created a situation for lawyers that is very different from that in Western capitalist societies. A legal profession lacking cohesion and prestige has developed in the past seventy years following the destruction of the entire Czarist legal apparatus. Its power follows from its proximity to the state rather than its claim to expertise in a specific body of knowledge.

This claim to distinctiveness lies not only in the unique experiences of Soviet jurists, but in the nature of the legal system itself and in attitudes towards law.

The legal system in the late *Perestroika* period spawned a great deal of new attention from Western lawyers and journalists as well as academics. As with the wider strands of social science scholarship, however, most of these studies looked at the centralized reform of the system rather than considering the transition.[39] The real boom for scholars during this period came from the opening of archives and permissiveness for field-work, which was to show results following the collapse of the Soviet Union. One example is Kathryn Hendley's analysis of how labour law actually worked in the Soviet Union (and

34. L. Shelley, *Lawyers in Soviet Work Life,* New Brunswick, NJ 1984.
35. R. Rand, *Comrade Lawyer,* Boulder 1991.
36. D. Kaminskaya, *Final Judgment: My Life as a Soviet Defence Attorney*, New York 1982 and K. Simmis, *USSR, The Corrupt Society: The Secret World of Soviet Capitalism*, New York 1982.
37. See for example, J. Azrael, *Managerial Power and Soviet Politics*, Cambridge, MA, 1966. In the legal sphere see E. Huskey, "Specialists in the Soviet Communist Party Apparatus: Legal Professionals as Party Functionaries", XL *Soviet Studies* 1988 No. 4, 538-555 (hereinafter "Specialists in the Soviet Communist Party").
38. L. Shelley, "Lawyers in the Soviet Union" in A. Jones, ed., *Professions and the State: Expertise and Autonomy in the Soviet Union and Eastern Europe*, Philadelphia 1991, 63, 85. Shelley argues that the functionalist model for lawyers is completely inapplicable and that while "conflict" theories are more applicable, they also miss the mark, since "[p]ower is not conferred because of professional characteristics but, rather, by proximity to the powerful Party apparatus". *Idem.*
39. Although there was some acknowledgement that the Republics were not all "marching to the same tune"; see Huskey, "Between Citizen and State", *op. cit.* note 33, 96. For the view of a practicing American lawyer see E. Griffith, "Law and Lawyers in the USSR", 61 *New York State Bar Journal* 1989, 18-23.

in the early post-Soviet period).[40] Through field-work based on interviews and observations she constructed a nuanced picture of how the *pro forma* aspects of legality were regularly used by managers and others in the work-place. She concluded however that ultimately the prescripts of the law were marginalized. While sometimes law "mattered" in a coercive sense (it forced citizens to modify behaviour) it more rarely mattered in a reciprocal sense (citizens did not see it as a "means of achieving justice or even solving problems").[41] Not surprisingly, the role of lawyers was also of marginal importance.

Post-Soviet Lawyers

In the 1990s scholars scrambled to reorient themselves to new country specialities (as diverse as Lithuania and Tajikistan) and a new research agenda. As Edward Walker put it in 1993: "No longer challenged to explain order, stability, institutionalization, or the function of the 'Soviet system,' we find ourselves confronted by dysfunction, fundamental and disjunctive institutional change, rapid attitudinal and behavioural adjustments to an ever-changing structure of opportunities, anti-regime mass mobilization, ethnic violence, and the driving force of intense nationalism."[42] Curiously there has been both convergence and divergence in the social sciences. On the one hand, there have been some fractures (dividing East European Studies from Soviet Studies) and the appearance of new country or regional specialities (accompanied by new academic programmes such as the University of California at Berkeley's Caucasus Program).[43] At the same time, the region-wide field of post-communist comparative politics and the multi-disciplinary field of "transitology" hold considerable sway.[44] These fields have produced inter-regional and intra-regional studies, based on the assumption that the post-communist space shares certain characteristics or at least certain problems (transition to market economy, human rights, state-building, de-militarization to name a few).

Post-communism also has normative significance for legal scholars.[45] The establishment of the rule of law faces common challenges throughout the

40. K. Hendley, *Trying to Make Law Matter*, Ann Arbor 1996.
41. *Ibid.*, 167.
42. E.W. Walker, "Sovietology and Perestroika: A Post-Mortem" in S. Solomon, ed., *Beyond Sovietology: Essays in Politics and History*, Armonk, NY 1993, 227.
43. In the Fall of 2000 it was announced that the Caucasus Programme would be joined with Central Asian Studies in a distinct programme within the newly formed Institute of Slavic, East European and Eurasian Studies (10 *Contemporary Caucasus Newsletter* 2000, 1).
44. And provoke considerable debate; see: P.C. Schmitter and T.L. Karl, "The Conceptual Travails of Transitologists and Consolidologists: How Far to the East Should they Attempt to Go?", 53 *Slavic Review* 1994 No. 1, 173-185 and V. Bunce, "Should Transitologists Be Grounded?", 54 *Slavic Review* 1995 No. 1, 111-127.
45. Although there is a growing recognition of the fact that speaking of one post-communist region in Eastern Europe and the Soviet Union is of little descriptive value: M. Krygier, "Traps for Young Players in Times of Transition", 8 *East European Constitutional Review* 1999 No. 4, 63-67.

former Soviet Union (attitudes towards law, corruption, human rights abuses, unfamiliar legal concepts) and some scholars have attempted to consider the entire post-Soviet space.[46] The nature of how the transition countries have legal model "shopped" has been a particularly fruitful field for comparative studies.[47] Generally, however, when consideration is given to the former Soviet Union, the focus remains on Russia as it was during the previous period, and specifically the centre of Russia (with increased interest in the former western republics). Law and legal institutions in Transcaucasia and Central Asia remain relatively unexplored by legal scholars writing in Western journals.[48] When references are made to Georgia, they usually concern a specific legislative development rather than any global or institutional analysis.[49] In this respect law has lagged behind other disciplines which have embraced a new post-Soviet research agenda throughout the former Soviet Union and have produced specialists in virtually all former republics.

Another feature of post-Soviet legal studies is that, beginning in the late *Perestroika* era, the small number of legal Sovietologists were joined by Western law reformers and practicing lawyers, attempting to influence the reform efforts underway or working in the system.[50] These newcomers have published studies of uneven character, some informative and analytical, while others represent what might uncharitably be called memoirs of legal tourists (accounts based on several weeks experience) or legal missionaries (self-congratulatory accounts of how aid and legal knowledge is transferred from the West to the East). Accounts of the legal profession in the region tend to examine trends in business law firms, particularly those with foreign connections, and ignore criminal and family law lawyers.[51] The field has also seen the appearance of

46. Those who have attempted to provide factual accounts for each of the republics have necessarily had to give a light treatment to each, given the number of republics and the breadth of experience. See for example J. Peter, *Freedom's Ordeal: The Struggle for Human Rights and Democracy in Post-Soviet States*, Philadelphia 1998.
47. See for example G. Ajani, "By Chance and Prestige: Legal Transplants in Russia and Eastern Europe", 43 *American Journal of Comparative Law* 1995 No. 1, 93-117.
48. Although recently this has been changing, with new interest in Central Asia in particular. In the national languages there is a great deal of literature available. In the Georgian case, see the numerous titles (in English) of the Georgian-language journal "Legal Reform" at http://www.geo.net.ge/reform/. The level of scholarship varies a good deal, however, a theme that will be returned to in Chapter 4 (Legal Education).
49. See W.E. Kovacic & B. Slay, "Perilous Beginnings: The Establishment of Antimonopoly and Consumer Protection Programs in the Republic of Georgia", XLIII *Antitrust Bulletin* 1998 No. 1, 15-43 and T. Jonas, "Georgia's New Investment Law", 25 *CIS Law Notes* 1997. As an exception, see F.J.M. Feldbrugge, "The New Constitution of Georgia", 22 *Review of Central and East European Law* 1996 No. 1, 9-17.
50. Examples include Griffith, *op. cit.* note 39 and S.M. Ryan, "Out from Under Soviet Rule: With the Help of C.E.E.L.I., Former Satellites Rebuild a Legal System", 11 *Criminal Justice* 1996, 11-19.

new journals financed by international actors actively interested in pressing the rule of law agenda.[52] International organizations, notably the World Bank, have also produced numerous technical examinations of individual countries' judicial systems as well as region-wide studies on law reform.[53]

As in the Soviet era, scholars studying post-Soviet lawyers in Russia stress the distinctiveness of that country's experience *vis-à-vis* the West. The distinct role of law (or lack of a role) in post-Soviet society is considered particularly important. As Michael Burrage puts it:[54]

> To Western observers it would seem self-evident that the development of a democratic political system and market economy will require the rule of law, sturdily independent courts, and activist lawyers. But Western expectations are colored by their own legal history and perhaps by tsarist Russia. There is, however, reason to wonder whether any of these experiences are relevant to postsocialist Russia.

Similarly I suggest in this book that the Western concepts of law and profession fit uneasily with the Georgian experience. I also argue, however, that the Georgian experience is distinct from the Russian, coloured by Georgia's particular legal past, informal laws, and attitudes towards law and lawyering. The next section introduces a legal pluralist perspective which can shed light on the nature of the Georgian experience.

51. L. Rogers, "Law Practice in Central and Eastern Europe", 6 *Journal of East European Law* 1999 No. 9, 91-95.
52. For example *Law in Transition* is a publication of the European Bank of Reconstruction and Development. A number of its articles are presented in the format of "report cards" on the performance of regional countries on various topics, such as insolvency law (see A. Ramasastry, S. Slavova and L. Vandenhoeck, "EBRD legal indicator survey: assessing insolvency laws after ten years of transition", *Law in Transition* (Spring) 2000, 34-42). The *East European Constitutional Review* is closely linked to the Soros network.
53. See for example, World Bank, "Georgia Judicial Assessment" (Report no. 17356-GE, 10 April 1998) (hereinafter "Georgia Judicial Assessment").
54. M. Burrage, "Russian Advocates: Before, during, and after Perestroika", 18 *Law and Social Inquiry* 1993 No. 3, 573-592, 587. Similarly Pamela Jordan argues that "[i]t is better not to fit professions into rigid categories (although the categories need not be totally ignored), but to investigate more broadly their unique historical contexts and the coexistence of such presumed inconsistencies as professionalization and bureaucratization, autonomy and external control, and professionalization (self-aggrandizement) and citizens' interests (public service). This more fluid approach is crucial to examining legal professions, where certain other factors, such as the *role of law in society* and differences between civil law and common law traditions, strongly influence professionalization in a given society". P. Jordan, "Russian Advocates in a Post-Soviet World: The Struggle for Professional Identity and Efforts to Redefine Legal Services" (unpublished Ph.D. dissertation, University of Toronto, 1997), 5 (hereinafter "Russian Advocates"). Jordan's thesis is the basis for a shorter, published article: P. Jordan, "The Russian *Advokatura* (Bar) and the State in the 1990s", 50 *Europe-Asia Studies* 1998 No. 5, 765-791 (hereinafter "The Russian Advokatura").

Accounting for the Georgian Difference

In reaction to the positivist reliance on central state law, the legal pluralist view is that "more than one legal order" can be present in a particular "social field".[55] These legal orders may compete with each other (Nigerian federal law versus the application of Islamic law in an individual state), they may inform each other (the use of sentencing circles to determine a culturally appropriate sentence for aboriginal offenders) or they may be unconcerned with each other ("the state has no place in the bedrooms of the nation"). But beyond the basic precept that polyjurality exists, there has been little agreement among socio-legal scholars as to its nature. Indeed, some have suggested the field has stagnated, with legal pluralists failing to establish a common conception of what law is and to distinguish law from social order.[56] As Sally Merry puts the central problem, "Where do we stop speaking of law and find ourselves simply describing social life?"[57] One response is that there need be no dichotomy between law and social order, that "all social control is *more* or *less* legal".[58] But this does not solve the central problem of defining law (is, for example, the potential for enforcement of norms a necessary element of law?). Others have suggested a non-essentialist view of law, rejecting the assumption that "law is a fundamental category which can be identified and described, or an essentialist notion which can be internally worked on until a pure (de-contextualized) version is produced".[59] While these non-essentialists differ considerably in their approach, they share the starting point that law cannot be what the theorists say it is.

"Critical legal plurists" posit that any attempt to capture what law *is* will fail, because laws have no independent existence outside of the imagination.[60] These pluralists suggest an approach which recognizes shifting conceptions of law by the *subjects* of law and does not attempt to reify the individual legal orders found in a social field (which is as bad as a state-centred approach). Law is seen as "autobiographical":[61]

55. J. Griffiths, "What is legal pluralism?", 24 *J. of Legal Pluralism* 1986, 1-56, 1. Other classics of legal pluralism include: S.E. Merry, "Legal Pluralism", 22 *Law and Society Review* 1988 No. 5, 869-896; G. Teubner, "The Two Faces of Janus: Rethinking Legal Pluralism", 13 *Cardozo Law Review* 1992 No. 5, 1443-1462 and M. Galanter, "Justice in Many Rooms: Courts, Private Ordering, and Indigenous Law", 19 *Journal of Legal Pluralism* 1981 No. 1, 1-47. Legal pluralism has also been called "the key concept in a post-modern view of law": B. de Sousa Santos, "Law: A Map of Misreading. Toward a Post-Modern Conception of Law", 14 *Journal of Law and Society* 1987 No. 3, 279-302, 297.
56. See B.Z. Tamanaha, "A Non-Essentialist Version of Legal Pluralism", 27 *Journal of Law and Society* 2000 No. 2, 296-321.
57. Merry, *op. cit.* note 55, 869-870.
58. Griffiths, *op. cit.* note 55 at 39.
59. Tamanaha, *op. cit.* note 56, 299 (in turn citing his article "The Folly of the 'Social Scientific' Concept of Legal Pluralism", 20 *Journal of Law & Society* 1993 No. 2, 192-218, 201).
60. M.-M. Kleinhans & R.A. Macdonald, "What is a *Critical* Legal Pluralism?", 12 *Canadian Journal of Law and Society* 1997 No. 2, 25-46.

> A *critical* legal pluralism presumes that legal subjects hold each of their multiple narrating selves up to the scrutiny of their other narrating selves, and up to the scrutiny of all the other narrated selves projected upon them by others. The self is the irreducible site of normativity and internormativity.

The "autopoietic" approach is to see law as what people say it is, by examining the binary discourse of what is legal or illegal.[62] This approach turns from the *function* of law to the *code* of law so that "[l]egal pluralism is then defined no longer as a set of conflicting social norms in a given social field but as a multiplicity of diverse communicative processes that observe social action under the binary code of legal/illegal".[63] Similarly, a conventionalist view sees law as "whatever people identify and treat through their social practices as 'law'".[64] In this scheme law is a cultural construct, without content in absolute terms, defined by social conventions which have "some minimal degree of continuous social presence" (*i.e.* there is a *de minimis* element to the definition; the social practice cannot be fleeting or that of the single madman).[65]

Turning now to the approach taken in this book, the first thing to note is that adopting *some form* of a legal pluralist perspective when studying Georgian law is not optional: to avoid the legal pluralism is to get it all wrong. There are few signs of formalized, centralized legal hegemony in any field of Georgian life. Even at the state level, two regions of the country (Abkhazia and South Ossetia) are *de facto* independent and a third (Ajara) pays little heed to the dictates of the centre. Where Parliament's laws do have relevance, they compete or combine with local practice to produce results different from the mythical "intention of the legislator". When we turn to the now formally regulated legal profession (which was entirely unregulated for several years of independence), state law is of limited use in examining how lawyers are ordered.[66] The more relevant question then is what form of a legal pluralist perspective to take.

In my view a broad non-essentialist perspective (drawing from all three approaches canvassed) is preferable to the traditional approach for two reasons.[67]

61. *Ibid.* at 46.
62. G. Teubner, "'Global Bukowina': Legal Pluralism in a World Society" in G. Teubner, ed., *Global Law Without a State,* Aldershot, UK 1997, 14.
63. *Ibid.*, 3, 14-15.
64. Tamanaha, *op. cit.* note 56, 313. I say "similarly", although Tamanaha argues that Teubner's version is ultimately essentialist, see Tamanaha, 311.
65. *Ibid.*, 319.
66. This is true even in states with better functioning governmental and bar institutions; see for example Arthurs, *op. cit.* note 15, 223-225 and W.B. Wendel, "Nonlegal Regulation of the Legal Profession: Social Norms in Professional Communities", 54 *Vanderbilt Law Review* 2001, 1955-2053.
67. Although the individual non-essentialist approaches canvassed each have their conceptual difficulties. Tamanaha (*op. cit.* note 56, 298) criticizes the critical legal pluralist view as "theoretical re-labelling, transforming the commonplace sociological observation that social life is filled with a pluralism of normative orders into the supposedly novel observation that social life is filled with a pluralism of legal orders." In turn the autopoietic approach

The first advantage is its usefulness for field-observation.[68] Laws are revealed by the subjects rather than pre-determined by the observer or theorists: law is what people perceive it to be, say it is or reveal through their behaviour. While the researcher cannot fully put aside pre-conceived notions of law, the potential usefulness of this perspective in a cross-cultural research field is obvious. Another advantage of this approach is that their contentless nature allows the researcher to avoid the tendency to romanticization of informal law evident in much of the literature. As Brian Tamanaha puts it, "many legal pluralists are anti-state law by inclination—as reflected in their attack on legal centralism—and consequently have a tendency to romanticize non-state normative systems".[69] Legal pluralists have often implicitly or explicitly mixed a celebration of the emancipatory nature of their method with their subjects, non-state laws and actors.

I do not wish to idealize informal Georgian law. On the contrary, it may well be that aspects of non-state law are hindering Georgia's democratic and economic development (a research agenda on this point is suggested in the Conclusion). But I see no inconsistency in recognizing this fact and in using a pluralist perspective to see Georgian law as it is.

is restricted by its insistence on language rather than behaviour as a code for determining law (are linguistic observations to be preferred to observations of coercive behaviour?). Finally the conventionalist approach suffers from a degree of circularity; if legal norms are whatever people recognize as legal norms through social practices, how do we know when a group is recognizing a norm as *legal*?

68. Although it is not clear how one actually conducts research in a critical legal pluralist fashion beyond the autobiographical (unless that is the point—for an example of how "law as autobiography" can be done well, see R.A. Macdonald, *Lessons of Everyday Law/Le droit du quotidien,* Montreal 2002). Beyond autobiography, amidst the shifting images and subjects of law, is it a legitimate (or realistic) exercise to make generalizations in even a single site (the factory, the club etc.)?

69. Tamanaha, *op. cit.* note 56, 305.

Chapter 2
Georgian Legal Histories

Introduction

Modern Georgian scholarship in legal history often reflects two purposes. First, indigenous law is presented as a cultural artifact and a source of national (and sometimes nationalist) pride to Georgians. Along with the Georgian language and Orthodox Christianity, legal history (and history generally) represents a badge of cultural distinctiveness, independence and a superior level of national development.[1] One historian describing an eighteenth century Georgian law code writes:[2]

> Ces lois sont l'expression d'une très haute conscience du droit, en particulier en ce qui concerne la liberté de l'individu. Elles sont d'un charactère infiniment plus humain que celles qui étaient en vigeur en Occident à la même époque.

Furthermore, Georgia's rich legal history is held with pride above the sham that was the Soviet legal system and is the Georgian legal system today. Writers are particularly keen to point out that Georgian law had achieved an advanced level prior to the Russian annexation of Georgia. As another author argues:[3]

> In the 18th century, particularly in its latter half, numerous, often highly important, prescriptive acts were published, and on the eve of the incorporation of Eastern Georgia into Russia (1801) vast legislative draft laws appeared, purporting to overcome feudal backwardness, to consolidate the unified state authority, and to effect decisive changes in economic and cultural development.

This view of pre-annexation Georgia challenges the notion that the subsequent Russian presence in Georgia was a needed civilizing or progressive force.

A second common use of Georgian legal history is to ground current legislation in the country's past. This serves to legitimize current laws as being within the Georgian legal frame of reference and not mere imports. Thus in a paper supporting the state's decision to ban capital punishment, the author points to the humaneness of traditional Georgian law and argues that capital punishment was historically an extremely rare form of punishment.[4] Similarly, in promoting a new civil code (drafted with German and other Western European models in mind) another author suggests that the new code represents a return to the European civil law family for Georgia, implying that Georgia had legal roots in Europe prior to foreign domination.[5]

1. On the use of religion and language by Georgian historians in the creation of national myths, see the chapters on Transcaucasia in G. Smith *et al.*, eds., *Nation Building in the Post-Soviet Borderlands: The Politics of National Identities,* Cambridge 1999.
2. A. Manvelichvili, *Histoire de Géorgie*, Paris 1951, 348 (n. 3), describing the 18th century code of Vakhtang VI.
3. D. Purtseladze, ed., *Zakony Vakhtanga VI*, Tbilisi 1980, 332 ("The Laws of Vakhtang VI").
4. J. Khetsuriani, "Death Penalty in Georgian Law", 1 *Georgian Law Review* 1999, 3-9.
5. B. Zoidze, "The System of the Civil Code of Georgia", 1 *Georgian Law Review* 1998, 3-14.

Regardless of its purposes, legal history is a live topic in Georgia. It is taught as a separate subject at the Law Faculty of Tbilisi State University, there is a section of Legal History at the official Institute of State and Law, numerous articles are published in the area each year and at least lip-service is paid to it in law reform efforts. Even some of the language of legal history has been revived. To take an example, the name of one lawyers' journal is *Meoxi*, the word for "defender" from prior centuries. Together the various understandings of Georgia's legal past represent a sort of collective legal memory. But questions remain as to whether these expressions of legal memory are purely hortatory, or whether there has been an institutional memory (broadly defined to include values).[6] Legal memory is one of the usual explanations as to why post-communist East European countries have had more success in legal reform than the countries of the former Soviet Union. Simply put, the European countries had fewer years of destructive communism and, through a parallel or second culture, memory of pre-communist, Western notions of law remained. The existence of this parallel culture allowed for an easier transition to democracy, regulated market capitalism and a rule of law based state.[7] But what do Georgian law and lawyers today "remember" of the legal past?[8] Now Georgia is, formally at least, in the European civil law family; are there any precedents for this? I argue that in fact Georgian lawyers had little historical memory upon which to rely in constructing an appropriate post-Soviet Bar (or indeed legal system) and that this partly accounts for the current confusion over what course to take.

The historical narrative can be divided into six fairly distinct periods: i) the pre-Tsarist period; ii) the Tsarist period; iii) Menshevik Georgia; iv) the Soviet period; v) *Perestroika*; and vi) independence regained. Particular attention will be paid to questions of legal continuity and disruption between the historical periods. This will assist in assessing the weak formal legal heritage of Georgian lawyers today. It should also be noted that there are few English language sources which sketch Georgian legal history to the present day; as a secondary aim, this chapter attempts to contribute to that neglected field.[9]

6. Using "institutional" here in the "new-institutionalist" sense, as defined by Douglas North to include "formal rules, informal constraints (norms of behaviour, conventions, and self-imposed codes of conduct), and the enforcement characteristics of both)..." (D.C. North, *Transaction Costs, Institutions and Economic Performance*, San Francisco 1992, 9).
7. R. Janda, "Something Wicked That Way Went: Law and the Habit of Communism", 41 *McGill Law Journal* 1995 No. 1, 253-267.
8. There is a subtle but important gloss which could be put on this question. Given the desire of most Soviet lawyers to distance themselves from anything political, how much can Georgian lawyers be expected to "remember" pre-revolutionary values? On the Soviet lawyer's distinction between law and politics, see "The Russian Advokatura", *op. cit.* chap. 1, note 54, 770.

Indigenous Georgian Law

It would be misleading to speak of "indigenous" Georgian law in the sense of "pure" law untouched by other legal systems. Georgia sat at the crossroads of empires (Byzantine, Persian, Arab, Mongol and Ottoman and later Russian and Soviet), was regionally fractured more often than not, and had few periods of sustained and centralized state-building. It is not surprising therefore that Georgian law, as it had evolved to the point of the Tsarist annexation of part of Georgia in 1801, was the result of "legal mixing" and reflected elements of various legal systems both of domestic and foreign origin.[10] Accordingly, by "indigenous", "Georgian" or "pre-Tsarist law" I intend only to denote the law as it developed on the territory of Georgia before the annexation.

The question of where to begin the story of Georgian legal history is a perplexing one, given that there is evidence of early human habitation from more than 50,000 years ago and forms of statehood from several centuries B.C.E. Nonetheless, for reasons of economy and the lack of sources on law in this period, I will handily skip Georgia's prehistory, early statehood (known as Colchis in the East and Iberia in the West), the period of competing Byzantine and Persian control and influence from the 3rd century, Georgia's conversion to Christianity in the 4th century under Byzantine influence, Arab occupation in the seventh century and finally the gradual process whereby Georgian lands were gathered culminating in a United Eastern and Western Georgia in the early eleventh century.[11] I will begin with Georgia's Golden Age, exemplified by the reign of King David the Builder or Restorer (1089–1125). This is not a completely arbitrary starting point, however, since the Golden Age continues

9. On formal legal developments up to the late Soviet period a useful source is L. Schultz, "Legal History, Georgia" in F.J.M. Feldbrugge, G.P. van den Berg & W.B. Simons, eds., *Encyclopedia of Soviet Law,* No. 28 *Law in Eastern Europe*, (F.J.M. Feldbrugge, ed.), Dordrecht 1985. A succinct article on the pre-Tsarist period is F.J.M. Feldbrugge's "A History of Georgian Law", 3 *Georgica* 1998, 2-5. The chapter on medieval Georgian justice in W.E.D. Allen, *A History of the Georgian People,* New York 1932, 1971, is essential reading for that period. There are numerous references to law in D.M. Lang, *A Modern History of Georgia,* London 1962 and. R.G. Suny, *The Making of the Georgian Nation,* Bloomington 1994. Suny's book is the best general history of Georgia available and is particularly strong on the Tsarist and Soviet periods and on the politics of identity during those periods. I rely heavily on it in this chapter. There are numerous studies in Georgian and Russian on Georgian legal history, some of which are referred to in this chapter. The starting point in the Georgian language sources are Chapters VI and VII of I. Javakhashvili, *Kartuli Samartlis Istoria,* Tbilisi, reprinted 1984 ("The History of Georgian Law").
10. On legal mixes generally see E. Örücü, "Mixed and Mixing Systems" in E. Örücü *et al.*, eds., *Studies in Legal Systems: Mixed and Mixing,* The Hague 1996.
11. In addition to the sources cited in note 8, *op. cit.*, some key sources on Georgian prehistory and early history are: C. Burney, and D.M. Lang, *The Peoples of the Hills: Ancient Ararat and Caucasus*, New York 1972, D.M. Lang, *The Georgians*, London 1966 and C. Toumanoff, *Studies in Christian Caucasian History,* Washington 1963.

to hold a powerful place in Georgia's national psyche. Indeed, during Georgia's weakened condition following the collapse of the USSR, symbols from this age were revived and the first President of independent Georgia, Zviad Gamsakhurdia, cloaked himself in the mantle of King David and other national heroes.[12] During David's reign, together with the reign of Queen Tamara (1184–1213), Georgian lands were unified, the Georgian Empire extended from the Black to the Caspian Seas, Tbilisi became an important capital and the authority of Georgian rulers "meant something".

The state of law during the Golden Age is not clear (many documents have been lost to historians), but it is certain that "ancient laws" of Georgian custom were in place.[13] To obtain justice under these laws was often a matter of petitioning the King and seeking his personal direction, as is demonstrated in a medieval chronicler's account of King David's travels through the kingdom:[14]

> [I]t was not easy for him to meet everybody who had a complaint to make, suffering from want or oppression—even though they were in such need of his royal judgment and aid that some would actually climb to a vantage point on his way...and whenever such persons were seen in a prominent place with a petition to present he would appoint men to find out the true facts and question the complainants, and it was from these they received redress.

Georgian-style feudalism reached its zenith during this classical period. Personal contacts and relationships between the sovereign and local princes began to be formalized in official decrees, hereditary tenure was put in place, and serfdom fully introduced. Feudalism was not, however, as structured in Georgia as it was in parts of Europe. It has been suggested that this is related to the lack of a Roman legal tradition in Georgia. One prominent author of Georgian history, R.G. Suny, writes: "Since the intellectual and juridical influences of Roman law were completely absent in Georgia, Georgian feudalism never developed an abstract theoretical framework."[15] This statement is problematic. First, it is not at all clear that no legal thought was transmitted during the many years of Byzantine control and influence in Georgia. According to

12. S. Jones, "Populism in Georgia: The Gamsaxurdia Phenomenon in D.V. Schwartz & R. Panossian, eds., *Nationalism and History: The Politics of Nation Building in Post-Soviet Armenia, Azerbaijan and Georgia*, Toronto 1994, 130-136 (hereinafter "Populism in Georgia"). Following the disastrous war in the breakaway republic of Abkhazia in the early 1990s, the government ordered the construction of a statue of King David to be placed in front of one of Tbilisi's Intourist hotels housing refugees from the war. The prominently placed statue stands in contrast to the blue tarpaulins hanging on the refugees' balconies. Its message is clear: Georgia will rise again.
13. A medieval chronicler writes that punishment did not take place under Tamara "except in accordance with the ancient law": S. Qaukhchisshvili, ed., *The Georgian Chronicle*, trans. K. Vivian, Amsterdam 1991, 85.
14. *Ibid.*, 37-38.
15. Suny, *Making of the Georgian Nation*, *op. cit.* note 9, 43.

one scholar of pre-Tsarist Georgian law, "l'activité juridique-législative paraît avoir débuté officiellement, en Georgie, sous l'influence byzantine, qui prévalait en ce pays aux environs du Xe siècle".[16] Second, we might quibble with the assumption that the absence of Roman law precludes the development of an abstract version of feudalism. Nonetheless, the fundamentals of Suny's position are indisputable; the influence of Roman law was not prominent and Georgian feudal relations were not highly abstracted.

If law was gradually becoming more structured during this period, the Mongol invasion of 1236 served to dampen its development. The invasion led to what has been called the "long twilight" of the Georgian Kingdoms, a period which lasted up to the Russian annexation in 1801.[17] The twilight was deepened by an Ottoman invasion at the end of the 14th century. During this time Georgia was divided into three kingdoms (Kartli, Kakheti and Imereti) and five principalities (Guria, Svaneti, Abkhazia, Samstkhe and Odishi). Each principality existed as a separate unit, and this disunity contributed to the inability to repel continued foreign domination as well as the continued lack of centralized lawmaking.

Despite Georgia's decline and disunity during this period, there were notable attempts at formal lawmaking. The law code of King Vakhtang VI of Kartli compiled during the early 18th century is especially noteworthy, both in its own right as a legal artifact and for the modern purposes to which it has been put. Vakhtang, who governed with interruptions from 1711 to 1724, has been called the "Georgian Justinian",[18] and his codification efforts labelled "the decisive landmark in the history of Georgian national law".[19] Though his scholarly pursuits ran to other areas, including literature and history, he undoubtedly saw his legal work as one of his greater achievements. His own epitaph written in exile read:[20]

> I hunted over the hills and slew deer and wolves.
> I wrote a book of laws, so that judges should have no cause for dispute.
> Also a commentary on *The Man in the Panther's Skin*, but to other writings I lay no claim.
> The knights of my entourage were known for their courtly manners.
> Finally the world took from me my riches and royal lineage.

Regarding the unhelpful patchwork of Georgian laws, Vakhtang established an advisory commission to collect Georgian laws and foreign laws which had been introduced to the Kingdom. This collection of laws would inform and supplement the ruler's own code, which was itself largely a codification of

16. J. Karst, *Littérature géorgienne chrétienne*, Paris 1934, 113.
17. Suny, *Making of the Georgian Nation*, *op. cit.* note 9, 42.
18. Interview with RR on 4 October 2000.
19. D. Purtseladze, *op. cit.* note 3.
20. D.M. Lang, *Last Years of the Georgian Monarchy, 1658-1832*, New York 1957, 118 (hereinafter *Last Years*).

custom.[21] Vakhtang's laws included comprehensive and nuanced scales of blood money in criminal matters as well as detailed civil provisions. The civil provisions touched matters such as weights and measures, interest rates, the rights and duties of nobles and peasants and land tenure. In terms of adjudication, resort to trial by ordeal was to be made in many cases. This included ordeal by combat, ordeals of torture and the making of a solemn oath on an icon. These practices were of course common in medieval Europe, although their origin in Georgia is likely some combination of indigenous invention and Persian influence, rather than a European import.[22]

Vakhtang's commission also included more recent Georgian laws, including canon law codes from the 16th and 17th centuries. Canon law paralleled the King's laws but was not restricted to spiritual matters. It reinforced the temporal powers of the church, as well as the King, making an affront against one an affront against the other. A number of criminal offences in Vakhtang's code, such as parricide or fratricide, were to be dealt with first under his code (for payment of *wergild*), and then treated under canon law for additional punishment. In the cases of parricide and fratricide the additional punishment was loss of a hand and banishment. The importance of Canon law was reinforced by the fact that the Orthodox Christian Church provided one of the few unifying forces over many of the territorially fractured, historic Georgian lands during this period.

The foreign laws collected by the Commission included the laws of Moses, those of the Byzantine Emperors Leo VI and Constantine Porphyrogenitus, and ancient Armenian law. Georgian scholars, however, have sought to minimize the influence of foreign law, suggesting that its use was extremely limited in actual application.[23] Indeed some have argued that in practice, more cases were decided by customary law than by Vakhtang's code (even though Vakhtang's code was itself built on custom). Part of the reason for this, they suggest, is that customary law had a wider scope than Vakhtang's code in various matters, including relations between nobles, and had significant regional variations.[24]

In addition to Vakhtang's code of laws, a code of administrative procedure was drafted under his authority (known as the *Dasturlamali*), which addressed matters such as the ordering of the royal court and taxation. Significantly, the *Dasturlamali* set out various positions in the royal court, including that of the *Mdivan-Begi*, or chief justice of the Kingdom. Other officials and local tribunals

21. According to a translator of Vakhtang's code "remontant aux origines même de la nation, elle se base sur les anciens us et coutumes, sur le droit primitif de la nation carthvélo-ibérique": Karst, *op. cit.* note 16, 116.
22. *Last Years*, *op. cit.* note 20, 37.
23. See Chapter 1 of M. Kekelia, "Sasamartlo Organizatsia da procesi sakarveloshi Rusettan sheertebis cin", Tbilisi 1970 ("Court organization and process in Georgia before joining Russia").
24. *Ibid.*

were also charged with the administration of justice. Despite the existence of permanent judicial figures, however, justice ultimately remained the prerogative of the king who heard appeals and important cases. Indeed cases decided by the *Mdivan-begi* were often submitted to the King for formal approval.[25] Significant for our purposes is that a recognized role for a defender—*meoxi*—began to appear around this time, although little is known about the role beyond the fact that he was able to make arguments to show an accused's innocence or mitigate punishment.[26] It is uncertain whether all accused persons could avail themselves of the services of a *meoxi* or whether they were only for the aid of the powerful. It is also unknown if the defenders were legally educated. Certainly, there is no evidence to indicate that there was any sort of professional body of defenders.

The system of blood money and the trials by ordeal lasted to the very end of the Georgian monarchy and, in some remote areas, continued well into the Tsarist and possibly Soviet periods. The subject of blood-money is particularly illustrative of Georgian law at the time. It represented a way of avoiding blood revenge—it was a replacement of blood revenge through compensation—rather than an abstract and prescriptive norm. One observer has hypothesized that:[27]

> Its persistence reflects the failure of the Georgian Kings to crush the feudal magnates and set up a centralized judicial and administrative machinery. In most of the countries of Europe, as well as in the Ottoman Empire, aristocratic turbulence had been thoroughly subdued. Kings and judges wielded power capable of striking terror into the most powerful malefactor. In Georgia, however, provincial separatism, with resultant anarchy, was the rule. It was hopeless for Georgian kings to try to assert regular powers of life and death over their unruly vassals. The traditional wergild system, consecrated by centuries of usage, offered the best hope of maintaining a semblance of law and order.

This observer, writing in the 1950s, goes on to argue that presence of blood money at such a late stage "must be regarded as a symptom of retarded political evolution".[28] That may be unduly judgmental, but what is certain is that the continued reliance on these methods is evidence that post-medieval European legal norms or institutions did not penetrate Georgia deeply. Following an early period of Byzantine influence and control (roughly 3rd to 6th century AD), contacts with Europe were largely insignificant for the rest of its pre-Tsarist history.[29] At its highest, Roman law was only one of several influences. As one historian suggests, "justice in the medieval Kingdom of Georgia

25. *Last Years, op. cit.* note 20, 31-32.
26. Javakhashvili, *History of Georgian Law, op. cit.* note 9, v. VII (Part 5, Chapters One and Two).
27. *Last Years, op. cit.* note 20, 38.
28. *Ibid.*
29. Though I do not wish to minimize the significance of these contacts entirely. "Colonies" of Georgian exiled royalty lived in Russia, Georgian church and other scholars visited foreign lands and Catholic missionaries were present in Georgia.

was based on certain primitive customary laws, combined with later accretions borrowed from the legislative principles of Byzantium and the Islamic world".[30] There is no evidence that Roman law ever became culturally embedded in Georgia or that the *idea* of a Roman social or legal order ever became a force in Georgian law-making as it did elsewhere.[31]

Indeed it is difficult to suggest that *any* comprehensive legal order was established during the pre-Tsarist period, let alone a Roman one. Despite attempts by Georgian historians to present essentialized versions of indigenous Georgian law (Vakhtang's code being the prime example), Georgia was a site of constant legal mixing before the Tsarist annexation.

The Tsarist Period

Faced with repeated Ottoman and Persian threats and occupation, Georgian rulers increasingly looked to Christian Russia for protection in the 19th century. Despite a number of broken promises to aid Georgia, Russian interest eventually did firmly turn south in 1801 with the outright incorporation of Kartli-Kakheti into the empire and the abolishment of the Bagrati monarchy. Needless to say, this was not the protectorate for which Georgians had hoped.[32] While it was not until decades later that Russia incorporated all the lands of historic Georgia into the Empire, Russia's dominant position in the Caucasus as a whole was complete by the end of the 1820s.

From the beginning of the incorporation of Georgia, it was decided that the applicable criminal law would be Russian, while civil law would remain Georgian, a fairly common division in other parts of the Russian Empire as well as other colonial contexts.[33] This distinction was reflected in the establishment of different administrative bodies for criminal and civil law, although both bodies were to be headed by Russians. However, conflicting legal norms, cultures and languages, Russian disregard for local custom and the fact that Vakhtang's code existed only in the Georgian language meant that the administration of justice was poorly conducted. In 1810 the nobility of Kartli Kakheti petitioned the Tsar:[34]

30. Allen, *op. cit.* note 9, 275.
31. See J.Q. Whitman, *The Legacy of Roman Law in the German Romantic Era,* Princeton, NJ 1990, an intellectual history which traces how "through law the cultural idea of Rome became a force in German society" (x).
32. The 1783 Treaty of Georgievsk stipulated that the Georgian Kingdom was to retain sovereignty under a Russian protectorate.
33. Even within Russia proper, local peasant customary law was tolerated: R. Beermann, "Pre-revolutionary Russian Peasant Laws" in W.E. Butler, ed., *Russian Law: Historical and Political Perspectives,* Leyden 1977.
34. Quoted by S.F. Jones, "Russian Imperial Administration and the Georgian Nobility: The Georgian Conspiracy of 1832", 65 *Slavonic and East European Review* 1987 No. 1, 53-76, 65.

> [T]he decisions of the courts are defined by Russian laws as by the laws of Vakhtang VI… Such a mixture of laws makes us blind in our own affairs and oppresses us terribly. Therefore, we ask that the judges be chosen by us, who if they follow Vakhtang VI's laws, will not prolong the business from year to year, and will judge in the Georgian language.

Early Russian policy towards Georgia was not consistently disrespectful of local tradition however. Much depended on the attitude of the governor.[35] Some wished to Russianize Georgia as quickly as possible, by administratively recreating the structure of a Russian province, including in justice matters, and by rooting out the peculiarities of the Georgian seigneurial system. The ignorance and contempt of some of the governors towards Georgian customs and laws earned the bitterness of the Georgian nobility. Other governors also had like-minded assimilationist goals but they believed it was necessary to work gradually towards that end by flexibly approaching local customs and structures.

The competing approaches are best contrasted between two governors, Generals Ermolov and Paskevitch who governed from 1816–1827 and 1827–1831 respectively.[36] Ermolov took a conciliatory approach towards the new subjects and attempted to balance Russian imperial norms with Georgian customs. For example, the problem of the inaccessibility of Georgian law to the new Russian administrators was eased somewhat by Ermolov's direction that Vakhtang's code be translated into Russian (a task completed in 1828). To this end he appointed a Russian-educated Georgian jurist as Procurator and charged him with the production of the translation. Paskevitch, on the other hand, was not as willing to adapt, as illustrated by Suny in the following example:[37]

> [Paskevich] ordered the call up of six thousand Georgians in March 1829 to fight the Turks, but not a single Georgian answered the call. Paskevich apparently had not been informed that Georgians traditionally responded only to the request of the *sardarebi*, their own local officials, to form militia. When the Russians requested that the *sardarebi* mobilize the Georgians, a militia was promptly formed. Paskevich interpreted this incident not as a warning to respect local traditions, but as a call to root out such disruptive influences.

During the mid-nineteenth century administration of Viceroy Vorontsov (1845–1854), generally considered to be the most "progressive" colonial administrator, the long-time demand that Georgians be judged by Georgian law was tackled head on. When none of the translated versions of Vakhtang's Code appeared reliable, Vorontsov appointed a commission of Georgian scholars to review the entire code. The commission surprisingly declared that the laws were outdated and recommended that only twenty statutes be kept. These twenty statutes were accepted by Vorontsov and were ultimately written into the Imperial Code, with application only in the Georgian provinces of the

35. See L.H. Rhinelander, "Russia's Imperial Policy—The Administration of the Caucasus in the First Half of the Nineteenth Century", 17 *Canadian Slavonic Papers* 1975, 218-235.
36. Suny, *Making of the Georgian Nation, op. cit.* note 9, 69.
37. *Ibid.*

empire.[38] Vorontsov also successfully co-opted Georgians into the administration of justice. In place of the separate departments of criminal and civil law he instituted provincial courts in every county. Some positions on each court were reserved for locals who were able to speak Russian and displayed knowledge of local traditions. Cases were referred to the courts by county justice boards, which consisted of Russian officials and their Caucasian deputies elected by the local gentry. Decisions were subject to the approval of the provincial governor, who in turn could refer cases up to the Central Council of the Caucasian High Commission—chaired by the Viceroy's Deputy, which served as a common court of appeal for the Caucasus.[39]

Regardless of the governor in power, Georgian social structures and customs were fundamentally affected over the course of the 19th century. This included a transformation of the Georgian nobility into a service gentry on the Russian model, the bureaucratization of the territory and the formal freeing of the peasantry. And there was undoubtedly a transfer of legal norms and institutions from Russia to Georgia. However, it is important to stress two points on this transfer. First, what Russia had did not fully represent European norms. Second, the transfer from Russia to Georgia was incomplete. The result was that by the end of the Tsarist era, Georgia was to a large extent only a formal member of the civil law family. This would have implications for its ability to "revive" the civil law tradition following the collapse of the Soviet Union.

Russia was undoubtedly more influenced by European law than Georgia at the time of the annexation in 1801.[40] But to say that Russia had a European system of law would be only a partial truth, as the transfer of European legal norms to Russia was far from complete. As one scholar puts it:[41]

> Russia had laws but no law. Until the nineteenth century there was virtually no legal scholarship, no theory or philosophy of law. Absent from people's experience was any notion of the rule of law, any sense of the ruler's accountability to the rules.

Despite some European influences, Russian law and Russian lawyering in the 19th century were not ideals to be transferred.[42] The Russian Imperial Code published in 1833 was a confusing tangle, and the courts and lawyers

38. L.H. Rhinelander, "Viceroy Vorontsov's Administration of the Caucasus" in R.G. Suny, ed., *Transcaucasia: Nationalism and Social Change,* Ann Arbor 1996, 97-98.
39. L.H. Rhinelander, *Prince Michael Vorontsov,* Montreal 1990, 158.
40. Almost at the same time as Vakhtang was entrenching traditional Georgian law, Russia's Peter the Great was importing ideas on legal reform along European lines, including a court system modeled on the Swedish.
41. Z. Zile, *Ideas and Forces in Soviet Legal History,* New York 1992, 3.
42. To take the mismanaged development of Russian corporate law as case study, see T.C. Owen, *The Corporation Under Russian Law, 1899-1917,* New York 1991. However, I do not mean to exaggerate the advancement of European law at this point. Indeed England's "Age of Reform" of the courts and the legal profession did not begin until the 1820s. See Part I of B. Abel-Smith & R. Stevens, *Lawyers and the Courts,* London 1967.

that dealt with the laws were largely unprofessional and tainted with corruption. Although by the 15th century Russian law codes made provisions for defenders, lawyering was essentially open to anyone (outside certain classes of individuals including members of the clergy, officials and those who had been criminally convicted) until the Great Reforms of the 1860s. Prior to the reforms, Russian lawyers were known—with some exceptions—for little but their chicanery.[43]

When Russian law was transformed through the Great Reforms launched in 1864, these changes were not fully transferred to Georgia. Among other things, the reforms attempted to create a new professional class of lawyers patterned on European models. One scholar has described the "birth" of the profession in 1864:[44]

> This was a particular birth. The Russian lawyer and the organization of the bar had no roots in the preceeding history of Russian legal institutions. The Russian lawyer's predecessors were not his ancestors. The institution created by the Laws of Nov. 20, 1864 was a complete innovation for Russia.

To be a lawyer after the reforms an individual required a higher legal education, a period of five years pupilage, admission to a Bar Council, registration with a regional appellate court (*Sudebnaya Palata*) and the taking of an oath. The Bar Councils were somewhat independent bodies responsible for the governance of lawyers which could be formed in court districts with sufficient numbers of lawyers willing to take the initiative in their formation. Councils of the Bar were elected in Saint Petersburg and Moscow in 1866 and in Kaharkov in 1874. Then, following an authoritarian "reaction" to the reforms, formation of new councils was blocked by the government until 1904. Lawyers outside the Council system were subject to governance directly by the courts. No Council was ever formed in the Caucasus.[45] Also under the reforms in Russia proper, local self-government was put in place and civil rights were expanded. In Georgia, however, peasant village councils remained directly responsible to the local Russian military commanders and police.[46] Similarly, the jury system, introduced in Russia in 1864, never came to Georgia. Of the Russian institutions that were put in place in Georgia, they were plagued by corrupt Russian officials, often the dregs of the civil service.[47] Following an inspection tour in 1830, Russian Senators Kutaisov and Mechnikov reported

43. See Chapter II on "The Emergence of Russian Lawyers" in S. Kucherov, *Courts, Lawyers and Trials Under the Three Last Tsars*, New York 1953.
44. *Ibid.*, 118-119.
45. B.L. Levin-Stankevitch, "Transfer of Legal Technology and Culture: Law Professionals in Tsarist Russia" in H.D. Balzer, ed., *Russia's Missing Middle Class, The Professions in History*, Armonk, NY 1966, 233.
46. Lang, *A Modern History of Georgia, op. cit.* note 9, 103.
47. *Ibid.*, 112.

that "[l]ocal administrators in Transcaucasia were more the example of breakers of the laws than guardians of the law".[48]

The transfer of ideas and institutions to Georgia was also hampered by the lack of a university in Georgia. Repeated requests for a university in Tbilisi (including those of Viceroy Vorontsov) were denied by a government fearing the establishment of new centres of dissent in the Caucasus.[49] On the other hand, the absence of a university in Georgia forced a growing number of Georgians to study in Russia, where they received more direct exposure to European ideas. Those returning to Georgia in the 1860s during the period of the Great Reforms were known as the *tergdaleulni*, or those who have drank from the Terek, the river dividing Georgia from Russia. Law students were among them.

The most prominent returning jurist was Ilia Chavchavadze, a Georgian from a noble family who was deeply affected by his legal studies in Saint Petersburg (1857–1861). Chavchavadze, who remains one of Georgia's most beloved intellectuals and writers for his poems and essays (he was canonized by the Georgian Orthodox Church in 1987), also held judicial posts within the Russian administration. At first upon his return he pressed reformist positions in fashion in Russia at the time, attacking, for example, the institution of serfdom and supporting local government and judicial reforms. He also deeply opposed capital punishment and addressed it in a short story entitled "On the Gallows", a tale of one man's revulsion at a public execution. Apparently "this abolitionist story was so influential on Georgian public morality that in 1906 the government could find nobody willing to act as a hangman in Tbilisi and terrorists had to be reprieved".[50] Niko Nikoladze was another "returnee" jurist of the 1860s.[51] He promoted a liberal reformist programme which pressed for, among other things, increased local self-government and court reform. What was the impact of these Russian or Western educated returnees? Certainly, their ideas were popularized mainly among the upper classes and small number of "progressives".[52] Nonetheless, Chavchavadze's ideas (which later turned into conservative nationalism[53]) and Nikoladze's liberal reformism dominated the intellectual life of Georgia in the 1860s and 1870s, limited as it may have been.

48. Cited in Suny, *Making of The Georgian Nation*, *op. cit.* note 9, 69.
49. Ultimately a polytechnic for Tbilisi was approved by the Tsar but no concrete moves were made to establish it before WWI: S.D. Kassow, *Students, Professors, and the State in Tsarist Russia*, Berkeley 1989, 366-367.
50. D. Rayfield, *The Literature of Georgia*, Oxford 1994.
51. Unlike Chavchavade, Nikoladze studied in Western Europe. In fact, he was the first Georgian to receive a doctoral degree from a European university (Zurich).
52. Suny, *Making of the Georgian Nation*, *op. cit.* note 9, 134.
53. Chavchavadze gradually turned towards a conservative nostalgic nationalism, arguing that Georgia should be preserved as an agricultural society with a renewed harmony between nobles and serfs. He also led a revival of interest in the Georgian language and literature.

By the time Georgian intellectual life became self-sustaining in the 1890s, with viable journals, full-time writers and a core of academics, there was only a quarter of a century left before the upheavals caused by the 1917 revolutions.[54] Furthermore this intellectual life was limited to a relatively small proportion of the population by literacy (only 20% of Georgians were able to read in 1914)[55] and cultural values. These values engendered mixed views of Russia and the West which have been described as follows:[56]

> The benefits of European civilization were greatly desired by a thin layer of Georgian society, and the road to the West lay through Russia. Generations of Georgian students trekked northward to Russian centers of learning to discover the latest intellectual advances of European thinkers. Enlightenment was the means by which Georgians could escape the past dominated by the Muslim East and join the Christian, modern West. At the same time, contact with Russia and the West worked to awaken consciousness of Georgia's unique culture and fears that Georgia would be overwhelmed by foreign values, by Russian political practice and by the alien economic operations of Armenian middlemen. This ambivalence toward "Europeanization" and Russian rule was a constant feature of Georgian intellectual life through the nineteenth century into the twentieth.

So far this section has focussed on questions of official law (mixed as it was between Russian and traditional Georgian norms) and formal legal institutions. But what of law beyond that enforced by courts? There is every reason to suspect that custom continued to be a primary method of social control and dispute resolution. This is particularly true in some of the more remote areas of Georgia, such as the mountainous Svaneti region, where formal Russian institutions barely penetrated. A number of anthropologists in the nineteenth and early twentieth centuries studied the mountain peoples of the Caucasus who had preserved ancient customs and laws.[57] These studies reveal tremendous regional variations among the various peoples of Georgia and suggest that legislative enactments such as Vakhtang's Code are only partial indicators of law as it was practiced. Take for example the case of selling land. The law of preferential treatment was apparently vigorously enforced by highlanders, so that if a man wished to sell property he first had to offer it to his relatives and secondly to his neighbours.[58] If neither relatives nor neighbours wished to purchase the land he was free to sell it to an outsider. Vakhtang's code did not specify that neighbours must be asked in addition to relatives. For the Svans of Northern Georgia, the land transfer was revocable, even after the sale, if the relatives or neighbours wished to purchase the land back from the outsider. The

54. Rayfield, *op. cit.* note 50, 204.
55. N. Grant, *Soviet Education*, Middlesex 1964, 19.
56. Suny, *Making of the Georgian Nation*, *op. cit.* note 9, 122.
57. See for example A. Grigolia, *Custom and Justice in the Caucasus: The Georgian Highlanders* (Ph.D. Dissertation, University of Pennsylvania, 1939) and D. Morgan, "The Customs of the Ossetes and the light they throw on the Evolution of Law", 20 *Journal of the Royal Asiatic Society* 1888, 364-412 (based on earlier work in Russian).
58. Grigolia, *ibid.*, 163-164.

sale itself was evidenced by certain formalities. Among one group, the deal was not legally binding until the seller and purchaser and at least one witness went to the land and the seller, stamping his foot on the land, said to the purchaser: "May the purchase of this land bring good luck to you."[59]

Traditional law remained a preoccupation of Georgian folklore in the 19th century urban life as well.[60] This is reflected in the works of the poet and ethnologist Vazha-Pshavela, who combined European and Georgian literary style with traditional dialect and stories. For example, in his poem *Host and Guest* (1893) he portrayed a clash between the laws of blood feud and those of hospitality.[61] In the poem a Georgian stumbles upon a Chechen enemy while hunting. The Georgian does not recognize his enemy and invites him home. When the Georgian's fellow villagers identify the Chechen they take him away and kill him. The Georgian hunter and his wife are outraged by the breach of the laws of hospitality and his wife guards the Chechen's body, causing the couple to be condemned by their fellow Christians. This literary nostalgia for traditional law can be contrasted with literary distrust of the official court system. For example, in *The Lawsuit or Semicolon,* a play launched in 1850 by Eristavi, corrupt Russian lawyers gain at the expense of the traditional gentry, in a play ostensibly about star-crossed lovers and their parents.[62]

By the start of the 20th century demands for reform, including judicial reform, broadly engaged Georgian society, including the peasantry in places. A striking example of peasant activism can be seen in Guria.[63] Peasant societies in this region of Western Georgia (somewhat atypical in that it had a relatively high education level and a long history of rebelliousness), along with social democrats from the cities, loudly began to demand reforms. Some of the demands were typical of agrarian popular protest and involved land distribution, relations with landlords and taxes. But the peasants also demanded governance reform along social democratic lines. For example, at one peasant society meeting which was attended by roughly 10,000 members, demands included freedom of speech and assembly, a constituent assembly, free compulsory education and a demand that "court and administrative officials should be responsible to the

59. *Ibid.*
60. A fascinating look at how, and why, Georgian and Russian ethnographers and folklorists told the story of the mountain peoples' customs and laws is A. Jershild, *Orientalism and Empire: North Caucasus Mountain Peoples and the Georgian Frontier 1845–1917*, Montreal 2002. At 8 he writes: "If mountain peoples were often the savage 'other' of the presumably civilized and Europeanized imperial imagination, mountain Georgians for Georgian educated society offered a glimpse into the past of a historically hardy and enduring Georgian identity."
61. See Rayfield, *op. cit.* note 50, 211.
62. *Ibid.*, 170.
63. See S.F. Jones, "Marxism and the Peasant Revolt in the Russian Empire: The Case of the Gurian Republic", 65 *Slavonic and East European Review* 1987 No. 3, 403-434.

people".[64] In 1905, discontent boiled over into armed rebellion. Tsarist officials were removed by peasants and elected representatives from among their own established what has been called the "Gurian Republic". Nicholas Marr, a half-Scot, half-Georgian linguist, travelling through Guria remarked on "the intense public life in the villages":[65]

> Meeting follows meeting, and you would be surprised how the peasants burdened by their work in the fields, hurrying everywhere, take active part in the debates, sitting for long hours, sometimes days, at meetings. Today the court, tomorrow discussion of the principal social questions with a well known travelling speaker, the day after tomorrow decisions about local affairs: schools, roads, land, etc., etc....

Another traveller described justice as handed down by the peasant societies, which also acted as "People's Courts" (a term unrelated to the later Soviet courts of the same name):[66]

> When a crime is committed, the whole community...co-operates in helping to apprehend the criminal, and brigandage and robbery have greatly decreased in consequence...the *Narodnyi sud* (People's Court) inquires into the private morals of the inhabitants. Any man committing adultery...is liable to prosecution and punishment...The usual penalty is a boycott.

This penalty was greatly feared as it involved complete social exclusion from the community. During the period of the People's Courts, not a single case was taken before the official courts. Apparently the Tsar's Viceroy considered legalizing the courts since they administer "justice far more honestly and efficiently than do the state tribunals".[67]

By February 1917, significant parts of both the urban and rural populations were politicized, market relations and new forms of communications had transformed the country, Georgian lands were unified, and modern European ideas of governance and law had partially been transferred to national elites. Georgia was arguably ready for statehood,[68] a proposition which was to be tested during a period of revolution and brief independence.

Menshevik Georgia (1918–1921)

Although brief, the independence period is revealing. It demonstrates concretely that at least a certain sector of society had internalized European norms transferred to Georgia. These values were certainly not shared by all Georgians, however, and the means to implement them were often absent.

The months following the February revolution were chaotic. The Special Transcaucasian Committee, set up by the Provisional Government in Petrograd to govern the Transcaucasus, was stillborn. Similarly the successor Transcauca-

64. *Ibid.*, 426.
65. Cited in Suny, *Making of the Georgian Nation, op. cit.* note 9, 166.
66. Cited in Jones, *op. cit.* note 63, 422.
67. *Ibid.*, 422.
68. Suny, *Making of the Georgian Nation, op. cit.* note 9, 180-181.

sian Republic containing Georgia, Armenia and Azerbaijan (roughly patched together in the wake of the Bolsheviks' October Revolution) was short-lived and Georgia declared its independence on 26 May 1918. The new provisional government of the Georgian Democratic Republic was primarily Menshevik, which handily took the majority of seats in the Parliament, directly elected in February 1919.[69] The Mensheviks under the leadership of Noi Zhordania believed Georgia would gradually evolve towards a Marxist state but meanwhile governed in what was essentially a social democratic manner. Remarkably, the Declaration of Independence contained no references to the class struggle which was ultimately central to the Menshevik programme. Stephen Jones explains the apparent contradiction as follows:[70]

> The Declaration, with its emphasis on Georgia's sovereign rights and her long history of independence, revealed a growing concern for the 'nation' rather than for class. A determination to enter the 'European Family of Nations' became the driving force in the new government's foreign policy. This was in line with the ideas long expressed by Georgian Menshevism. This was a bourgeois revolution, where national development, at least in Georgia's case, was a prerequisite of socialism. They had to follow the European path of development; no other road was possible. They had to pass through all the stages set down by Marx including that of bourgeois constitutionalism.

Preoccupied with foreign relations, and indeed survival, the Menshevik government did manage to lay out a progressive programme, although circumstances meant that many goals would never be fully implemented.

The Menshevik programme included laws on an eight-hour day, child labour and trade union rights (although this was combined with strict labour discipline as the economy worsened). In the judicial sphere, the Menshevik position was quite different from that of Bolshevik Russia. In contrast to the latter's view of law as a tool of the bourgeoisie to be subordinated to the workers' interests, the Mensheviks had a bourgeois view of law. The Menshevik-drafted Constitution expressed ideals on judicial independence, limits on state power and equality before the law, although it was formally adopted only three days before the Red Army occupied Tbilisi.[71] Other legal reforms included setting up a Council of Advocates to supervise the profession, the use of juries (which could decide both guilt and sentence), the election of lower level judges and the establishment of Georgian as the language of the courts.[72] The pride of the

69. Of the 130 parliamentary seats the Mensheviks took 109. Thirteen of the deputies were jurists. See R. MacDonald, "La Répubique Géorgienne Socialiste" in *L'Internationale Socialiste et la Géorgie*, Paris 1921, 18.
70. S.F. Jones, *Georgian Social Democracy 1892-1921: In Opposition and Power* (unpublished Ph.D. dissertation, University of London, 1984), 389. Jones' thesis is the key source for the brief period of Georgian independence.
71. *Ibid.*, 506.
72. *Ibid.*, 506-508 and A. Inghels, "Une République Sociale à l'Oeuvre" in *L'Internationale Socialiste et la Géorgie*, Paris 1921, 140-142.

justice sector reforms was the creation of a Senate in July 1919. Its members, who were to be elected by Parliament, would "supervise the observance and defence of laws and to ensure strict adherence to them by all organizations, persons, and local government organs".[73] This legal watchdog was to act as a final appellate court but also had the power to quash any government decision contrary to law and to deal with complaints against courts.

Despite the expressed liberal values of the government, however, the ideals were often not reflected in practice. Rule by decree, military courts and revolutionary tribunals continued. Russian imperial laws remained in force in civil and criminal matters, and Russian officials and the Russian language dominated in the courts. The Senate itself appears to have been largely inactive. There was recognition of these failings even from within the government, as Jones describes:[74]

> The Minister of Justice complained that while the anarchy in administration continued, effective reform was impossible, and that proper training, better wages and a strong executive arm to carry out court decisions was necessary, otherwise many of the reforms would remain on paper.

As we will see in the next chapter, these complaints resonate in contemporary independent Georgia. Certainly the fledgling republic did not last long enough to nurture an indigenized European-style legal system or profession.

Soviet Period

Independence would last until 25 February 1921 when the Red Army, together with Georgian Bolsheviks, occupied the country and the Sovietization process began. Georgia became a formal member, along with Armenia and Azerbaijan, of the Transcaucasian Federative Socialist Soviet Republic (although the Republican legal institutions were never fully implemented).[75] The Transcaucasian Federation was a constituent member, along with the Russian, Belorussian and Ukrainian Soviet Republics, of the USSR formed in 1922. In 1936 the Transcaucasian Federation was dissolved and Georgia, Armenia and Azerbaijan each became full constituent republics of the USSR. While some regional peculiarities appear in Soviet Georgian legislation, the Republic's constitutions and laws were overwhelmingly consistent with Union and Russian Federation norms.[76] This uniformity in legislation extended to legal institutions and

73. Law on the establishment of Georgian Senate regulations as cited in Jones, *ibid.*, 507.
74. *Ibid.*, 508.
75. For example, a planned Supreme Court of the Transcaucasian Federation was never created: J.N. Hazard, *Settling Disputes in Soviet Society*, New York 1960, 209.
76. The similarity in the 1978 constitutional texts of Russia and Georgia—with the Georgian document eschewing even cosmetic differences made in many other Republican Constitutions—can be seen by comparing texts in F.J.M. Feldbrugge, *The Constitutions of the USSR and the Union Republics: Analysis Texts and Reports*, Alphen aan den Rijn, NL 1979.

the organization of the legal profession. This section will first briefly outline the historical development of Soviet law and lawyering. While there are some Georgian "twists" here, the commonality is clear. The second part of this section will then turn to a more fundamental point of Georgian departure from the Union norm—namely the use of informal law.

Soviet Law and Lawyering (with Georgian Twists)[77]

The Bolsheviks saw Tsarist era lawyers, and indeed lawyering itself, as a bourgeois threat to the communist programme. Following the October Revolution the Imperial Russian Bar was quickly dissolved, and anyone with the correct political consciousness was permitted to act as a representative for accused persons. Some advocates who had practiced before the revolution were deprived of the right to practice or restricted in their practice and some were persecuted as enemies of the people. Others, however, managed to maintain the semblance of a practice and even professional autonomy. Georgia of course missed the earliest years of Bolshevik rule, but in April 1921, promptly after the Soviet takeover, the Georgian Bar was dissolved. For a year and a half there was an institutional void but new direction came in 1922 under the dictates of the New Economic Policy (NEP)—Lenin's attempt to kick-start the failed economy by permitting some forms of capitalist activity. Lawyering as an occupation was revived and semi-autonomous colleges of defenders were opened in 1922—including in Georgia. The sworn advocates from the Tsarist era continued to represent clients in some criminal cases (albeit under restraints, including lack of access to clients and mistreatment from the court) and found new sites of employment in enterprises or in state-run legal consultation bureaus (LCBs). At the same time, however, communists began infiltrating the colleges, and party and government officials frequently interfered in college decisions.

The reprieve of the NEP was short-lived, however, with the Stalinization of the Bar beginning in the late 1920s and culminating in the 1939 "Statute on the Advokatura". The 1939 statute substituted "Colleges of Defenders" with "Colleges of Advocates" and forced all advocates into Legal Consultation Bureaus. The managers of the LCBs were to answer directly to the Colleges' presidiums. The presidiums themselves answered to the Commissariat of Justice. Fees for legal services were to be paid to the LCBs rather than to the advocates, who began to resemble state employees. During this time advocates were under strong pressure to join the Communist Party, and a number of advocates throughout the USSR were purged. Formal and informal barriers to lawyers' professional work, including work assessment methods which led to "vanishing acquittals" in criminal cases, also hampered lawyers' work.[78] Paradoxically, during this period, the measures which increased state authority also served to

77. For the general narrative of the development of the Soviet Bar, I rely on Huskey (see references *op. cit.* chap. 1, notes 32-33).

institutionalize the *advokatura*; although stripped of much of their autonomy it became clear during the Stalin years that lawyers were to be a permanent feature of socialist justice. This was reflected not only in a comprehensive legislative regime governing legal practice, but in the re-establishment (and in Georgia the establishment) of legal education at the university level.[79]

During the Khruschev era, with the emphasis on "socialist legality", advocates gained new respectability. The informal norms which led to low acquittal rates continued (and indeed would continue into the late-Soviet period), but debate over the importance of a defence was revived and advocates were formally given more scope for their activities. Changes in the 1958 criminal procedure codes, for example, allowed advocates to represent persons under a disability from the beginning of a preliminary inquiry. Legal scholarship was also promoted through a uniform five-year curriculum, legal publishing and a push towards "scientific" research. In Georgia this involved the establishment of a Department of State and Law in 1958 in the Economics Institute of the Academy of Sciences.[80] Some structural reforms allowing advocates a greater role in the criminal process were made, although the process was in law and in fact still weighted heavily in favour of investigators and prosecutors.

Despite continuing legislative impediments to their work—and state and party control over the colleges—the *advokatura* was further institutionalized during the Brezhnev era. The right to a defence was enshrined in the 1977 USSR Constitution and a 1979 Union law on the *advokatura* (followed by similar Republican versions) set down the Bar's place in the legal system. Among other things, the law strengthened the autonomy of the colleges (although they still could not decide on important matters of internal policy) and permitted representation by advocates before administrative tribunals. Georgian legal science flourished during this period, and numerous texts were published in all areas of contemporary law and on Georgian legal history.[81] Advocates' writings also reveal increased self-assuredness during this period. In a 1974 book celebrating fifty years of advocacy in Georgia, the author traces the progressive evolution

78. To recap from Chapter One, acquittals became increasingly unacceptable during the Stalin period; generally the most lawyers could hope for was to mitigate their client's sentence, have lesser charges substituted or have the case returned for preliminary investigation (Solomon, *op. cit.* chap. 1, note 30).

79. As of 1935 higher legal education was provided at Law Faculties in Tbilisi, Yerevan and Baku and Law Institutes in Moscow, Leningrad, Saratov, Kazan, Sverdlovsk, Minsk, Kharkov and Tashkent: S. Kucherov, "Legal education" in F.J.M. Feldbrugge, G.P. van den Berg and W.B. Simons, eds., *Encyclopedia of Soviet Law*, No. 28 *Law in Eastern Europe*, (F.J.M. Feldbrugge, ed.), Dordrecht 1985, 451.

80. The Department became a separate institute in 1990. See the web site of the Institute at www.acnet.ge/stlaw.htm.

81. See V. Makashvili and D. Purtsiladze, *Iuridicheskaia nauka v Akademii Nauk Gruzinskoi SSR*, Tbilisi 1983 ("Legal Science at the Georgian SSR Academy of Sciences").

of institutional arrangements for lawyers in the Soviet Union generally and in Georgia and points out the importance of the Republic's 500 advocates for the legal system.[82] He also highlights some of the "great men" of the Georgian Bar—a literary tradition prominent among professions in the West and one which serves to "reinforce their professional and social identity".[83]

Tellingly, a number of the "great men" of the Georgian Bar had gone on to become high ranking members of the government or had entered the procuracy or judiciary. Despite institutional improvements and stability during the Brezhnev era, advocates continued to be the "poor cousins" to prosecutors and judges. In Georgia at least, the best and most connected law students went into the procuracy, the *KGB* or the somewhat less prestigious judiciary.[84] The remainder went into the *advokatura* or into enterprises as jurisconsults. Indeed prosecutors or judges were sometimes sent to work as advocates as punishment for poor work performance.[85] In terms of prestige, advocates also ranked lower than prosecutors and judges in the eyes of the public throughout the Soviet Union.[86] And it was perceived by many that advocates in the Caucasus (along with Central Asia) were the worst in the Union in terms of legal ability.[87] If an accused or his/her family could, they sometimes sought to obtain a lawyer from Moscow rather than rely on local talent.[88] In fairness, however, Caucasian advocates were trained in much the same manner as their counterparts in other republics (the failings of Soviet legal education generally—including the lack of emphasis on critical thinking—are addressed in Chapter 4).

82. M. Komaxidze, *Sabchota Advokaturis Ormotsdaati Tseli*, Tbilisi 1974 ("Fifty Years of Soviet Advocacy"). There appears to have been a trend to write such histories in the period 1972–1975 in the non-Russian Republics (see the references in Huskey, *Russian Lawyers, op. cit.* chap. 1, note 32 , 7, ft. 3).
83. V. Masciotra, "Quebec Legal Historiography, 1760-1900", 32 *McGill Law Journal* 1987 No. 3, 712-732, 724.
84. This may represent a departure from the pattern in large Soviet Russian cities where the best students from day faculties went into government work or the defence bar, while the procuracy and judiciary admitted more graduates of the night faculties and correspondence schools.
85. For an example of this type of demotion see Solomon, *op. cit.* chap. 1, note 30, 537.
86. A nuanced account of relative prestige among legal occupations is D.D. Barry and H.J. Berman, "The Soviet Legal Profession", 82 *Harvard Law Review* 1968 No. 1, 1-41. On the prestige of advocates in the late Soviet period see P.H. Solomon, Jr., "The Role of Defence Counsel in the USSR: The Politics of Judicial Reform Under Gorbachev", 31 *Criminal Law Quarterly* 1989, 76.
87. Interview with I on 18 May 1999. Shelley's comments are also telling: "In the Transcaucasus and Central Asia there is wider latitude [than in Moscow, Leningrad, Kiev and the Baltics] for corruption in arbitration, because the level of legal competence is generally lower. Arbitrators in the republics of these areas can take gifts with impunity because even a poorly constructed decision does not arouse suspicion." (Shelley, *Lawyers in Soviet Work Life, op. cit.* chap. 1, note 34, 94.)
88. Interview with I, *ibid.*

In addition to a reputation for shoddy lawyering, Georgian advocates, along with prosecutors and judges, were widely seen to be corrupt. Numerous interviewees suggested that the common view of Georgian lawyers was that they were "middlemen" to bribe the judge or prosecutor. Corruption among legal actors was far from unknown in the RSFSR, but it may have occurred with greater frequency in Georgia and other "Southern republics".[89] Indeed corruption in the legal system in Soviet Georgia was openly publicized in campaigns against the evil. For example, shortly after taking office in 1979 the new Georgian Prosecutor removed seven district prosecutors, four of their assistants and two investigators for "unprincipled" behaviour.[90] One former Russian advocate who frequently visited Georgia said he "[c]eased to be amazed when a client said that he needed a lawyer who was considered a specialist on such-and-such a judge. I realized he was talking about a lawyer through whom the judge in question would accept a bribe without fear."[91] Official reports occasionally criticized Georgia's justice organs, including the courts, for a lack of professionalism. One stinging criticism was that "the Leninist principle of the inevitability of punishment for crimes committed or for violations of public order and socialist legality has still not been excluded once and for all".[92] Corruption and cronyism at the single law faculty was also rampant, with bribes given for entrance as well as grades.[93]

While Georgia never experienced the degree of ethnic or religious discrimination that has been documented in the Soviet Russian legal professions,[94] there was an ethnic dimension to legal careers. The Faculty of Law at Tbilisi State University—the only one in the Republic—had a disproportionately low number of ethnic minorities.[95] This was reflective of the University as a whole (which was known as a seat of nationalist sentiment) and the general trend in the 1960s and 1970s towards the "Georgianization" of higher education. In 1969-1970, Georgians, who comprised roughly 67% of the Republic's population, accounted for 82.6% of the students in higher education. By contrast, Armenians, with 9.7% of the population, accounted for 3.6% of higher education students.[96] After law school, entry into the procuracy and judiciary were

89. *Ibid.*, and see Solomon, *op. cit.* chap. 1, note 30, 548 and 553 (n.76).
90. Huskey, "Specialists in the Soviet Communist Party", *op. cit.* chap. 1, note 37, 550. The pattern appears similar in Azerbaijan and Armenia (Huskey, 551).
91. K.M. Simis, *USSR: The Corrupt Society*, New York 1982, 114. Simis also details corruption in the other republics of the USSR.
92. Cited in E. Scheetz, "Criticsm of the Administrative Organs in Georgia", *Radio Liberty* 60/77, 14 March 1977.
93. Interview with PP on 11 September 1998.
94. On anti-Semitism in the Russian professions see the references in Shelley, *Lawyers in Soviet Work Life, op. cit.* chap. 1, note 34.
95. L. Alexeyeva, *Soviet Dissent,* trans. C. Pearce and J. Glad, Middleton, CT 1985, 107.
96. R.B. Dobson, "Georgia and the Georgians" in Z. Katz, ed., *Handbook of Major Soviet Nationalities*, New York 1975, 177.

understood to be for the titular nationality, namely ethnic Georgians.[97] Armenians, Jews, Russians and others had more chances as advocates or jurisconsults. Non-Georgian lawyers were also at a linguistic disadvantage outside of areas where their ethnic group formed the majority. Although the use of Russian in official and legal work was widespread, Georgian remained predominant.[98]

Other peculiarities among Georgian advocates were the high numbers of advocates relative to the republic's population and the low numbers of females. In 1987 Georgia had one advocate per 6,000 people, compared to one advocate per 13,000 for the Union average.[99] This higher number of lawyers, however, seems to be related more to corruption and cronyism in the ranks of the "advocate producers", the Law Faculty and the Collegium, than to a higher demand for legal services compared with the other Republics.[100] Many interviewees were clear on the need for bribe passing or connections for entrance to these two institutions, although there were exceptions made for the brightest students. Similarly, it has been suggested that corruption at the Medical Faculty may account for the fact that Georgia had the highest number of doctors per capita in the world, at least according to Soviet statistics.[101]

Not surprisingly, the Georgian legal professions (along with their Armenian and Azerbaijani counterparts) had the lowest proportion of women in the Union.[102] According to Soviet statistics, 16% of the total number of judges in Georgia were women in 1975. This compares with the figure of 36.9% in Russia. That same year, 27.8% of advocates in Georgia were women compared to 44.5% in Russia and only 7.5% of procurators were women compared with

97. Interview with I, *op. cit.* note 87.
98. Shelley, *Lawyers in Soviet Work Life, op. cit.* chap. 1, note 34, 41.
99. W.E. Butler, *Soviet Law*, London 1988, 83. This compares with a ratio of one lawyer for 380 persons in the US at roughly the same time (L.M. Friedman, "Lawyers in Cross-Cultural Perspective" in Abel & Lewis, eds., *Lawyers in Society* (v. 3), *op. cit.* chap. 1, note 10, 5, though on the conceptual difficulties of comparing the size of professions see Friedman, 5-6).
100. The question of "demand for law" is not easily determined by statistics of litigiousness. Nonetheless these statistics may provide one tool to measure demand. Soviet figures reveal, for example, that in 1979 there were 1.5 divorce suits per 1,000 inhabitants in Georgia, compared to 4.2 suits per 1,000 inhabitants in Russia and a Union average of 3.6 per 1,000 inhabitants. In other types of civil cases, Georgia appears closer to the Union average. See Table 35 and other statistics in Appendix II of G.P. van den Berg, *The Soviet System of Justice: Figures and Policy*, Dordrecht 1985.
101. See Suny, *Making of the Georgian Nation, op. cit.* note 9, 307.
102. It would be simplistic to say that Georgia was (or is) a patriarchal society as, for example, motherhood is highly esteemed. But with respect to work life outside of the home (and outside of the education and health sectors), it is uncontroversial to say that Georgia is traditionally male-dominated. See UNDP, *Human Development Report: Georgia 1997*, Tbilisi, 8 and UNDP, *Human Development Report: Georgia 1998*, Tbilisi, 73. The following statistics are from "Female Lawyers", 16 *Soviet Law and Government* 1977 No. 2, 87-95, reprinting data prepared by the USSR Ministry of Justice.

27.3% in Russia. In addition to demonstrating the overall low numbers of women in the legal professions, the statistics reveal comparatively more room for careers for women in the *advokatura* than in the more prestigious and powerful procuracy and judiciary.

Beyond Soviet Law and Lawyering: Georgian Non-State Law

During the Soviet period, Georgia was perceived to be one of the most corrupt Republics in the Union, if not the most corrupt. This fact was known to observers in the West through reports from émigrés, as well as from monitoring the Soviet media, which publicized the corruption problem in Georgia and the other "Southern republics". Writing in 1977, one Western observer stated that "in form this activity may not differ greatly from what takes place in other regions, but in Georgia it seems to have been carried out on an unparalleled scale and with unrivalled scope and daring".[103] Not only was the second economy known to be large, but the connection between the second economy and the Communist Party in Georgia was also clear; the same observer wrote that "eyewitnesses report significant control by the largest underground entrepreneurs over major party appointments within the republic".[104] In a reaction to the extent of corruption (and resultant poor economic performance), Moscow replaced the long-time First Secretary of the Georgian Communist Party, Vasili Mzhavanadze in 1972 with the forty-four-year-old Minister of Internal Affairs, Eduard Shevardnadze. The "new broom" led a number of purges and anti-corruption drives, including some high profile prosecutions. However, as the next Chapter will address, Shevardnadze's efforts were as unsuccessful then as they are today.

There are various explanations as to why Georgia was so corrupt. Some have suggested that a partial answer lies in Georgia's climatic advantage in the production of fruit, especially citrus where the Republic had a monopoly.[105] Peasants would only receive a fraction of the worth of the oranges through official channels and so the temptation was great to market the fruit in the other economy. Presumably, however, every republic had its comparative advantage which it could exploit. A more convincing explanation is to be found in the political relationship between Tbilisi and Moscow. In consistently nationalistic Georgia, party leaders rested their legitimacy in part on the ability to "deliver"

103. G. Grossman, "The 'Second Economy' of the USSR", 26 *Problems of Communism* 1977 No. 5, 24-40, 35.
104. *Ibid.*
105. *Ibid.* This explanation seems especially weak in light of the persistence of Georgian black marketeering following the collapse of the country's fruit industry in the 1990s (see A. Lotuashvili, "The Food Processing Sector in Georgia" (US Embassy to Georgia, 2001), available online at http://www.bisnis.doc.gov/bisnis/country/010322gaagribus.htm).

benefits from Moscow and shield Georgians from Moscow's interference.[106] Apparently some legal decision-makers had a similar view, favouring Georgian enterprises in arbitration over their Slavic counterparts.[107] But other republics also had strong nationalist tendencies and it has been well-documented that the creation of a "spoils system" for the elite of the titular nationalities was a Union-wide phenomenon.[108] It seems to me that the explanation for the Georgian difference is to be found largely in culture.

In a 1983 study, researchers attempted to describe the cultural forces supporting the second economy, through interviews with Georgian Jewish émigrés.[109] Mars and Altman portrayed Georgian men (the primary movers of the second economy) as bound by family ties and personal networks. Concepts of honour and shame, trust, obligation, and competitiveness (with those outside of the family or network) govern these relationships. A loss of trust can lead to social as well as economic exclusion.[110] A Georgian man is constantly on show, even on social occasions such as the ritualized feast, during which he must develop good personal relationships. Business follows the personal relationships. The researchers contrasted these values with formal Soviet values.[111] For example, the Soviet value of separation of private life from work life is contrasted with the Georgian fusion of work life and private life. Furthermore, since for Georgians "private concerns are dominant, work roles and resources are therefore subordinate to private concerns".[112] Whereas in the formal Soviet system recruitment for employment should be based on universalist and meritocratic ideals, in Georgia "nepotism [is] a moral duty". With respect to official roles, Mars and Altman write:[113]

106. Suny, *Making of the Georgian Nation*, *op. cit.* note 9, 304.

107. Shelley, *Lawyers in Soviet Work Life*, *op. cit.* chap. 1, note 34 , 70-71, writes that "[a]lthough many lawyers prepared with extra care for arbitration in these highly nationalistic republics [of Transcaucasia and Central Asia], even where evidence overwhelmingly favored the non-Asian organizations there was little chance that Slavic and Baltic lawyers would win their cases".

108. V. Zaslavsky, "Success and collapse: the traditional Soviet nationality policy" in I. Bremmer and R. Taras, eds., *Nations and Politics in the Soviet Successor States*, Cambridge 1993, 34-38.

109. Mars & Altman, *op. cit.* chap. 1, note 23.

110. Simis, *op. cit.* note 91, 155 reports that murder was also the punishment for some unfulfilled contracts.

111. There is no doubt that the "Soviet man" was in many ways a fiction, and it has been well-documented that "private reciprocity systems" were used to cope with the inefficiencies of the command economy throughout the Soviet Union (see for example, J.R. Millar, "The Little Deal: Brezhnev's Contribution to Acquisitive Socialism" in T.L. Thompson and R. Sheldon, *Soviet Society and Culture*, Boulder 1988). Nonetheless it appears that private reciprocity—especially that focussed on kinship—was more culturally engrained in Georgia than in the European Republics.

112. Mars & Altman, *op. cit.* chap. 1, note 23, 555.

113. *Ibid.*, 549.

> In this kind of 'honour and shame' society where peer approval is so important, hierarchical official relations are resented and resisted and are the source of perpetual conflict. The individual Georgian sees honour accruing to families and sees families linked by a common honour. In such a context there is little role for the state or for any centrally organized hierarchy. Relationships need always to be personalized and abstraction has no place.

The Mars and Altman study is not without its difficulties. First, it tends to portray a reified version of Georgian cultural attitudes (Georgians *are*...) which does not account for the diversity of the Georgian experience. Secondly, by nature of the fact that their informants are Georgian Jews, they fail to capture the dynamic relationship between ethnic Georgian elites involved in both the state and the second economy. Their view needs to be supplemented by linking the second economy to the semi-official brand of Georgian nationalism which tolerated a "spoils system" for well-connected ethnic Georgians. Despite these flaws, the Mars & Altman study does provide valuable insight into some dominant tendencies in unofficial business culture.

Another study has shown how Soviet laws were avoided or perverted in a rural context. In fact, in her study of rural Georgian families, Tamara Dragadze suggests that villagers used Soviet laws to *reinforce* Georgian customs and family patterns:[114]

> [R]ather than hasten the end of tight rural communities, the state control has fostered their persistence. These state controls have reinforced the traditional range of informal controls used by villagers because people are forced to rely on their family, kin and sense of Georgianess.

For example, each household was entitled to own a small number of livestock "privately". In order to increase the number of livestock, a member of the family, usually the eldest son, would be declared a separate household, and half-hearted attempts to construct a house on the surrounding land might be made. The reality, however, is that the household remained whole and the declaration was essentially a fiction.[115] To take another example, under Soviet law it was residence rather than kinship which was the main determinant of inheritance. However, if the sole occupant of the house was an elderly person, family members who did not live in the house were nonetheless registered to ensure traditional inheritance of a house which may have been in the family for generations.[116] Often the falsely declared relatives may have moved to towns and cities. Through the manipulation of inheritance rules, the rural—and regional—ties of urbanized Georgians were reinforced.

If Georgian peculiarities are evident in how unofficial business was conducted or laws avoided, they are also evident in how disputes were resolved. The first method of dispute resolution was direct person-to-person, or family-to-

114. T. Dragadze, *Rural Families in Soviet Georgia*, London 1988.

115. *Ibid.*, 36-37.

116. *Ibid.*, 33-34.

family negotiation. Failing that, respected persons in the community (generally known to both parties) might be asked to mediate. In mountainous areas such as Svaneti, where resort to the official court system was especially rare, these persons were village headmen or elders. In underworld cases, "thieves in law" were often used. It is estimated that in Soviet times roughly 20,000 such individuals were in operation throughout Georgia.[117] These were respected figures in the second economy or former prisoners who had gained the respect of fellow prisoners and prison authorities by mediating disputes in prison. They would mediate disputes between the underworld and authorities, or between parties in the second economy or in criminal cases in their communities.[118] Some of the thieves also ideologically grounded themselves in opposition to the state and held themselves out as "symbols of freedom and independence".[119] Finally, it should be noted that self-help was also used and, in rare cases, murder was the punishment for unfulfilled contracts.[120] There is little role for the lawyer in this sort of contract enforcement.

In sum, in addition to the marginalization of lawyers by Soviet legalism, a legal pluralist perspective suggests that Georgian lawyers' roles were limited by the pervasiveness of non-state law.[121]

Perestroika

Gorbachev's early rule, which began in 1985, was characterized by attempts to bring in limited reforms and end the Soviet Union's long economic decline. Wholesale or systematic change had not been originally contemplated.[122] But reform soon took on a life of its own and core Soviet values and practices began to be questioned. Dissidents, who had previously been of marginal influence, began to have mass followings and civic groups began to appear with programmes contrary, at least by implication, to the continued existence of the regime. In a number of republics the dissident movement had a decidedly nationalist character. This was particularly true of Georgia, where the nationalist—although not outright separatist—movement had started much earlier than in other parts of the Soviet Union.[123]

117. "Georgia Judicial Assessment" *op. cit.* chap. 1, note 53, 24.
118. *Ibid.*
119. G. Glonti, "Problems Associated with Organized Crime in Georgia", 9 (undated, online on the website of the Institute of Legal Reforms (Center to Study Organized Crime, Corruption and Legal Reforms in Georgia): www.geo.net.ge/reform/eng/publication).
120. Simis, *op. cit.* note 91, 155.
121. Although trusted jurisconsults were often important to maintain legal form during second economy transactions.
122. For example, it has been documented how Gorbachev's reform of the legislature was intended to reinvigorate communist politics, not to replace the central role of the party: F. Foster-Simons, "The Soviet Legislature: Gorbachev's School of Democracy" in D.D. Barry, ed., *Toward the 'Rule of Law' in Russia?*, Armonk, NY 1992, 115.

In 1986 open opposition to the regime was psychologically boosted by a protest over a proposed direct rail link with Russia over the Caucasus mountains. Protesters claimed that the railway would threaten Georgian heritage sites, the environment and the mountaineers' traditional way of life. Undoubtedly there was also discomfort over the prospect of closer ties to Russia and easier access for non-Georgian migrants into the Republic. Plans for the railway were eventually abandoned, spurring the fledgling dissident movement. In 1986 and 1987 historians and artists began producing works that pushed the limits of official tolerance and new civic groups sprang up. Among the civic groups, nationalist groups formed such as the Ilia Chavchavadze society, rallying under the slogan "Language, Religion, and Fatherland".

In contrast to the historians, philologists and artists, and their protests over heritage and the environment, Georgian advocates played a passive role in the politics of the period. While many Russian advocates, like their Georgian counterparts, prided themselves on their aloofness from politics, some Russian advocates and institutions, including the Presidium of the Moscow City College of Advocates, openly criticized law enforcement organs.[124] Dissent among Georgian jurists was visible only among a small group of law students. At the end of 1987 students at Tbilisi State University complained about the Soviet army's use of land near a monastary as a firing range. After student meetings with government officials proved useless, the student leaders went on a hunger strike, and the army declared in the summer of 1988 that it would suspend use of the land as a firing range. The army reneged on its commitment, however, and in the Autumn of 1988 open student demonstrations took place at Tbilisi State University.[125] Apparently at one point, the Rector ordered the Dean of the Law Faculty to use 50 law students to clear the protesters.[126] Law students were seen as the most "politically reliable" and in the past had been used as volunteer guards at the University. Four of the law students went to the Dean, however, to complain about the use of law students to clear the protesters. The students suggested that even if the protesters were incorrect, it was more appropriate to use police than law students to clear them. Despite the law students' modest demands this was considered a radical move that earned them condemnation at a Party meeting at the University later that term. Each of the students would go on to hold key positions in the reform movement of the 1990s (particularly

123. See J. Aves, *Paths to National Independence in Georgia, 1987-1990,* London 1991. It is important to recall, however, that dissidents were not only nationalists. The solidarity of the communist elite has been described as having had "a complex ethnic colouration to it, directed upward against Russians and downward against minority nationalities living in the Republic". (Suny, *Making of the Georgian Nation, op. cit.* note 9, 318.)

124. Jordan, "Russian Advocates", *op. cit.* chap. 1, note 54 , 86.

125. See Aves, *op. cit.* note 123 , 11.

126. Interview with H on 21 September 1999.

in NGOs), and one interviewee reported that this experience was the defining moment for him in terms of protest against the regime.[127] With another of the four protesters he wrote an article critical of a draft law on elections to the Supreme Council. They attempted to have their article published in a journal edited by an esteemed law professor (later appointed to the Republic's Supreme Court), who refused it on the grounds that it was too critical and would harm the law students' careers. They were eventually able to publish the article in a literary magazine.

Despite their low level of political engagement, Georgian advocates and their counterparts in other republics did see an improvement in their professional lives. Advocates gained more autonomy over colleges, as well as increased control over setting fees for some services. The *advokatura*'s prestige was raised, at least in the eyes of Gorbachev's reformers, as their specialized legal knowledge and perceived ability to socialize clients with the new socialist legality were seen as important elements of the reform process. They were to have an expanded role in the justice system, including greater access at the preliminary investigation stage. Finally, they were permitted, or even encouraged, to criticize the faults of the legal system.

Early Independence

In the Gorbachev years regional pressures in Georgia intensified and intersected with the resurgence in Georgian nationalism. In the "autonomous republic" of Abkhazia, ethnic Abkhaz had long expressed a desire to separate from Georgia.[128] By successive waves of ethnic Georgian migration, the Abkhaz felt they had become a minority in their own land and they resented Georgianization policies in areas such as education. Similarly, resentment flared in South Ossetia and other ethnic minority areas. Georgian reaction to the calls from the regions was one of "wounded pride" and resentment. These regional questions and a desire for ethnic Georgian control began to colour the move towards democratization and independence.[129] A flashpoint came when Abkhaz nationalists called for separation from Georgia during a mass rally on 18 March 1989. The separatist rally provoked a sharp outcry from Georgian protesters who quickly took to the streets. The street protests grew, and on 9 April 1989 Soviet troops attacked protesters in Tbilisi with sharpened shovels and tear gas, killing nineteen people, mostly women. Instead of stifling dissent, this act cost the communist regime any remaining legitimacy. The Republic's leadership was immediately

127. *Ibid.*

128. For a look at some of the cultural roots of the conflict in Abkhazia, see the chapters on Transcaucasia in Smith *et al.*, *op. cit.* note 1. S. Goldenberg's *Pride of Small Nations: The Caucasus and Post-Soviet Disorder*, London 1994, is an excellent journalistic account of the conflict.

129. Suny, *Making of the Georgian Nation*, *op. cit.* note 9, 322.

put on the defensive by radicalized nationalist groups with mass followings and independence from the Soviet Union began to appear inevitable.

Under pressure from the opposition, the Supreme Soviet of Georgia called elections for 28 October 1990 and some nationalist blocs competed with the communists. The communists were defeated by the "Round Table" bloc headed by the writer Zviad Gamsakhurdia, a well-known Georgian dissident and human rights activist. Gamsakhurdia, who was elected chairman of the Supreme Soviet, declared his intention to lead Georgia to full independence and to restore Georgian authority over the regions. A referendum was held on 31 March 1991 in which nearly 90% of the voters supported a "restoration" of Georgia's independence. The declaration of independence by the Georgian Parliament (which did not follow the procedure for secession provided for formally by the laws of the USSR, thus adding an element of legal ambiguity to the transition)[130] took place on 9 April 1991, the anniversary of the Tbilisi killings. On 26 May 1991, the seventy-fourth anniversary of the first declaration of Georgian independence, Gamsakhurdia was elected president of the independent republic. Although Gamsakhurdia was known as a human rights crusader, with links to Western human rights non-governmental organizations, his version of rights centred on the collective rights of the ethnic Georgian nation. His rule was marred by hostility towards ethnic minorities (whom he saw as Moscow's stooges and a demographic threat to "pure" Georgia) and violence in South Ossetia and Abkhazia. Increasingly he demonstrated an autocratic streak as he stifled opposition, imposed censorship and attempted to create a cult of personality by portraying himself as a modern day David the Builder—unifier of Georgia and reviver of the Golden Age.[131]

Despite the autocratic nature of Gamsakhurdia's time in office, and his "parliament of amateurs" which shut out many members of the Tbilisi elite,[132] a number of decent laws were enacted. As Stephen Jones puts it: "Gamsaxurdia's legislative programme showed a concern for democratic forms. Within one year he had introduced laws on citizenship, the press, political associations and the judiciary which, on paper at least, laid the groundwork for a genuine 'Rechtstaat'."[133] The reality, however, was that power became increasingly centred on Gamsakhurdia. He ruled by decree and changed or manipulated laws to suit his ends. For example, he extended the permissible detention period without charge from three to nine months in order to continue the detention of one of his political opponents. In a similar vein he made frequent changes to the

130. See F.J.M. Feldbrugge, "Law of the Republic of Georgia", 18 *Review of Central and East European Law* 1992 No. 4, 367-375, 369-370.

131. See Jones, "Populism in Georgia", *op. cit.* note 12.

132. Goldenberg, *Pride of Small Nations, op. cit.* note 128, 97.

133. Jones, "Populism in Georgia", *op. cit.* note 12, 137. And see S.F. Jones, "Georgia: a failed democratic transition" in Bremmer & Taras, *op. cit.* note 108, 301-304.

constitution and disregarded and manipulated the procuracy and judiciary. One positive move came in the area of legal education, with the establishment of a new International Law and Relations Faculty at Tbilisi State University. Eager to establish diplomatic relations with foreign countries as a badge of independence, and distrustful of the communist and corrupt Faculty of Law, Gamsakhurdia ordered the establishment of the new Faculty to train people capable of managing Georgia's foreign relations.[134] However, even this reform should be seen in the light of Gamsakhurdia's decision to strip the university as a whole of its autonomy.

In December 1991 a coup was launched against Gamsakhurdia and for several weeks the President retreated to his bunker in the basement of Parliament while gun battles raged around the building. Gamsakhurdia was eventually toppled by a rough coalition of opposition leaders and paramilitary forces (known as *Mekhedrioni* or horsemen), although he managed to escape and continued to direct his supporters from abroad for a short while before his death. Whether or not politically justifiable, the deposition of his democratically elected government, and its replacement by an unelected alliance of opposition figures in a "military council", added another element of uncertainty to Georgian law.

The Military Council was quickly reconstituted as the State Council and the former Soviet Minister of Foreign Affairs and leader of the Georgian SSR, Eduard Shevardnadze, was invited to take up the chair of the Council. He returned in February 1992 and over the next few years, despite the absence of real constitutional legitimacy,[135] managed to consolidate power and bring some stability to the country. He built a base of support from the fractious coalitions, received a popular mandate from the electorate in October 1992, defeated the "Zviadists" (followers of the deposed Gamsakhurdia) in their power base in Western Georgia and disarmed the paramilitaries on whom he had initially relied. He also ended the separatist wars, although the after effects are still being felt, as the next chapter describes.

During the dark years of the early 1990s, advocates "laid low". As one lawyer interviewed put it, lawyers had no place during this period of "rule of the gun".[136] Some courts continued to operate although they were forced to take orders from paramilitaries or from the "legitimate" authorities. Even if courts were interested in deciding cases according to the law, the legal uncertainty made this difficult. There were several possible sources of law: the 1921 Constitution, the laws of the USSR and the Georgian SSR and the laws of

134. Interview with PP on 9 September 1998.

135. The Georgian Constitution of 1922 was reinstated, but this had largely symbolic importance only. See Feldbrugge, "Law of the Republic of Georgia", *op. cit.* note 130, 372.

136. Interview with H, *op. cit.* note 126.

independent Georgia from before and after the coup against Gamsakhurdia. Following a visit to Tbilisi in 1992, one prominent Sovietologist reported that "the state of Georgia's law at the present time borders on the chaotic", a fact "frankly admitted by almost all Georgian lawyers whom I met during my recent visit".[137] There were also brave attempts to carry on. The head of an LCB located close to Parliament—the centre of the civil war violence—came regularly even in the midst of the fighting to check on the office and as a symbolic refusal to close.[138] On one visit to his workplace, this Second World War veteran was wounded by a stray bullet. Following Shevardnadze's return, some progressive lawyers were quickly engaged by his administration, including young jurists who suddenly found themselves in unexpected positions of importance. They began work in destroyed offices and libraries during a period when the main preoccupation of Georgians not involved in the fighting was simply survival. By late 1993 the worst of the violence abated and Georgia began its slow recovery, including the legal recovery which will be addressed in the next chapter.

This chapter can be summed up as follows. The sources of Georgian law in the centuries prior to the Russian annexation were shifting and mixed, and there were few periods of sustained and centralized indigenous law-making. Georgia's legal heritage from the last two centuries has been that of foreign "occupiers" (Russian and Soviet), often resented by the population and limited in scope by pervasive non-state laws. As a result of these facts, the country regained independence in the early 1990s with few established indigenous or European formal legal traditions or institutions,[139] including traditions and institutions of lawyering.

137. Feldbrugge, "Law of the Republic of Georgia", *op. cit.* note 130, 373.

138. Interview with B on 22 September 2000.

139. I have focussed more on the way law was practiced than on formal Soviet law. For an argument that Soviet "law on the books" was in the civil law family, see J. Quigley, "The Romanist Character of Soviet Law" in F.J.M. Feldbrugge, *The Emancipation of Soviet Law*, Dordrecht 1992. But also see the editor's foreword on the difficulties in categorizing Soviet law in this way.

Chapter 3
The Legal Environment

The purpose of this chapter is to portray the contemporary legal environment within which Georgian lawyers operate. In subsequent chapters I will show how this environment constrains the process of professionalization by limiting the scope of legal practice and shaping the choices of legal actors. The first section addresses the fact that, despite its stability relative to the early 1990s, Georgia remains a partly failed state.[1] It lacks effective government and large parts of the country *de facto* remain outside of the centre's authority. The second section describes the failure to adequately implement the formal legal reform process launched in the mid-1990s and highlights corruption and human rights problems. The third section of this chapter explores the continued use of informal law, which sometimes intersects with formal institutions and at other times appears entirely unconcerned with formal legal values and institutions.

Regionalism

The end to the separatist wars came at a price. Georgia was militarily defeated in Abkhazia and the territory is now *de facto* a separate republic with its own president. Although lacking official international recognition—a primary badge of statehood—Abkhazia continues to receive at least tacit support from Russia. In addition the Abkhaz have ongoing relationships with North Caucasian peoples and loose relations with some other states such as Armenia.[2] Since the cease-fire and the presence of Russian "peacekeepers" and international observers under a UN mandate, there have been skirmishes along the boundary between Abkhaz forces and Georgian irregulars. Tbilisi is adamant that Abkhazia remains Georgian, and a rump ethnic Georgian government still exists. Despite statements from the Georgian government promising Abkhazia a high degree of autonomy, there is little prospect of the territory returning to the Georgian fold in the near future. In South Ossetia, an ambiguous truce was reached and continues to involve the presence of Russian peackeeping troops and ongoing internationally mediated efforts to find a lasting solution. Courts continue to function to a limited extent in both Abkhazia and South Ossetia, applying a mixture of Russian Federation law, "Presidential" decrees, newly locally enacted laws including self-styled constitutions, and some remnants of law from the Georgian era.[3]

1. For a good typology of failed states, see D. Thürer, "The 'failed state' and international law", *International Review of the Red Cross* 1999 No.836, 731-761.
2. See "Tbilisi criticizes Armenian visit to Abkhazia", *RFE/RL Caucasus Report*, Vol. 3(45), 16 November 2000.
3. See for example, Amnesty International's comments on the application of the death penalty in the two territories. "Georgia: Summary of Amnesty International's Concerns" (August 1998, *AI Index* EUR 56/02/98). On 8 April 2001, South Ossetian voters approved a new constitution for the territory (see L. Fuller, "South Ossetian President Strengthens his Position", *RFE/RL Caucasus Report*, Vol. 4(14), 10 April 2001).

A small number of the ethnic Georgian internally displaced persons (IDPs) created by the conflicts have returned to South Ossetia and an insignificant number to Abkhazia. Several former Intourist hotels in Tbilisi and elsewhere remain filled with IDPs from these two breakaway regions. Among them are jurists and law students who have experienced difficulties in finding work in their field or continuing their studies.[4] The IDPs have distinct legal needs (social and housing rights for example) which are inadequately served, although several foreign funded legal advocacy initiatives have been undertaken.[5] Many IDPs are hostile to the Georgian government, which they consider to have inadequately addressed the issue of returning Abkhazia to Georgia or of improving their lot.[6] In addition, the rate of criminal activity among the population is reportedly quite high.[7] The presence of the IDPs in Tbilisi and other regions represents a continuing source of potential instability.

In return for the shaky peace in Abkhazia and South Ossetia, Georgia has had to rely on Moscow's good will not to fan the flames of conflict. This includes continuing membership in the Commonwealth of Independent States (CIS), which both Gamsakhurdia and initially Shevardnadze had refused to join, and tolerating the continued presence of Russian military bases on Georgian soil. One military base in particular has become a "hot" issue in recent years. The base in the predominantly ethnic Armenian area of Akhalkalaki in Southern Georgia is the largest employer in the region. Reports that it may close have caused a great deal of consternation among the local population and have fuelled ethnic Armenian resentment towards the Georgian government.[8] There are fears that Russia continues to use the base—and its possible closure—as a lever in its bid to retain authority in the South Caucasus. Turning North, Russia has repeatedly accused Georgia of tolerating incursions into Chechnya from its territory and has even bombed some villages in what were alleged to be accidents. There are fears that Russia will become even bolder with respect to the Georgian border as US tolerance for Russia's actions in the Caucasus increases following the terrorist acts of 11 September 2001.[9] Russia has also imposed a visa regime on the 500,000 to 700,000 Georgians working in Russia,

4. Interview with C on 16 December 1998.
5. For example, the Horizonti Foundation has provided grants to an NGO operating in Eastern Georgia for the production of a guide to IDPs' rights and the provision of legal consultation.
6. Some IDP spokespersons have called for Shevardnadze's expulsion from Georgia: L. Fuller, "Georgia appears to backtrack on Abkhaz accords", *RFE/RL Caucasus Report*, Vol. 4(5), 2 February 2001.
7. G. Glonti, "Problems Associated with Organized Crime in Georgia", undated article published online by the Institute of Legal Reforms (Tbilisi) at www.geo.net.ge/reform/eng/publication1.html.
8. "Fate of Russia's Akhalkalaki base still unclear", *RFE/RL Caucasus Report*, Vol. 3(45), 16 November 2000.
9. R. Giragosian, "The War on Terrorism: Implications for the Caucasus", *Eurasia Insight* 29 September 2001.

hampering the remittance of hundreds of millions of dollars to their families in Georgia.[10] With some 50% of the population living below the poverty line, this economic pressure can be ill afforded.[11]

Although not as serious as Abkhazia and South Ossetia, it should also be noted that effective control of the Ajara region (on the Black Sea, bordering Turkey) is held by a local strongman, Aslan Abashidze. Elections in that region have been consistently tarnished with heavy irregularities (the rest of the country has also had its share of manipulated elections, but not to this degree) and media and local police forces are tightly controlled by Abashidze. It is unclear if and to what extent the regional government has attempted to manipulate the judiciary, but there have been public skirmishes between the Georgian and Ajaran prosecutors' offices over jurisdictional matters.[12] While Abashidze in the past has made vague threats of separation, more recently he has backed away from any discussion of separation and has attempted to reincarnate himself as a politician on the national stage.

The regionally fractured nature of the country has made the effective implementation of laws difficult in some areas and impossible in others. As we will see in subsequent chapters, regionalism has also hampered the development of nation-wide lawyers' associations and the state-mandated bar structure.

Formal Law and Its Implementation

Constitutional and Judicial Reforms

As indicated in the previous chapter, constitutional uncertainty reflected the political uncertainty of the early independent years. The need for a new constitution was evident early on and drafting began in February 1993 (through a commission headed by Shevardnadze). In the end, a number of drafts were submitted, including one by a group of young lawyers. However, lawyers by no means dominated the drafting process, with scientists and literary figures playing a more important role. After long and bitter debates inside and outside of Parliament, a compromise draft was reached in August 1995.

The 1995 Constitution is fully democratic in form and has ushered in a period of law-making which has left Georgia with a relatively comprehensive series of "laws on the books".[13] The Constitution recognizes a division

10. See "Is Russia seeking to impose an economic stranglehold on Georgia?", *RFE/RL Caucasus Report*, Vol. 3(46), 30 November 2000.
11. *Ibid.*
12. "General Procurator's Office is Taking Over the Case", *Svobodnaia Gruziia* 14 July 1999. In another legal battle, Ajaran authorities refused to release a prisoner who had been pardoned by President Shevardnadze: "Supreme Court Demanded to Release Tengiz Asanidze Immediately", *Sarke Information Agency* 29 December 1999.
13. Constitution of Georgia adopted on 24 August 1995 (hereinafter "Georgian Constitution"). For an English translation see Feldbrugge, "The Constitution of Georgia", *op. cit.* chap. 1, note 49. An English version of the Constitution can also be found at the Georgian Parliament's web site: www.parliament.ge.

of powers between the legislature (Parliament), executive (President) and an independent judiciary. Perhaps as a harbinger of things to come in the sphere of law reform, the American—as well as West European—system of government was looked to as a model. In the end an American-style presidency was selected, with the President being both head of state and chief executive.[14] The Parliament is composed of both constituency and proportional representatives, with the speaker playing a key role (there being no Prime Minister at the time of writing, though one is being actively considered).[15]

The civil and political rights common to Western constitutions are contained in the Georgian Constitution, but there are also a number of Georgian departures from a "boilerplate" democratic constitution informed by Enlightenment ideals.[16] The Georgian Constitution contains economic, social and cultural rights, continuing in the social democratic tradition of the first independent Georgian constitution (as well perhaps as the Soviet heritage). The document lists duties for citizens as well as rights, including an obligation to respect the cultural and environmental heritage of the country.[17] Other Georgian peculiarities include explicit references to Georgia's independent past, traditions and culture, although these are generally of a symbolic nature. For example, the preamble declares that the Constitution is "based upon many centuries of state tradition and the main principles of the 1921 Constitution".[18] Article 9 "recognizes the special importance of the Georgian Orthodox Church in Georgian history" while simultaneously protecting freedom of religion for all. With regard to the importance of motherhood in Georgian culture, Article 36(3) states that "[t]he rights of mothers and children are protected by law". An understandable obsession with territorial integrity is reflected in the Constitution,[19] with the insistence that Abkhazia and South Ossetia remain part of Georgia (albeit to be given distinct status).[20] The outstanding territorial issues also give the Constitution a provisional nature, since some institutions (including a bicameral legislature) are not to be established until the "full restoration of the jurisdiction of Georgia over the entire territory".[21]

14. On the American influence over the form of government chosen see G. Papuashvili, "Presidential systems in post-Soviet Countries: the Example of Georgia", *Georgian Law Review* 1999 No. 3, 3-23.
15. Although the governing Citizens' Union Party has agreed to reintroduce the post of Prime-Minister: L. Fuller, "Papering Over the Cracks in Georgia", *RFE/RL Caucasus Report*, Vol. 4(16), 26 April 2001.
16. Much of the language of the Universal Declaration of Human Rights (Adopted and Proclaimed by UN General Assembly Resolution 217 A(III) of 10 December 1948) appears in the Constitution.
17. Georgian Constitution, *op. cit.* note 13, Art. 34(2).
18. *Ibid.*, Preamble.
19. See for example, *ibid.*, Art. 38(2) which states that "the exercise of minority rights should not oppose the sovereignty, integrity and political independence of Georgia".
20. *Ibid.*, Art. 1.

Of particular importance for our purposes, the Constitution provides for an independent judiciary.[22] The Constitutional Court began operations in September 1996 with nine justices, three appointed by Parliament, three by the President and three by the Supreme Court, for non-renewable ten-year terms.[23] Of the nine original judges, all worked as jurists during Soviet times, many having done graduate studies in Moscow.[24] This is in fact not surprising given that Georgia has never gone through a process of ridding top state positions of former communists (lustration). None of the judges are career advocates or judges, although prosecutors and legal academics are represented on the bench. There is one woman on the bench. The judges are assisted by competent young lawyers,[25] and the court is adequately staffed by administrative assistants. The court occupies a historic and impressive building on Rustaveli Avenue and the physical state of the Court is good. Security is very tight. These conditions are in marked contrast to those of the lower courts.

The 13 June 1997 Law on the Judiciary establishes the judicial framework within which most court lawyers operate. It is a comprehensive road map for reform with three main planks: i) unifying and rationalizing the court system; ii) ending the authority of the Ministry of Justice over the courts; and, iii) professionalizing the judiciary. This reform was clearly a priority for the reformers in government and the international community. A June 1998 World Bank-Government of Georgia public opinion survey revealed that the public had little confidence in the judiciary.[26] In fact, of the 15 public institutions which were ranked for quality of service, local courts were ranked lowest, followed closely by local prosecutors and police, but well behind state educational and

21. *Ibid.* Arts. 2, 4 and 108. For a discussion on ways of resolving Georgia's territorial disputes through constitutional change, see B. Coppieters, D. Darchiashvili & N. Akaba, *Federal Practice: Exploring Alternatives for Georgia and Abkhazia,* Brussels 2000.
22. *Ibid.* Chap. 5. Many aspects of the judiciary's organization were left to Parliament however.
23. In addition to Chapter 5 of the Constitution, the relevant pieces of legislation are the Law on the Constitution of Georgia (31 January 1996) and the Law on Procedure in the Constitutional Court (22 March 1996). The Court follows the German model with jurisdiction to hear cases in three ways. The first is to be petitioned by the elected representatives to rule on the constitutionality of legislation or state actions. The second is to decide on constitutional issues in cases referred to it by lower courts. Finally individuals can challenge the validity of legislation violating their constitutional rights before the Court.
24. Judges' profiles are contained in an undated (c. 1997) court pamphlet entitled "Constitutional Court of Georgia". The composition of the bench has changed only slightly since its inception.
25. Author's observations during an address to judges' assistants at the Court ("Lessons from Canadian Federalism", June 1998, Tbilisi).
26. "Coordinating Reforms in the Public Sector: Improving Performance and Combatting Corruption", Briefing notes for the World Bank workshop held on 21-23 June 1998 in Tbilisi, 10 (hereinafter "Coordinating Reforms").

medical institutions.[27] In households which admitted making "unofficial payments", payments to the courts were highest. Perhaps this was to be expected with judges receiving a monthly salary of 40-50 Laris a month and court staff receiving 12 to 15 Laris a month[28] (1 US$ is worth roughly 2 Laris[29]).

The 1997 law unifies the court system by putting all civil, criminal and administrative cases under the courts of general jurisdiction. Any cases handled by the Soviet-era arbitration courts (which were charged with resolving disputes between state enterprises) or military courts were transferred to the courts of general jurisdiction. In addition to rationalizing the court system, unification has the goal of underlining the constitutional prohibition against "special courts" and increasing transparency.[30] First instance courts are either district courts sitting with one judge in minor cases (or two in administrative cases) or circuit courts sitting in panels of three judges for more significant cases. There are 84 district courts and nine circuit courts. The law provides for appellate courts in Tbilisi, Kutaisi, Ajara and, fictionally, Abkhazia. Finally the 39-judge Supreme Court sits atop the court structure as a cassation court. The latter has politically significant tasks as well, including appointing some Constitutional Court judges and deciding on issues related to impeachment of the President. The law also ended Soviet-era supervision of the courts by the Ministry of Justice and transferred it to the newly created Council of Justice. The Council consists of 12 members with the President, Parliament, and the Supreme Court each appointing four members. The Chairpersons of the Supreme Court of Georgia and the High Courts of Ajara and Abkhazia are *ex officio* members of the Council.

The judiciary reform was to be done by setting qualification examinations for judges, initiating disciplinary cases against corrupt sitting judges, nominating candidates for judicial office and proposing further reform measures. The government also intended to combat corruption in the judiciary by increasing

27. *Ibid.* So as not to unduly pathologize the Georgian experience, it should be stated that courts are held in poor esteem throughout much of the former Soviet Union; as Russian President Vladimir Putin told Parliament in April 2001: "We badly need judicial reform today. The country's judicial system is lagging behind real life and is not very helpful in carrying out economic transactions. Not only for entrepreneurs but also for many people who are seeking to restore their rights in law, the courts have not been quick, fair, and impartial." (Cited in T. Frye, "The Two Faces of Russian Courts: Evidence from a Survey of Company Managers", 11 *East European Constitutional Law Review* 2002 Nos. 1-2, 125-129, 125.)
28. "Georgia Judicial Assessment", *op. cit.* chap. 1, note 53, 15.
29. To give some sense of the purchasing power of the Lari, a short return trip on a mini-bus (a common form of urban transportation) costs 1 Lari, as do two loaves of bread. The UN estimates that a subsistence wage is 102 Laris per month (see UNDP, *Human Development Report: Georgia 1999*, Tbilisi, 16).
30. Georgian Constitution, *op. cit.* note 13, Art. 83(4).

judges' salaries to 500 Laris per month.[31] Exams were prepared in secret, printed in California and shipped using a diplomatic pouch (to avoid leaks), with the assistance of the German Technical Co-operation Agency and the American Bar Association's Central and East European Law Initiative (ABA-CEELI, hereinafter ABA). The first round of exams was held in the Spring of 1998. More than 1,000 persons took the exams and only 270, many in their early 30s, passed, a large number of them women.[32] Most incumbents failed the test or refused to write it. A temporary setback to this aspect of the reforms was met in a decision of the Constitutional Court. The judgment satisfied a claim brought by a sitting judge who refused to write the exam on the basis that it infringed his rights to finish his ten-year appointment to the bench made in 1991.[33] The irony of the decision was that the former communist, corrupt and legally incompetent "old guard" had won a victory over the liberal reformers by using the language of reform: constitutionalism, the rule of law and judicial independence. The decision provoked angry responses in the media and protests occurred in front of the Constitutional Court and the offices of the Judges' Association. The most vociferous protesters, members of the Liberty Institute (a reform-minded NGO), demonstrated outside the Constitutional Court, burning in effigy the three judges of the majority decision (one judge dissented) and carrying a coffin entitled "Justice".[34] Through some dexterous legislative drafting—carried out with broad public support—the effect of the Court's decision was muted and applicants who passed the exams were sworn into office a year later.

The Justice Minister's hope when the judicial reforms were launched was that qualified and properly paid judges would create an "island of totally uncorrupted people who can serve as an example to all of society."[35] There undoubtedly have been improvements in the judiciary since the exams. The number of complaints to the Public Defender's Office regarding court decisions dropped significantly,[36] and there are qualitatively observable indications that

31. Presidential Order No. 726 of 30 December 1998. Although this was subsequently reduced by 20-30% due to budget cutbacks.
32. See S. Kinzer, "Georgia, Judging That Most Judges Shouldn't, Readies Replacements", *New York Times* 12 July 1999, A4. On women passing the exams in disproportionate numbers to their previous composition on the bench: A. Tskitishvili, "Elite Judges Punished for their Offences Against Citizens", *Resonance* 2 November 1998 (cited in CIPDD Monitor, 2 November 1998).
33. *Avtandil Chachua v. The Parliament of Georgia* (heard 3 November 1998), Constitutional Court of Georgia. Unofficial English translation of decision on file with the author.
34. The protests prompted the judges of the court to complain to the prosecutor, who in turn charged the leaders of the Liberty Institute with insulting a judge, hooliganism and holding a protest without a permit. G. Kapanadze, "Zhvania and Saakashvili May Be Arrested", *Resonance* 31 March 1999, 1 (cited in *CIPDD Monitor*, 31 March 1999).
35. Kinzer, *op. cit.* note 32.
36. 170 complaints were received in 1999 compared to 715 in 1998: *Annual Report—Public Defender of Georgia*, Tbilisi 1999.

improvements have been made. For example, signs have been posted centrally in courthouses and on some judges' doors indicating that litigants should not approach judges directly, as was the norm.[37] And in a refreshing concordance between the formalism of signs and actual practice, judges are increasingly refusing to meet alone with one party in the absence of the other party or the party's lawyer. Some have even taken to locking their doors from the inside to prevent access.[38] The judges are also more knowledgeable about the law, although complaints persist that exam standards are still not high enough and that some judges use only a subjective "reasonableness" standard in deciding cases rather than applying the law to the facts of the case.[39] Public opinion has shifted slightly since the reforms, with a survey from early 2000 revealing a roughly 7% increase in the level of trust in courts and judges since the reforms were launched.[40]

It must be recalled, however, that the judges' exams tested for competence, not honesty, and there has been no serious screening of judges for "moral" fitness or vigorous disciplinary action taken against errant judges.[41] The reforms are further undermined by the failure to pay judges their salaries for months at a time and a reduction in their salaries due to budget cuts.[42] Even if the salary issue is resolved, there is a series of other issues which must be addressed to promote the continued reform of the judiciary. These challenges, common in many parts of the former Soviet Union, include the abysmal facilities of first instance courts as well as the inappropriate location of some of the courts.[43] For example, the Vake District Court, located in one of the wealthiest areas in Georgia, is poorly lit and there are no library facilities and little modern

37. The sign in Vake District Court reads: "Judges will not accept visits from citizens regarding their cases. You will be notified the day of your case through the secretary and cases are filed directly in the secretarial office." (Observed 21 May 1999.)
38. Interview with EE on 2 May 1999.
39. Interview with BB on 7 June 2000. The concern about resort to "reasonableness" may partly reflect the mechanical view of judicial interpretation (judges should simply apply the law) common in the former Soviet Union and indeed in many civil law jurisdictions. Lawyers also complain that judges are unfamiliar with new areas of law such as bankruptcy.
40. Georgian Opinion Research Business International (GORBI), *Judicial Reform in Georgia: A Study of Public Opinion* (final report prepared for the World Bank, Spring 2000), 16. On a scale of trust from 1 (no trust) to 4 (much trust), courts and judges scored 2.2 in 2000, up from 1.98 in 1998.
41. For an analysis of recent Russian moves in this regard—and the necessary balancing involved—see P.H. Solomon, "Putin's Judicial Reform: Making Judges Accountable as well as Independent", 11 *East European Constitutional Review* 2002 Nos. 1-2, 117-124.
42. See C. Stefes, "Debilitating Georgian Corruption", *Transitions On-Line* 2 October 2000 and "Economic and Social Rights", *South Caucasian Human Rights Monitor* (January) 2000.
43. Happily, infrastructure rehabilitation is one of the aims of the World Bank's US$ 13.4 million Judicial Reform Project for Georgia: World Bank, "World Bank Approves US$ 114.9 Million for Georgia" (*News Release* No. 99/2288/ECA, 29 June 1999).

office equipment.[44] Judges' offices open directly on to the corridors, crowded by litigants, lawyers and police, many of them attempting to speak with the judges. The courtrooms are inhospitable, contain damaged furniture and have a layout designed to correspond to Soviet notions of justice.[45] The court is directly above an LCB and a police station occupies an attached building. Poor case management, lack of training for judges, limited distribution of new legislation, and underpaid and poorly trained court staff should also be mentioned as impediments to continued reform.

Unlike the Soviet system where the procuracy was a part of the executive, the 1995 Constitution formally makes the procuracy a part of the judiciary.[46] The intention was to establish an independent organ with, among other roles, supervisory powers over investigations. In reality there is a close connection between the procuracy and the executive, both at the central level and in each region (where typically the prosecutor, the police chief and the local representative of the executive are the "local bosses").[47] While the procuracy's power was somewhat curtailed in a 1996 law, it remains a powerful—and heavily corrupted—institution.[48] Furthermore, in contrast to the judiciary, the procuracy remains largely unreformed. In fact, a number of judges who failed the judicial exams were appointed as local prosecutors, leading to opposition demands that the prosecutor-general be impeached.[49] Generally speaking, independent defence counsel receive little co-operation from the procuracy.

Lawmaking

Having looked at the constitutional and judicial framework within which lawyers work, I will now turn to the area of legislation. Recent years have seen quite active lawmaking as the government has sought to modernize the legislative regime, gain entry into international organizations such as the World Trade Organization and the Council of Europe, and implement treaty obligations.[50]

44. Personal observations from visits in 1999 and 2000.
45. J.N. Hazard, "Furniture Arrangement as a Symbol of Judicial Roles" in A.D. Renteln & A. Dundes, *Folk Law: Essays in the Theory and Practice of Lex Non Scripta,* Madison 1994, 459.
46. Georgian Constitution, *op. cit.* note 13, Art. 91.
47. In fact in some regions, the prosecutor's job is divided up between "clans". For example, the Georgian media has suggested that in Akhalkalaki four Armenian clans have divided up all powerful positions (prosecutors, judges, police chiefs, political party leaders and criminal bosses): see "Inter-Clan War in Akhalkalaki: The Only Idea They Share Is That of Autonomy", *CIPDD Monitor* 21 September 1998.
48. Like other jurists, however, prosecutors are familiar with the rhetoric of human rights: interview with E on 17 April 1999.
49. See L. Fuller, "Embattled Georgian Prosecutor-General Resigns", *RFE/RL Caucasus Report,* Vol. 4(6), 8 February 2001.
50. On Georgia's treaty law see K. Korkelia, "Treaty Law and Practice in Georgia", 25 *Review of Central and East European Law* 1999 No. 3, 445-457.

A number of these new laws have been drafted in close co-operation with the European Union (EU) under a Partnership and Co-operation Agreement, which states in part that the EU will provide technical assistance to Georgia in reforming its legislation along European lines:[51]

> The Parties recognize that an important condition for strengthening the economic links between Georgia and the Community is the approximation of Georgia's existing and future legislation to that of the Community. Georgia shall endeavour to ensure that its legislation will be gradually made compatible with that of the Community.

The agreement emphasizes approximation in, among other areas, competition and banking law.

Three concerns are raised by all this legislative activity (in addition to the fact that enacted laws are often ignored "on the ground").[52] The first is that while a good deal of progressive legislation has been passed, some of it lacks coherency. Civil Code reform was given a high priority by lawmakers and, after five years of drafting and consultation, a new code was passed by Parliament on 26 June 1997. The law is heavily influenced by the German Civil Code, with French, Dutch and Swiss influences as well. But there are also Anglo-American legal concepts, such as the trust, which have found their way into the Georgian code.[53] Other areas such as oil and gas legislation, antimonopoly and consumer protection have been influenced by American lawyers operating under grants from the United States Agency for International Development (USAID).[54] These Anglo-American laws fit uneasily within the larger civil law scheme and may contribute to confusion in the legal system. Part of the blame for the incoherent aspects of Georgian legislation may be attributed to Georgia's refusal to more closely follow the harmonization movement in the Commonwealth of Independent States.[55] The movement, which has been sponsored by the Dutch and other Western governments, has presented an alternative to each small republic attempting to "find its own way", although

51. Art. 43 of the Partnership and Cooperation Agreement Between the European Communities and Their Member States, of the One Part and Georgia, of the Other Part. The agreement, which entered into force on 1 July 1999, is available online at http://www.eu-delegation.org.ge/pao.html.
52. On some of the system dangers inherent in "top down" international harmonization of law movements, see P.B. Stephan, III, "Institutions and Elites: Property, Contract, the State, and Rights in Information in the Global Economy" (*University of Virginia Law & Economics Research Paper* No. 01-9, 2001). Among other things, he cites the possibility that unification reduces healthy competition among legal rules.
53. See B. Zoidze, "The Influence of Anglo-American Common Law on the Georgian Civil Code", I & II *Georgian Law Review* 1999, 10-19. For a broader discussion on the role of legal imports see Ajani, *op. cit.* chap. 1, note 47.
54. To take two examples, oil and gas legislation was promoted by USAID contractor Hadler Baxley, and advisors were provided to Georgia's anti-monopoly service by USAID through the Center for Economic Policy and Reform.

it has been criticized as Russia-focussed and a means for Moscow to reassert legal hegemony over the region.

The second concern is that even where the law is coherent, it may be of a character which is incomprehensible to Georgian jurists and the public. A number of laws have essentially been translated from Western sources (or based on Russia's approximation of Western sources) without real debate. Of course in the drafting of most legislation in Western countries, the public is typically not engaged, but there are at least stakeholders who put forth various positions. In Georgia a good deal of legislation for the regulation of market capitalism has been passed by Parliament without real understanding by legislators, stakeholders, the public or most jurists. At times it appears the only people who are familiar with the legislation are the foreign experts and their counterparts in the relevant government ministry. This lack of conceptual understanding has contributed to the difficulties in implementing the legislation.[56] Assessing Georgia's insolvency laws in 1999 as "inadequate", one report states: "[w]hile Georgia's insolvency law became effective in January 1997 and cases have been brought under this law, none of these cases has yet been concluded".[57] The authors suggested that this may be attributable to the judges' "lack of understanding of their powers under the law".[58]

The third major concern in the lawmaking field is that some key acts do not meet international standards. The criminal procedure code is the most blatant example.[59] In 1998 Georgia adopted a new criminal procedure code to replace the old Soviet one. While the new code did not fully correspond to international standards, it was perceived to be a significant step forward. It was reviewed by experts from the Council of Europe and passed in a period when Georgia was lobbying hard for access to the Council. Georgia became a member of the Council on 27 April 1999, but shortly after accession the act was amended to effectively repeal many of the earlier reforms. The most significant change is the removal of provisions allowing defendants access to court at the pre-trial stage to make complaints of procedural and human rights

55. For a full discussion of this issue, see W.B. Simons, "The Commonwealth of Independent States and Legal Reform: The Harmonisation of Private Law", *Law in Transition* (Spring) 2000, 14-24. As early as 1992 Feldbrugge noted that "[a]mong leading Georgian lawyers a certain tendency is noticeable towards 'legislation shopping', selecting models for various branches of law...which seems most suitable for Georgia..." ("Law of the Republic of Georgia", *op. cit.* chap. 2, note 130, 374.)
56. On the difficulties in implementing one legal regime, including the need for legal expertise, see Kovacic & Slay, *op. cit.* chap. 1, note 49. The inadequacy of simple legal transplants is also addressed in the Conclusion.
57. See Ramasastry, Slavova & Vandenhoeck, *op. cit.* chap. 1, note 52.
58. *Ibid.*
59. This discussion of criminal procedure draws heavily on Human Rights Watch, *Georgia—Backtracking on Reform: Amendments Undermine Access to Justice*, Tbilisi, October 2000.

violations, including a lack of access to counsel. Instead complaints must be made to investigators or prosecutors, the very individuals who may be abusing the rights of detainees, or who allow the abuse.[60]

Human Rights and Corruption

As pointed out in the previous chapter, Georgia had a remarkable reputation for corruption during Soviet times. Little has changed and virtually all aspects of Georgian political and bureaucratic life are tarnished by corruption. As a result of the territorial and political instability of the early 1990s, the power ministries (interior, defence and state security) and local strongmen have been heavily relied upon by the state. In turn, some have exploited this reliance. To take the most blatant example, it was widely asserted that long-time Interior Minister Kakha Targamadze was corrupt.[61] He had been heavily criticized by parliamentarians and journalists alike for reported smuggling of cigarettes and other commodities. Nevertheless, after his re-election in April 2000, President Eduard Shevardnadze reappointed Targamadze and the Minister remained in power bolstered by 30,000 uniformed policemen under his control. Ultimately Targamadze was forced to leave his post, but only after massive street protests in October 2001 over a government raid on an independent media outlet led Shevardnadze to sack his entire cabinet.[62] It is unknown what the orientation of the new minister—once a deputy minister under Targamadze—will be.

The sale of offices is also widespread. For example, US$ 5,000 is the going rate for the purchase of the position of traffic policeman and a position of customs official at the Russian-Georgian border costs roughly US$ 100,000.[63] Despite the high costs, money is quickly re-couped by pressing citizens and businesses for bribes. Portions of this re-couped money, however, must be passed both up and down the chain; up to supervisors and ultimately into ministries, and down to families or patrons who helped the "applicant" put up the money in the first place. One frequent rationale offered to justify the bribe-taking is the low (and frequently late or unpaid) salaries of officials. It is doubtful, however, that an increase in salaries, without structural reform, will change the nature of systemic corruption.[64]

Two watchdogs set up in the mid-1990s to combat corruption have proven ineffectual. Parliament's temporary Anti-Corruption Committee and the Chamber of Control can only inform the public prosecutor of cases of corruption; they cannot press charges on their own accord. Generally speaking the public

60. *Ibid.*
61. Stefes, *op. cit.* note 42. See also "Georgian Majority Parliamentary Faction Renews Criticism of Interior Minister", *RFE/RL Caucasus Report,* Vol. 3(43), 3 November 2000.
62. J. Devdariani, "Georgia's new ministers of interior, state security grapple with legacy of mistrust", *Eurasia Insight* 28 November 2001.
63. Stefes, *op. cit.* note 42.
64. *Ibid.*

prosecutor takes no real measures in response to the cases which are referred to it. In fact, it is often the whistle-blowers who are themselves dismissed or punished, such as the policeman who was immediately fired by the interior ministry after accusing Tbilisi's police chief of misuse of public funds.[65]

Corruption has also placed a burden on enterprises and represents a disincentive to foreign and domestic investment. The tax inspectorate is perceived to be particularly corrupt with vast sums of potential tax revenue sorely needed by the state budget remaining uncollected.[66] It is estimated that 80% of all imports are smuggled, and Georgia has the worst record of all the ex-Soviet Republics in terms of tax collection.[67] A joint World Bank-Georgian government study estimates that businesses spent an average monthly amount of 230 Laris on unofficial payments to state officials (individual households pay an estimated average of 109 Laris per year in unofficial payments).[68]

The poor human rights situation in Georgia is related to the corruption issue.[69] The most obvious manifestation of this interconnectedness is the behaviour of the traffic police, which is symptomatic of more general trends in policing.[70] Arbitrary stops by traffic police are commonplace. Generally a flimsy excuse for the pull-over is given: failure to obey barely visible lines in the road, etc. Drivers are given a choice: pay a small "fine" on the spot or receive an official ticket which would result in a much larger fine. Drivers generally opt for the immediate payment. On one hand, the behaviour of the traffic police could be seen in a positive light: the state cannot afford to pay police officers a decent wage yet requires traffic to be regulated; bribes remedy the needs of both the state and the police. Unfortunately even with the personal gain, police officers do not adequately regulate traffic.

Three brief points illustrate this. First there is often no discussion between police and the stopped drivers. The driver may simply step out of the car, press a few Laris into the policeman's hand and get back in the car without a word having been spoken. This is nothing more than a toll; the driver does not know which if any traffic regulation has been broken and there is no deterrent to bad driving. Secondly, the police select targets based on likelihood of gain rather than bad driving. If the car is an expensive model, police will be reluctant to

65. *Ibid.*
66. UNDP, *op. cit.* note 29, 25-35.
67. "La Géorgie saignée par les trafics et la contrebande", *Le Monde* 9-10 April 2000, 3.
68. "Coordinating Reforms", *op. cit.* note 26.
69. On the effects of corruption on democratization more generally, see C.H. Stefes, "The Incompatibilities of Institutionalized Corruption and Democracy in the Former Soviet Union: The Case of Georgia" (unpublished Ph.D. dissertation, University of Denver, 2002).
70. This discussion on the traffic police, which is based on personal observations and a UNDP report, *op. cit.* note 29, 39, reflects a common pattern in many parts of the former Soviet Union.

pull the car over, regardless of how bad the driving is. The driver is likely to be a wealthy and well-connected individual who may create trouble for the police officer if pressed. On some occasions police officers have been beaten for pulling over the wrong driver. In fact, the police can generally tell the influence of a driver by a quick glance at the license plates. The initial figures on the plate will reveal if the driver is in the government, procuracy or police. Even when there is no official code, plates can be purchased or gained through influence which are patterned by repetitive figures revealing influence or power to the police. Finally, police are much more likely to be found at traffic lights which are working than those which do not (an all too frequent case in Georgia, which has regular power cuts). Where the lights are working they can watch carefully for excuses to pull drivers over ("you didn't stop at the line") and when the lights are not working there are fewer excuses as drivers necessarily contravene traffic regulations to safely navigate an intersection. The perversion here of course, is that the traffic police could usefully be employed at the intersections without working lights to direct traffic.

There are some bright spots on the Georgian human rights landscape. For example, the public can find robust denunciations of government policies in the media. Even in this sphere, however, there are attempts to stifle journalists. Examples include harassment by tax authorities, spurious defamation claims, the firing of independent-minded journalists from the state broadcaster and police beatings of journalists attempting to cover sensitive court cases.[71] Another general bright spot is freedom of religion for the established religions (Orthodox Christianity, Armenian Grigorianism, moderate Islam and Judaism), although the attitude towards recent religious imports is often one of extreme intolerance.[72]

In the area of criminal investigations, there is a clear and persistent pattern of abuse by police or the failure of the state to protect vulnerable individuals.[73]

71. Z. Anjaparidze, "The Impact of Media and Information Exchange on Georgian State-Building", *UNDP Discussion Paper* 1999 No. 2, 13.
72. The worship services of Evangelical Christians and Jehovah's Witnesses are frequently disrupted by police. At other times, police have looked on as radical Orthodox Christian Georgians have violently attacked worshippers. See Amnesty International, "Georgia—Continuing allegations of torture and ill-treatment" (*AI Index*: EUR 56/01/00, February 2000).
73. A brief description of the investigation procedure, more familiar to Europeans, may be useful. Briefly, in Georgian Criminal Procedure an investigator (in most cases from the Ministry of Internal Affairs) may conduct inquiries into suspected crimes. Then, with the sanction of the Procuracy, charges may be laid and an individual taken into custody. Within 72 hours a judge must rule on the lawfulness of the detention. Once a suspect is charged, a formal investigation, known as the preliminary investigation, is commenced. The preliminary investigation may take up to nine months to complete and involves the preparation of a case file which is then presented to the defence and the competent court.

Torture and ill-treatment at the hands of police during pre-trial detention are consistently reported.[74] Beatings with a view to exacting confessions or money are commonplace, and several deaths have occurred in police custody. While in police custody, detained persons are often denied access to their families and—as described above—their lawyers. The lack of pre-trial access to counsel squarely reveals some of the structural impediments to criminal lawyering in Georgia. Access is restricted in a number of ways. Prosecutors and police may simply deny access to counsel without reason. Often absurd reasons, such as that the accused person cannot be located, are used. Sometimes counsel are made to wait for hours and then told to return on another day. In other cases, suspects are intentionally misclassified and detained as witnesses rather than suspects (only suspects have an explicit right to counsel). Suspects are also pressured into accepting counsel not of their choice. The police-nominated lawyers may be working in collusion with the police to obtain confessions or bribe money—they rarely vigorously pursue their clients' interests. Finally other "tricks" have been used, such as not informing defence counsel of upcoming court dates or naming the counsel of choice a witness in the case in order to disqualify the lawyer from acting. Given the fact that pre-trial torture and ill-treatment regularly occur in Georgia, lack of access to a lawyer at the earliest stages of detention is particularly troubling and contrary to international human rights standards.[75]

When complaints of torture are made, it is very difficult to obtain a forensic medical report.[76] The Procuracy has sole, unreviewable discretion to order such an exam. Exams are rarely ordered and, when they are, the impartiality of state-appointed physicians is questionable. Many complaints to the Procuracy about police ill-treatment are simply ignored, and it is thought that other cases of ill-treatment go unreported for fear of further reprisals or with the assumption that authorities will not act on complaints. There are also frequent reports of unfair trials, especially in politically significant cases.[77] Lawyers—through intimidation by state authorities and the occasional beating—have themselves been the victims of human rights abuses in their attempts to defend their clients.[78] In one case, a defence lawyer discovered the prosecutor and investi-

74. Amnesty International, *op. cit.* note 72.
75. For example, Principle 17(1) of the UN Body of Principles for the Protection of All Persons under Any Form of Detention or Imprisonment (Adopted by General Assembly Resolution 43/173 on 9 December 1988) states: "A detained person shall be entitled to have the assistance of a legal counsel. He shall be informed of his right by the competent authority promptly after arrest and shall be provided with reasonable facilities for exercising it."
76. Human Rights Watch, *op. cit.* note 59.
77. Amnesty International, 1998, *op. cit.* note 3, 11.
78. Z. Mikatadze, "I'll Seat You and Your Lawyer on a Broken Bottle", *Resonance* 28 January 1998.

gator meeting alone with the judge, without notice having been given to the defence. The lawyer alleged that when he attempted to disrupt the meeting, the prosecutor threatened him with a gun.[79]

Human rights advocates had hoped that Georgia's accession to the Council of Europe would bring a human rights dividend. During its tenure with guest status at the Council, the 41-member regional body promoting democratization and human rights, Georgia lobbied hard for its "return" to the European family.[80] Among other things it touted the new Criminal Procedure Code as an example of its willingness to combat human rights abuses.[81] As outlined above, however, regressive amendments to the Code were made shortly after accession. Furthermore, although much of the Council's human rights regime has been formally adopted, including the European Convention for the Protection of Human Rights and Fundamental Freedoms, no effective measures seem to have been taken to implement the guarantees contained in those treaties.[82] In its recommendation on Georgia's application for membership to the Council, the Council's Parliamentary Assembly declared:[83]

> Georgia is a pluralist democratic society, respectful of human rights and the rule of law, and is willing, in the sense of Article 4 of the Statute, to continue the democratic reforms in progress in order to bring all the country's legislation and practice into line with the principles and standards of the Council of Europe.

One can only assume that the decision to accept Georgia into the Council on the basis of its record on human rights and rule of law issues was a political one, perhaps influenced by President Shevardnadze's considerable international (although not domestic) prestige. As one observer puts it:[84]

> While Europe and the United States will undoubtedly continue to laud the achievements of President Eduard Shevardnadze, "our man in the Caucasus", Georgia appeared frighteningly close to settling into the Eurasian model of development already adopted by several of its compatriots in the Commonwealth of Independent States (CIS)—sluggish economic growth, systemic corruption, weak and asymmetrical center-regional relations, and impotent democratic institutions.

79. "Life of a lawyer under threat in court", *Human Rights in Georgia Monthly Bulletin* Nos. 22-23/2000, 27 November 2000.
80. In a 1997 speech at a Council summit, President Shevardnadze declared, "[w]e are reuniting with Europe, as an offshoot grafted into a life-giving stock, to contribute to the salvational message of European culture and find within it our own salvation". Second summit of heads of state and government, Council of Europe, Strasbourg 11 October 1997. Text of speech available online at www.coe.fr/cm/sessions/97summit2/georgia.htm.
81. Human Rights Watch, *op. cit.* note 59, 7.
82. *ETS* No. 5, 11 November 1950. Ratified by Georgia on 20 May 1999. Among other treaties, Georgia has signed and ratified (on 20 June 2000) the European Convention for the Prevention of Torture and Inhuman or Degrading Treatment or Punishment, *ETS* No. 126, 26 November 1987.
83. Council of Europe, P.A. Opinion No. 209 (1999).
84. C. Welt, "Georgia Annual Report 1999: 'A Return to Eurasia'", *Transitions Online*.

Following the removal of the carrot of membership in the Council, it is unlikely that there will be major changes to Georgia's human rights record in the near future. The admission of Georgia certainly adds credence to the argument that enlargement of the Council's membership to states that do not yet have their human rights "houses in order" has led to a dilution of standards.[85]

Non-State Law

> There is currently much conversation about the lack of self-discipline and disrespect of the law as something characteristic of Georgians. Some even declare that Georgian's [*sic*] traditions, strong kinship among them, are outdated in these new times. This does not look like a fair assessment. Our language, songs, poems, meals, all these things are Georgian traditions. They are good today and will continue to be good tomorrow. Are laziness, negligence, corruption and many other vices really Georgian? These look like wrong habits unfortunately adopted in another time (Soviet time), habits that still continue to be with us. Those habits and relations are the ones really outdated, not the Georgian traditions.[86]

While the importance of kinship and personal connection seem little diminished in post-Soviet Georgia,[87] some aspects of unofficial law have changed. The institution of "thieves in law" has broken down, although apparently some cases are still resolved by respected underworld figures.[88] The main reason given by my interlocutors for this breakdown is that "even the criminals are corrupt now"; the thieves work closely with the corrupted police and officials in the power ministries and their independence has been eroded.[89] In addition, the economic basis of the thieves—the perversions of the command economy—has been destroyed and this has contributed to the demise of this "institution" (though many have gone into other forms of criminal activity).[90]

There is also interplay between the official law—or its near complete failure to deliver justice—and unofficial law. The most extreme example of this interplay is the apparent increase in "mob justice" in Georgia, with 50 recorded lynching attempts during the first decade of independence.[91] The lynchings appear to be a manifestation of public mistrust in the ability of law enforcement agencies to properly prosecute crime. At least one Georgian observer of the

85. See P. Leuprecht, "Innovations in the European System of Human Rights Protection: Is Enlargement Compatible with Reinforcement?", 8 *Transnational Law & Contemporary Problems* 1998 No. 2, 313-336.
86. UNDP, *op. cit.* note 29, 61.
87. For example, one study has shown that kinship provides a strong "safety net" for the internally displaced: J.L.V. Pol, "Stable Instability of Displaced People in Western Georgia: A Food-security and Gender Survey after Five Years", 12 *Journal of Refugee Studies* 1999 No. 4, 349-366, 361-362.
88. Some of them representing a threat to the central government were arrested or killed in the early 1990s. Others have moved to Russia: Glonti, *op. cit.* note 7.
89. Interview with AA on 19 September 1998.
90. Glonti, *op. cit.* note 7.
91. G. Chikhladze, "Fear Makes Justice Wild", 4 *Georgia/Caucasus Profile* 2000, 22-23.

lynchings has argued that the practice is alien to Georgian national tradition or is a perversion of the tradition to which people have been driven by fear and frustration:[92]

> To kill out of passion was considered as something quite common to the genetic code of the region. However, it was associated with a sense of national pride or point of honor over a love relationship or loss of a family member and it was not something associated with misdirected fear and anxiety. The revengeful taking of life was always considered in Georgia to be not in the category of sin, but an obligation. Such an ordained spilling of blood was to be carried out by either a close relative or a friend. But in spite of seemingly common features, vendetta and lynch are by no means identical. This type of societal-sanctioned activity where one carefully and premeditatedly carried out a vendetta was reflective of what one stood for in this culture. An angry and fearful mob is a creature of a different colour.

Less extreme measures of popular justice are of course available. In cases of theft, a beating is not uncommon. In domestic violence cases, neighbours may intervene (although frequently not, as many consider such incidents to be in the private domain). Similarly, fathers and brothers of a woman may mete out physical justice to an abusive husband. Few (including the victim) would consider calling the police, as the likely result would be detention of the man (perhaps the breadwinner) and extortion by the police for his release.[93] In other cases, such as negligent or impaired driving, monetary restitution may be tendered on the spot to victims.[94] The general attitude towards the police is that they are not there to protect—they are there simply for their own gain, and they should be avoided whenever possible.

In short, many cases simply never go to police or courts because of a combination of traditional ways of doing things and a distrust of the official legal system. And, of course, as long as citizens continue to avoid the official legal system, the need for court lawyers will remain limited. As we will examine, however, lawyers are being used more frequently in a "private law world" which avoids state institutions.

92. *Ibid.*, 23.
93. In sexual violence cases the "shame" factor would also make the victim and others reluctant to report to police.
94. In one case reported to me, a Kurdish mother was offered cash shortly after her son was killed by a senior military official driving drunk. The mother never reported the case to police as it is considered foolish for Kurds (a minority widely discriminated against) to seek police assistance. Interview with LL on 1 June 1999.

Chapter 4
Legal Education

Educating Lawyers

The Numbers Boom

There has been a tremendous increase in the popularity of legal education following independence. In Soviet times, legal education was only offered at law faculties in the three main state universities—the universities of Tbilisi, Kutaisi and Batumi. By the late 1980s Georgian law faculties graduated a combined total of a couple of hundred students each year. By itself the Faculty of Law at Tbilisi State University (TSU) now graduates roughly 800 people each year.[1] More dramatic is the fact that since 1991 over 200 private institutions offering a legal education have opened, with a combined enrollment of over thirty thousand students.[2]

What explains this rise in the popularity of legal education? First, enrollment in higher education in general increased in the mid-1990s.[3] By the late 1980s supply had not kept pace with demand and thousands of students who wished to attend university, but who did not have connections or high enough grades, were turned away. In the early to mid-1990s private institutions began opening under lax licensing requirements of the Ministry of Education.[4] These private colleges largely catered to students who were unable to gain admission to state institutions. Also in the 1990s demand for higher education increased as young people attempted to avoid a difficult job market and some young men attempted to avoid military service. But the increased numbers of students and private institutions do not by themselves explain the rise in the popularity of legal education.

In terms of number of applicants per place, statistics from the University of Tbilisi reveal that law is clearly the most sought after subject (more than double the demand for hard sciences for example).[5] Along with subjects such as economics and foreign languages, which have also seen rises in enrollment,

1. Georgia Judicial Assessment, *op. cit.* chap. 1, note 53, 25. The law faculties at Kutaisi and Batumi graduate roughly 80 students a year each.
2. Putting exact numbers on the number of private law schools and students is a difficult matter. The Georgia Judicial Assessment indicated that in 1998 there were 240 private law schools in Georgia with an enrollment of 40,000. The Georgian office of the American Bar Association's Central and East European Law Initiative's suggests 280 law schools have opened [see www.abalawyersource.org/ceeli/countries/georgia.html under legal education]. However, these numbers appear suspect as they closely resemble the total number of private educational institutions. Accordingly, I have suggested lower figures. One of the difficulties is that many non–law faculties offer law courses and there is no functioning accreditation body determining which institutions are actually offering what might be called a programme of legal education.
3. In 1990 there were 103,900 students in higher education. Eight years later there were 127,900 students (UNDP, *Human Development Report: Georgia 1998*, Tbilisi, 89).
4. "Georgia Judicial Assessment", *op. cit.* chap. 1, note 53, 25.

students (and parents, who in many cases choose for their children) see law as the key to success.[6] It is a ticket both to study overseas and, following graduation, to lucrative and "clean" employment with foreign organizations, law firms or companies dealing with foreign investors. Some students remain drawn to the traditional "power" career paths such as entering the Procuracy or the Ministry of Internal Affairs. Other attractions include the increased prestige of lawyering as a profession and a desire to be involved with the law reform agenda. The explosion of demand has had a profound impact on the quality of formal legal education in Georgia, the need for supplementary practical education and access to the profession (or the "supply" of lawyers), topics which are examined below.

Formal Legal Education

Higher education institutions in many parts of the former communist bloc face similar problems.[7] These include deteriorated facilities, low salaries for professors and the related problem of corruption, outdated teaching methods and materials and, outside of capital cities, scholarly isolation and stagnation. In law and the social sciences, there is the additional problem that many professors trained in the Soviet period are unable or unwilling to adapt to new realities in their fields.[8] In this section these issues will be examined with respect to Georgian legal education.

In terms of facilities, the situation is mixed. The Faculty of Law and the Faculty of International Law and Relations at Tbilisi State University occupy stately, impressive buildings. And, although there are physical problems—a lack of heating in winter, poor chalkboards, filthy restrooms—the situation may be described as adequate for teaching purposes. Most other law departments inside and outside of the capital occupy more decrepit buildings (often non-descript "Stalinist" structures) and are beset with a host of physical plant problems including frequent power cuts (with corresponding darkness), broken windows and doors, very cold temperatures in winter and malfunctioning

5. Cited in Fig. 4.8 of the UNDP, *Human Development Report, Georgia: 2000*, Tbilisi (online at http://www.undp.org.ge/). This increase in the popularity of law is a larger post-communist trend. In Russia in 1997 for example, it was reported that there were 18 applications for every one position in law schools. See G. Ajani, "Legal Education in Russia: Present and Future—An Analysis of the State Educational Standards for Higher Professional Education and a Comparison with the European Legal Reform Experience", 23 *Review of Central and East European Law* 1997 Nos. 3-4, 267-300, 270.
6. Based on numerous discussions with students between 1998 and 2000.
7. These problems have been well documented. See for example the articles under the title "Higher Education on Trial" in 9 *East European Constitutional Review* 2000 No.3 and P.L.W. Sabloff, ed., *Higher Education in the Post-Communist World: Case Studies of Eight Universities*, New York 1999.
8. Some students suggested that their professors be examined before being allowed to continue teaching: interviews with U and M on 16 December 1998.

elevators. In these schools, the deteriorated physical plants are impediments to the educational enterprise. At the Georgian Technical University for example (despite its name, a law department opened there in 1992), students are visibly cold and demoralized during the winter months. Both attendance and concentration drop during this period, and there is little willingness to have after-class discussions.

In some schools the situation improved in the late 1990s, in one of three ways. At times these improvements have been made possible through Western assistance.[9] For example, the German Technical Co-operation Agency (GTZ) renovated classrooms and offices for the newly-created Faculty of Business and Law at the Georgian Technical University. The Faculty, which is jointly run by Germans and Georgians (with Germans distinctly in a leadership position) has created Western-standard facilities which exist beside the unimproved classrooms and offices of the rest of the university. In other improved faculties and private universities, particularly those catering to the children of wealthy parents, the improvements have come about through high tuition fees.[10] Finally, private enterprise is making its debut in Georgian universities, often on a small scale. For example, in 2000 an elevator at the Georgian Technical University was repaired and decorated and students charged a small fee for using it. The alternatives were to use the filthy, dilapidated elevator for free, when it worked, or to take the 11 flights of stairs. What is lacking are state funds, and perhaps the will, to undertake general repair to higher educational institutions.[11] In fact, universities are beginning to resemble the patchwork of standards that one finds in apartment buildings in Tbilisi. Many buildings lack collective management and have fallen into disrepair, with dirty halls, slowly crumbling walls and no lighting. And yet one can find floors which have been freshly renovated and lit by a wealthy resident or a few neighbours acting together. Slowly, bit-by-bit, parts of the buildings improve, but unevenly and without core improvements.

Underfunding has caused a corresponding deterioration in library and other resources. In Soviet times, central, interdisciplinary university libraries were maintained. In the last decade, however, shared university resources have been neglected as individual departments attempted to survive largely on their

9. One consequence of academic corruption, a topic addressed below, is that Western donors have refused to offer large sums of money to certain institutions for reconstruction. For example, on the condition of anonymity, several USAID employees indicated to me in 1999 that the international funds and interest existed to renovate the Faculty of Law but that the money would not be granted because of pervasive corruption in that faculty.
10. An example is the International Business Faculty of Tbilisi State University (which offers a specialization in international business law).
11. In the late 1990s, budgetary allocations to higher education decreased to US$ 15 million in 1999: Chap. 4 of the *Human Development Report, 2000, op. cit.* note 5.

own. Central libraries continue to exist but have made few recent acquisitions and remain stocked with Soviet-era books (which in the social sciences and law are obviously outdated). Furthermore, as in most of the former Soviet Union, the libraries have not been automated and continue to rely on a cumbersome request procedure (browsing is not permitted in most libraries, so students must know what they are looking for). Most students and professors do not use the central university libraries at all. To compensate for this, departments have established their own discipline-specific libraries, which often consist of nothing more than a couple of shelves in a faculty office. The collections are comprised of uncatalogued Western donations, and many of them, because of language or content (books on the common law, for example) are of limited use to students or professors. In some cases, donated books are kept by professors in their own offices and are practically speaking not available to students at all.

Underfunding also impacts on the availability of computers. No law school in Georgia of which I am aware provides instruction in computer-assisted legal research, a consequence of both lack of funds to purchase computers (many faculties have only one computer which is used for administrative purposes and some have no computers at all) and a lack of expertise in this area. To some extent library and computer deficiencies are mitigated by the presence of resources outside of the university. Computer centres (with internet access) have been established at several locations in Tbilisi and some regional centres by Western organizations. The Georgian Young Lawyers' Association has an excellent law library which its student members can use, and the United States Information Service in Tbilisi has a decent library as well (naturally with an American bent to the materials).

Although the universities are visibly underfunded, there are people who, through corruption, draw good incomes from their university positions. Corruption on the part of many professors and most administrators was widely reported to me by students of various institutions offering a legal education. Similar levels of corruption are reported in high-demand subjects such as economics, and markedly lower levels in the humanities and hard sciences, which have seen a drop in their popularity in recent years. Corruption takes place when students wish to gain access to the institutions (buying your way in) and for passing courses (buying your way through). Not all students pay bribes. Those who perform exceptionally well on the state exams may successfully compete for a non-fee paying position at the university. They generally do not pay bribes (although one student who was very successful on the state exam reported paying anyway, "just to make sure").[12] And, if they display true academic excellence throughout the programme, they may pass their exams without paying bribes. At Tbilisi State University's Law Faculty, roughly

12. Interview with FF on 15 April 2000. A popular joke reports a sign at TSU stating: "Entrance Exams Will Not Be Held: All Places Have Already Been Sold."

one-eighth of the places for students are non-fee paying.[13] Theoretically the remaining students are also admitted, albeit as fee-paying students, on the basis of their examination scores. In reality, the selection of the fee-paying students is based largely on buying their way in (bribing administrators) or by relying on connections. During the course of the programme itself, some professors are known to require bribes for giving a passing grade in the course. Opportunities for this sort of bribery are enhanced through the widespread use of oral examinations (a common Soviet, post-Soviet and Western European practice), with questions varying from student to student during individual testing. With many departments already charging from US$ 400 to US$ 1000 in official tuition fees, legal education in a good school can be quite costly and beyond the reach of most, a fact that has implications for access to the profession as will be discussed below.[14] In fact, even those students who win non-fee paying positions through state exams are generally wealthy, since they typically have paid hundreds of dollars to tutors (university professors who wish to supplement their income) in their final years of high school.[15]

Low professors' salaries are related to the corruption problem. While wages are a problem throughout former Soviet universities, at an average of 40 Laris per month Georgian academic salaries are particularly low.[16] This is an inadequate living wage and for many professors provides the justification for their bribe-taking activities. Some professors—often the most qualified—have left academia (or the country) and represent an outright "brain drain" from the universities. Some of the remaining ones have adopted coping strategies to remain in academia without taking bribes. They may teach at several different universities, tutor, and take second jobs, resulting in a partial drain from the state faculties.[17] Others have looked to Western funders to support their teach-

13. Chap. 4 of the Human Development Report, 2000, *op. cit.* note 5.
14. *Ibid.* The state provides stipends to some students but this is roughly 12 Laris per month. In Russia some corporations have established fellowships and scholarships for students who agree to work for them following graduation (see P.H. Solomon, Jr. and T.S. Foglesong, *Courts and Transition in Russia: The Challenge of Judicial Reform*, Boulder, CO 2000, 101) but this has not occurred in Georgia.
15. The *Human Development Report, 2000, ibid.*, reports that students may pay US$ 2000-3000 for a thorough tutoring in the required subjects.
16. For example, by the mid-1990s Ukranian professors were already receiving roughly 180 US$/month: figure cited in J. Stetar and A. Pohribny, "Towards a New Definition of Quality: Taras Shevchenko National University (Kyiv University), Ukraine" in Sabloff, *op. cit.* note 7, 177.
17. Apparently in Russia, there has been a "brain drain" of professors from state to private universities. In the Georgian context I have observed only a partial "brain drain", as professors at the state schools maintain their positions in those schools (which is a source of prestige) but may spend only small amounts of time there (with corresponding low involvement in the general academic life of the faculty). On the Russian "brain drain" see Ajani, *op. cit.* note 5.

ing and research activities. For example, an NGO called the Civic Education Project provides young academics who have studied in the West and returned to a full-time academic position in their former-communist homelands with a stipend and teaching support.[18] But many of the Western-funded supports require a knowledge of English (or sometimes German or French) and international educational experience, requirements which exclude the majority of professors.

It is clear that until professors' salaries are raised to at least the subsistence level, corruption will continue to exist. At the same time, it would be naïve to think that corruption will end with the raising of professors' salaries alone. Many administrators have grown rich through corruption and undoubtedly wish to grow richer still. This wealth-creating activity is supported by a network of patron-client relationships that will not easily be broken. Professors pass money up to department heads who pass money up to deans who pass money up to vice-rectors and rectors, in a system which many students call "academic mafia". While such a "mafia" is pervasive in Georgian universities, it is a phenomenon observed in other parts of the former communist bloc. As one author puts it, a "new university hierarchy emerged after the fall of Communism, dominated by senior professors who wish to maintain their power, as well as control over hiring, promotion, the granting of diplomas, elections to university representative bodies and elected offices, budgets that can be embezzled and entrance exams that can be sold".[19] It is well known who the largest beneficiaries of bribe-taking are on campus, as their latest model Western luxury cars are often parked outside of their offices.

The quality of teaching in Georgian law departments varies significantly. Georgians themselves appear to place the law departments in three tiers. In the first tier are the Law, and International Law and Relations Faculties at Tbilisi State University. Second are the law faculties at the state universities in Batumi and Kutaisi, along with those of the best private universities. Third are the law departments in the other private universities.[20] While I would generally concur with this ranking, there are some wrinkles. As noted above, teachers at the state universities often teach courses at the private universities as well, thus blurring the public-private divide. In addition, law specializations are being offered in a

18. For information on the Civic Education Project's "Eastern Scholar" programme see www.cep.org.hu. Other Western organizations providing teaching opportunities for local professors are the GTZ (which sponsors the Business and Law Faculty at the Georgian Technical University) and, curiously, the University of Hawaii (with a small campus in Tbilisi).
19. A. Tucker, "Introduction: Higher Education on Trial", 9 *East European Constitutional Review* 2000 No. 3, 88-89, 88.
20. The perception that private law schools are of very poor quality is shared in Russia: see A.M. Lomonosov and R.W. Makepeace, "Legal Education in Russia—Present Challenges and Past Influences", 31 *Law Teacher* 1997 No. 3, 333-347.

number of business faculties of which some are quite good. Finally, the Faculty of Law at Tbilisi State University has a large number of correspondence students (more than half of its almost 4,000 students), whose education is of questionable quality.[21] But there are also commonalities between the three tiers. These include teaching methodology and content, which remain largely unchanged despite formal changes in academic programmes (from a 5-year to a 4-year bachelor's degree[22]) and bold pronouncements that Georgian universities are now "European-style".[23]

The Soviet-style passive-learning environment, in which students are expected to memorize the law and any critiques as passed down by the professor, remains predominant. Class discussion during lectures is generally not encouraged (although there is also a tradition of holding seminars aside from the lectures, under the guidance of teaching assistants). There are some exceptions to the static teaching method. In a departure from the strong Soviet-era distinction between academics and practitioners, the latter are increasingly being asked by law departments (burgeoning with new students) to teach courses. While these courses tend to be more interactive, my observations suggest that many of the newly appointed lecturers do not prepare for class and the format seems to be that of telling "war stories" or providing "question and answer" sessions.[24] Another exception is that professors who have studied abroad are introducing interactive learning into the classroom and are holding debates or moot courts.[25] Foreign lecturers are also now teaching in universities in the capital, and have introduced new teaching styles.[26] Their efforts are limited

21. There is a long pedigree of legal education by correspondence in the Soviet space: W.E. Butler, *Soviet Law*, London 1983, 71.
22. In the Soviet period a full-time law degree at a university was a five-year programme. The first post-graduate degree was the Candidate of Legal Sciences which has its equivalent somewhere between a North American Masters and Doctorate. In 1994 TSU adopted the "four plus two" model of a Bachelor's Degree followed by a Master's Degree. In this regard Georgia is already in line with the European Union's "two-cycle" higher education as expressed in the Bologna Declaration (Joint Declaration of the European Ministers of Education Convened in Bologna on 19 June 1999).
23. A promotional pamphlet from TSU (c. 1997, on file with the author) states: "After a pause of several centuries in higher education the teaching of all branches of science at a high level in Georgian at a European style university became possible against the great cultural and educational background created by the educated ancestors of the Georgian people."
24. In one business law class I observed at the TSU International Business Faculty in May 1999, the lecturer-practitioner took questions from the class on topics ranging from debt collection to inheritance to the impending divorce of one member of the class.
25. Interview with DD and observation of DD's class on 14 November 1998.
26. Some examples are the placement of visiting lecturers by the Civic Education Project in Tbilisi's universities, courses on humanitarian law offered by delegates of the International Committee of the Red Cross (ICRC), and German Professors at the Faculty of Business and Law, Georgian Technical University. There are also American Fulbright scholars teaching in Tbilisi.

by language and content barriers and the reluctance of administrators to fully incorporate foreigners' courses into the curricula. Finally, legal clinics are starting to become a part of the law school curriculum, starting in 2000 with the introduction of a legal clinic at Tbilisi State University's Law Faculty. Though it appears that the reaction of students, professors and even potential clients to the clinic has been lukewarm (with more enthusiasm shown for the clinics outside of the universities), clinical legal education has the potential to provide practical skills training while at the same time aiding vulnerable citizens.[27]

Besides the common characteristic of static teaching methods, the content of Georgian legal education tends to be abstract and theoretical. Comparative Law courses (formerly "Bourgeois Legal Systems"), for example, involve an articulation of rules and structures in an essentialist form ("the common law/civil law says...") rather than an examination of how different legal systems handle similar problems. Indeed, second and third year students at the International Law and Relations Faculty, who had taken international and comparative law courses, reported never having read a case from an international, European or foreign court.[28] This is in keeping with the general emphasis placed on what the lecturer says, rather than self-study through readings and regular assignments. In fairness, this is partly due to the lack of translated international or comparative materials and the lack of quality Georgian-language textbooks. The textbook problem is compounded by the fact that while upper-year students are generally able to compensate for the lack of Georgian-language materials by relying on Russian-language books, Georgian students just entering university are increasingly unable to read in Russian.[29] Furthermore, while the knowledge of English is growing, it remains uneven in many faculties and English-language texts (where they exist in sufficient numbers) cannot yet be assigned as mandatory reading.

In terms of subject matter, law school curricula tend to exhibit the Soviet feature of state-centrism. Indeed, the single most important course is "Theories of State and Law". This emphasis on public law comes at the expense of private

27. The clinic, which is funded by the Constitutional Law and Policy Institute based in Budapest, has "sister" clinics at universities in Yerevan and Baku.
28. Reported to me by students in my Comparative Law class at the International Law and Relations Faculty of TSU in Spring 1998. It should be noted that there are remarkably different approaches to the use of case law among Western European countries as well, even in the teaching of European Community law: N. Cohn & A. Garde, "Mutual Influences of English and French Legal Cultures Through Legal Education", 3 *European Review of Private Law* 1999, 381-387.
29. The lack of materials in the national languages of smaller post-communist nations is a common problem (see for example E. Spaho, "Dire Straights: Albanian Legal Education", 9 *East European Constitutional Review* 2000 No. 3, 90-93, 92). Given the small markets, publishing in this area is not very profitable, though granting agencies are increasingly funding publishing activities of academic textbooks in national languages.

law courses.[30] Georgia is certainly not alone in this statist approach, and perhaps such an approach is reasonable for the country given its legal development and current need for state-building. As the lack of consensus on legal education within the European Union shows—particularly in wake of the Bologna Declaration—there is no one "Western" model to simply import, were that ever a desirable plan.[31] But it is noteworthy that the statist direction in Georgia continues by inertia or force of habit—there has never been a significant debate on the nature or aims of legal education.[32] A lack of (an) articulated vision(s) of legal education may also account for the continued presence of criminalistics on the curricula in many schools, a throwback to the time when one of the aims of law school was to prepare students to be investigators or secret police. Finally, it should be noted that legal clinics have the potential to link law schools to the community and to present a vision of law which is different from the predominant state-centred orientation.[33]

Challenges in teaching are also matched by various barriers to scholarship. A primary difficulty, noted above, is the lack of academic material given the poor shape of libraries.[34] And, on their salaries, professors are unable to purchase books or to devote much time to their research or teaching.[35] Georgian legal publishing has been slow off the mark (though this area improved in the late 1990s, with the appearance of new journals and more thorough, better referenced articles),[36] and Russian books are expensive and difficult to

30. See for example the curriculum of the Law Faculty at Grigol Robakidze University, which includes the following courses: "State and Law", "The History of State and Law in Georgia", "State and Law Theory" and "Georgian State Law" (http://www.gruni.kheta.ge/).

31. On post-Bologna discussions, see N. Reich & W. Stoffel, "Legal education in a unifying Europe", 1 *European Law Faculties Newsletter* 2000, 16-20 and the other articles in that issue of the Newsletter.

32. Unlike Russia, which has seen some debate over legal education, and the publication of state standards for law school curriculum (*Gosstandarty*), Georgia has not had such a debate, consensus or regulation on what constitutes the essentials of a legal education. On the Russian curriculum see Ajani, *op. cit.* note 5.

33. As it has been argued that American legal clinical education provides an alternative vision of legal practice to the predominant business law stream (see M.J. Kotkin, "The Law School Clinic: A Training Ground for Public Interest Lawyers" in J. Cooper and L.G. Trubek, eds., *Educating for Justice: Social Values and Legal Education,* Aldershot 1997).

34. This also applies to the Institute of State and Law. Despite the fact that researchers at the Institute are working on important issues of the day, such as organized crime and corruption, they are hampered by a lack of up-to-date material. This has been helped by external funders, including a grant of US$ 27,000 from the Eurasia Foundation in 2000 to support the Institute's legislative reform efforts.

35. Students in various faculties reported that some professors come to their lectures only sporadically.

36. Generally the new journals have been launched by Western organizations or though sponsorship by international donors. For example, the *Georgian Law Review* is published by the Georgian European Policy and Advice Centre, which is a TACIS/European Union Project. The *Georgian Journal of International Law* was launched with the financial assistance of the United Nations High Commissioner for Refugees.

obtain in the absence of properly functioning postal services. As mentioned, academic isolation is another challenge, particularly outside of Tbilisi. While in the capital there is a degree of synergy between universities, the Institute of State and Law, foreign organizations and legislative drafters, this is not the case in the regions. Furthermore, scholarly networks in Transcaucasia, strong in Soviet times (particularly between the state universities in Tbilisi, Yerevan and Baku), were all but broken by the mid-1990s, though there are encouraging signs that they are being re-established.[37] As the political situation stabilized in the late 1990s there were increased exchanges between the state universities in the three countries, including invitations to attend thesis defences and sit on the editorial boards of journals. Many of these exchanges are based on individual initiatives and past connections, though exchanges are also occurring at the behest of Western aid programmes. For example, the Constitutional Law and Policy Institute based in Budapest has funded legal clinics at a main university in each of the three Transcaucasian countries. Conferences and meetings involving clinic directors and staff are regularly held in Tbilisi.[38] Likewise the Civic Education Project, which has activities in all three Transcaucasian states, holds annual regional student conferences in Tbilisi. The regional emphasis of many of the aid programmes is not purely administrative, but rather reflects the stated policy goal of funders to promote regional co-operation.[39] At the same, time, grants from the Open Society Institute (a part of the "Soros network"), Muskie Fellowships and other Western (heavily American-funded) programmes have allowed for growing numbers of professors to study in the West. If and when they do return from the West, they not only bring new teaching methodologies, but also resources for their own scholarship.

Financial and logistical difficulties aside, it should be noted that some professors and administrators have simply been intellectually unable to retool themselves to operate as legal scholars or law teachers in a democratic, capitalist society. The UNDP's 1996 *Human Development Report* addressed the "human capital" issue in these terms:[40]

> Among the higher rank professorship there is no motivation for change and many of the more dynamic and innovative have left to teach abroad or to pursue some other employment. Those who were teaching a few years ago Marxist-Leninist political economy and

37. The reasons for the breaks in relationships are various and include deteriorated transportation routes, lack of funding for travel and conferences and heightened animosity between the countries on a variety of issues.
38. Georgian academics and those in the NGO sector have benefited from the conflict between Armenia and Azerbaijan, in the sense that conferences involving participants from all three countries are nearly always held in "neutral" Georgia.
39. For example, the Eurasia Foundation launched its South Caucasus Co-operation Programme in 1998 to fund projects initiated by partners in each of Georgia, Armenia and Azerbaijan.
40. UNDP, *Human Development Report, Georgia: 1996*, Tbilisi, 117.

"scientific communism", currently teach market economy or political science. The departments and faculties do not plan their activities on the basis of defining priorities and needs in society, or on the basis of market demand, but rather following inertia...

Although this statement is no longer as true today, "inertia" continues to carry the day in many faculties.

Given the challenges in teaching and scholarship, perhaps it is not surprising that Georgian law students often have initial difficulties (which they are able to overcome fairly quickly) when faced with critical thinking exercises. In my teaching experience, requirements that they link legal principles with hypothetical facts or case studies proved a challenge. While students were excellent at identifying and articulating the legal issues, they were often unable to apply the law to the facts in a meaningful way. Dispassionate discussion of sensitive issues was also difficult. On questions pertaining to the Georgian identity (minority rights, religious rights for "non-traditional" religions), some students would quickly fall into "blood and soil" rhetoric which did not lend itself to civil (or legal) discourse. On questions of domestic or international politics, the lens was usually that of *realpolitik*. For example, in a class discussion on the legitimacy of NATO's air campaign against Serbia during the Kosovo conflict, the students in my international law class universally saw NATO's attacks as an action against Russia ("to show the Russians who's boss"). They were initially unwilling to consider other geopolitical, legal and moral issues involved. As I have written elsewhere, however, this *realpolitik* view can be seen as a reaction to the ideological interpretations of history and politics from Soviet times, and in this respect is an improvement on previous thinking.[41]

Until very recently, students' trained passivity in the classroom had its counterpart in student politics. At Tbilisi State University power had been carefully handed down to "new" councils from the communist-era student government. General student elections were not held and there was an air of mystery about how the student councils were run.[42] Student leaders were seen as self-interested "toadies" of the university administration. This appears to be changing, with increased student activism in late 2000 and early 2001, including demonstrations at Tbilisi State University.[43] There is hope among students that the new student leaders will be "change agents" in higher education.

41. See C. Waters, "Georgian *Realpolitik*", 28 *Peacekeeping and International Relations* 1999 No. 4, 2.
42. Observations of student discussions on student government held at the Civic Education Project's Caucasus Conference (Tbilisi, April 2000).
43. The new student activism was sparked by a tuition fee increase at TSU, leading to demonstrations: "Students of Tbilisi State University Against the Increase of the Education Fee", *Sarke Information Agency* 1 October 1999.

Beyond Law School: Preparing Law Graduates for Practice

In its assessment of Georgian legal education, the World Bank criticizes Georgian legal education for the fact that it does not adequately train students for the practice of law. The report states that "[i]t has been reported that most graduates of the state schools need significant additional study to be able to assume a legal job".[44] While this is without doubt the case (though a surprising number of Georgian jurists were unwilling to admit this "on the record")[45] it is not peculiar to Georgia. In many civil law jurisdictions a university legal education is not considered to be professional training; law is an undergraduate education in which students also take non-law courses in order to have a well-rounded education.[46] And in North America there is a tension (or at least duality) between legal education as an academic enterprise in its own right and lawyer training. In all jurisdictions, though the numbers vary widely, there are more law graduates than lawyers (however widely defined).[47] The fact that thousands more persons will graduate from Georgian law schools than will practice, and that law school is not simply training for law practice, is not in itself alarming. But that does not mean that a broad-based undergraduate degree in law is unrelated to practice either. As Reueschemeyer puts it: "Even with a rather diffuse and academic education, however, graduates bring a certain level of knowledge and understanding to their work that is difficult to quantify but hardly irrelevant to an overall assessment of the uses of legal expertise in the political economy."[48] In Georgia, in the absence for the first decade of independence of a licensing body, bar admission course, examination or mandatory internship which could be used to screen law graduates for adequacy of knowledge or skills, legal education remains particularly relevant to law practice. Until a law was passed in June 2001 anyone with a law degree (and even that was not a formal requirement) could act as a lawyer.[49] As will

44. "Georgia Judicial Assessment", *op. cit.* chap. 1, note 53, 25.
45. At the beginning of my interview with a law professor (V) on 3 December 1998, I asked her if students graduating from her department were ready to practice law. She replied that they were, though later, when reassured that her remarks would not be attributed suggested that only one quarter of students should be licensed to practice.
46. For example, in addition to law courses, law students at the International Law and Relations Faculty (TSU) take political science, philosophy, sociology, economics and language courses.
47. Brazil is perhaps an extreme example in this regard: J. Falcão, "Lawyers in Brazil" in R.L. Abel and P.S.C. Lewis, eds., *Lawyers in Society: The Civil Law World,* vol. 2, Berkeley 1989, 412 (hereinafter *Lawyers in Society* (v. 2)).
48. D. Rueschemeyer, "Comparing Legal Professions: A State-Centred Approach" in *Lawyers in Society,* vol. 3, *op. cit.* chap. 1, note 10, 295.
49. Law of Georgia on the Bar (20 June 2001, hereinafter Law on the Bar). The Georgian language version can be found online at www.parliament.ge/LEGAL_ACTS/976-IIs.html (unofficial translation on file with the author).

be explored in the next chapter, the current law sets up a mandatory bar association and requires an examination as well as a law degree. The examination will likely not be a stringent one, however, and candidates have until 2003 to pass the exams. Accordingly, legal education will continue to be of primary importance in determining the number and character of lawyers.

Although the World Bank report may be accurate in stating that Georgian students *need* further study, many students leave law school directly for practice without additional training.[50] It is perhaps not surprising that the public believes educating lawyers and judges is the best ways to improve the judicial system (more so than other factors including higher judges' salaries).[51] If Georgian law graduates do receive additional training, it comes in the form of study or working internships abroad, voluntary continuing legal education (CLE) or mentoring. The primary deliverer of CLE is the Georgian Young Lawyers' Association (GYLA), which has offices in Georgia's major cities and offers evening seminars to its practicing and student members (including foreign language courses). In fact GYLA is the only consistent provider of CLE which reaches sizeable numbers of lawyers. Other lawyers' groups, namely the Collegium of Advocates and the Lawyers' Union, appear to do little CLE, although the Collegium still formally has an internship programme for new members. A number of foreign or international organizations also provide CLE, notably the ABA and USAID contractors, often in collaboration with a local NGO.[52] The experts brought in by these programmes are generally Americans who do not speak local languages and sometimes lack awareness about the civil law system. It should be noted that the June 2001 law establishes an "Advocates Training Centre" at the Bar Association, but given the institutional challenges which will face the Association (explored in the next chapter), it is doubtful if the Training Centre will become an effective body in the near future.[53]

It is difficult to gauge the extent of informal mentoring in Georgian legal practice, though some "progressive" law firms have established mentoring programmes with a degree of formality. The Georgia Consulting Group (GCG) is not a typical law firm—one of its early principals was an American lawyer and its roughly ten Georgian lawyers all have foreign training. However it is worth looking at for its importance on the Georgian legal landscape

50. By contrast, Russian law students must complete internships in different branches of the legal system before graduating: Solomon and Foglesong, *op. cit.* note 14, 102.
51. GORBI, *op. cit.*, chap. 3, note 40, 23.
52. On ABA activities in Georgia see http://www.abalawyersource.org/ceeli/countries/georgia.html. On the activities of US organizations in Russian legal education—many of which are duplicated on a smaller scale in Georgia see J.M. Picker & S. Picker,"Educating Russia's Future Lawyers—Any Role for the United States?", 33 *Vanderbilt Journal of Transnational Law* 2000 No. 1, 17-77.
53. Law on the Bar, *op. cit.* note 49, art. 23(3).

(there are no multinational law firms active in Georgia and GCG is the main legal "conduit" for foreign investment) and because it reveals what mentoring needs exist. The American principal described the training he gave to new lawyers joining the firm as follows.[54] Improving their legal writing was a priority. He wanted them to write in a tight, "American style" which "gets to the point", not the "abstract meandering which they were taught".[55] To this end he bought each of the lawyers the well-known American book *Elements of Style*, and instructed them how to write memoranda containing the facts, a statement of the legal issues and rules and an application of the law. He also trained them in practice management (filing systems and docketing) and legal ethics on a case-by-case basis.

On the non-business side, one of the bright spots in mentoring can be found in a local NGO called Article 42. Through its "Fundamental Rights Centre" the NGO acts as a legal clinic, which, as the name implies, focuses on human rights cases (particularly those involving wrongdoing on the part of the police). The founder, who was one of the student dissidents at the Faculty of Law of Tbilisi State University in the late 1980s, set up the Centre with a grant from the American Bar Association. There are now several practicing lawyers and a dozen or so law students who volunteer at the clinic.[56] The volunteers do the client interviews and have a degree of "ownership" over the cases, but they regularly seek the advice of the senior lawyers and have group sessions where they share work in progress and seek advice from their peers. Foreign lawyers are also asked to give seminars to the volunteers on a regular basis. The student volunteers are enthusiastic about their work at the clinic and appear to skip classes, believing that they have more to learn at the clinic than in law school.[57] The students see the training they receive at the clinic as good preparation for a move to private practice following graduation. Student volunteers also receive practical skills development through GYLA's telephone consultation service.[58] Through the week students research legal issues assigned to them by the GYLA lawyer who takes the call and discuss the legal issues with the lawyers. On Sundays students themselves answer the calls and conduct the initial telephone interviews.

Access to the Profession

Formal education is seen by Weberians as one of the principal mechanisms for controlling the supply of lawyers.[59] In some countries a degree from an accred-

54. Interview with OO on 14 May 1999.
55. *Ibid.*
56. Interviews with AA on 19 September 1998, 10 March 1999 and 9 June 2000.
57. Discussion with student volunteers at Article 42's offices over several days in October 2000.
58. Interview with PP on 11 September 1998.
59. See R.L. Abel, "Comparative Sociology of Legal Professions" in *Lawyers in Society* (v. 3), *op. cit.* chap. 1, note 10, 85-90.

ited law school is a mandatory requirement to practice law, and the number of places for students at the schools is restricted. Particularly in Canada and the US—where a law degree is typically a student's second degree—competition to enter law schools is strong. In other countries, where law is an undergraduate programme and not one which delivers professional training *per se*, large numbers of students are accepted into the first year of the programme. In these jurisdictions, however, the difficulties in completing the law degree (with high failure and drop-out rates) are significant. Once through law school, law students in most jurisdictions also face barriers in the form of professional examinations or apprenticeship requirements. For a decade in Georgia there was no formal requirement of a law degree to practice law, no professional examination and no mandatory apprenticeship. As will be discussed, the efficacy of the legislation now in place is questionable. In spite of this lack of regulation, or more accurately, because of it, a good formal legal education plays an important role in determining access to employment in law. But what does a student need to get into law school and then use the law degree to get a job?

As noted, comparative wealth (and/or connections) is needed by most students to get into and through law school. But having this wealth is not the only barrier to professional employment. The reputations of the law school and the student are also potential barriers. Those in what are considered to be the first tier of law schools (the Faculty of Law and the International Law and Relations Faculty at TSU) have the easiest time in finding work. In fact their work often begins during the course of their studies, with internships in government ministries or, for those with foreign language skills, employment with foreign organizations. After graduating, students from these faculties receive the plum jobs of Georgian legal society, such as clerkships with the Constitutional Court, employment with the Procuracy or business law firms, or, for students from the International Law and Relations Faculty, employment with the Ministry of Foreign Affairs. There is still a good deal of unemployment or underemployment for these graduates (entry level positions at the Ministry of Foreign Affairs often pay token amounts only), but it is clear that the best jobs that are available go to them. This is due not only to the fact that the first tier of law school is or is considered to be the best. Rather, the students who attend these law schools are generally children of the elite and are better connected.[60] While some students in the other two tiers of law schools will find law-related work, many others will not or will find work only at the margins of their occupation.

In addition to what school a student attends, grades also count. Grades are given on a five-point scale (five being the highest score) and recorded

60. They also become better connected while at elite institutions. Needless to say, "school ties" matter in every society; see for example D. Marmaros & B. Sacerdote, "Peer and social networks in job search", 46 *European Economic Review* 2002 Nos. 4-5, 870-879.

in individual booklets which students carry throughout their degree. Some employers ask to see students' booklets during interviews, and the grades are considered when applying for study abroad possibilities (which in turn make students more marketable). But in a system of pervasive corruption, the face value of grades in a booklet is a potentially unreliable indicator of a student's academic performance. Here individual reputation comes into play. At the end of the day, students generally know who has studied for and who has only paid for their degrees among their classmates. While paying bribes in addition to studying is considered to be somewhat acceptable, merely paying is not. Sometimes professors themselves publicly make it clear who does and does not have a real grasp of the material. For example, it was reported to me that during final oral exams before an examining board at a private law school in Kutaisi, the chair of the board confronted one student who appeared to have learned absolutely nothing during the course of his degree. Before granting the student his degree—the student had paid for it after all—the chair of the examining board ridiculed the student before his peers.[61] In a reputation-bound society (particularly in law where there are few other controls), students who are known to have simply bought their degrees are thought of poorly and may have their career options limited. Thus, despite the lack of control over numbers of law schools and numbers of places for law students, law school education does matter and *de facto* restricts the supply of students who might realistically be offered employment in law.

Two other points need to be made here with respect to access to legal education and in turn access to the profession. The first is that the law schools in the first tier are both in Tbilisi. Thus in order to send their children to one of the best law schools parents in the regions must have the ability to bear the additional travel and living expenses which living in the capital entail. Few can afford this. Accordingly, the concentration of well-educated lawyers in Tbilisi continues and contributes to the legal underdevelopment of the regions *vis-à-vis* the capital. As will be discussed in the chapter on legal practice, the regions lack legal talent and clients are often forced to travel to Tbilisi to obtain decent legal advice and representation. The second point is that there are few minorities among the students in the first tier of law schools. This is due to linguistic barriers, factors of national chauvinism (recall the "Georgianization" of higher education during Soviet times) and the fact that on average minority students are less well connected and less wealthy than their Georgian counterparts. The lack of minority access to the elite institutions in turn plays a role in limiting minority access to the legal profession.

61. Interview with C, *op. cit.* chap. 3, note 4.

Educating the Public

Thus far in this chapter we have examined how law students or junior lawyers are educated about the law. However, as has been pointed out in different contexts, law teaching is not only for or by jurists.[62] This was certainly true of the Soviet period when "legal propaganda" was delivered in workplaces and schools and knowledge of socialist law was considered essential for each citizen.[63] Advocates and jurisconsults had a special role to play in this regard, and were expected to devote a set portion of their time to such activities. But if the idea of spreading legal knowledge to the citizenry was not new in the 1990s, the form and content was much changed. In the mid-1990s public affairs shows (including those with a call-in format) increasingly dealt with the leading-edge constitutional and legal issues confronting Georgia. And television programming dedicated to legal knowledge made an appearance with series such as "The Georgian Constitution" and "Democracy and Self-Government". Indeed television and newspapers appear to be the primary source of legal information for citizens though the cost of newspapers and frequent power cuts limits their effectiveness somewhat, especially in the regions.[64]

Understandably, the most popular issue for the population as a whole has been the rights of citizens *vis-à-vis* the police (though questions as to tax and family law are also popular). Various NGOs staffed by lawyers have distributed pamphlets setting out citizens' rights in summary form, such as a pamphlet from Article 42 entitled "If you are arrested!!!"[65] These groups also hold seminars or publish materials targeted at the general public or at specific segments of the population (women and internally displaced persons in particular). International organizations have also launched public awareness campaigns, several in the area of electoral rights. Finally, as a mandatory part of the curriculum, secondary schools provide tenth grade students with one hour per week on law.[66] The lack of emphasis on this subject has been criticized, one report stating:[67]

> What may be surprising from the current...curricula is the low emphasis on the subject "Fundamentals of Justice", an area in which the whole of Georgian youth seem to be inadequately prepared. This issue is all the more important given the current efforts to move towards a new social system with a new approach to understanding justice and how it is to be dispensed. In fact, "Fundamentals of Justice" receives the same attention

62. See for example N. Kasirer, "Apostolat Juridique: Teaching Everyday Law in the Life of Marie Lacoste Gérin-Lajoie (1867-1945)", 30 *Osgoode Hall Law Journal* 1992 No. 2, 427-470.
63. See Butler, *op. cit.* note 21, 71.
64. See Anjaparidze, *op. cit.* chap. 3, note 71, 10.
65. Tbilisi 1999 (unofficial translation on file with author).
66. *Human Development Report, 1999, op. cit.* chap. 3, note 29, 43.
67. *Ibid.*

> as "Astronomy" and half the number of hours of "Drawing". In the current curricula, teaching our youth "Primary Military Training" is four times as important as teaching them concepts of justice.

This criticism appears to echo public sentiment. A public opinion poll conducted in 2000 found that 68% of those surveyed said that "the education system does not provide adequate knowledge of rights, liabilities and laws".[68] In some areas, however, the curriculum has been supplemented by additional presentations put on for students by NGOs (including GYLA) and international organizations.[69] The International Committee of the Red Cross (ICRC) was particularly active in the late 1990s in disseminating principles of international humanitarian law in schools.[70] Through a co-operation agreement with the Ministry of Education, the ICRC developed an illustrated textbook which drew on Georgian history and literature to demonstrate humanitarian principles (Georgian kings sparing civilians in times of war, for example).

These public opinion campaigns have not fundamentally transformed the legal culture of Georgia. To start with, citizens complain that they do not have enough legal information to insist on respect for their rights. As a report on public perceptions of law concluded in 1998:[71]

> Focus group participants believe that most of the population of Georgia has little knowledge of developments in the legal sphere, including what rights and responsibilities individual laws and codes grant them. The little information which is available often seems to lack clarity, depth and accuracy. Participants also spoke of legal knowledge discrepancies between people living in Tbilisi and other regions. Finally, participants emphasized that the education system in Georgia lags behind changes in the legal system and hence, is weak in raising educated and responsible citizens.

At the same time the public opinion survey revealed that citizens do have *some* rudimentary knowledge about their rights, albeit incomplete and sometimes with a sense of apathy towards their rights.[72] Furthermore, this knowledge seems to be growing, giving credence to what some respondents to the 1998 survey called "an awakening in Georgian society to laws and one's rights and responsibilities".[73] For example, in the 1998 survey 41% of respondents believed they had the right to appeal to a court against a state official's decision, while

68. GORBI, *op. cit.* chap. 3, note 40, 4.
69. *Human Development Report, 1999, op. cit.* chap. 3, note 29, 42.
70. ICRC, *ICRC in Georgia/Abkhazia: Information Sheet,* Tbilisi 1998. And see S. LeVine, "A Lesson in the Caucasus: Even War Has Rules", *New York Times* 14 February 1999, 15.
71. *Georgia Legal Reform Baseline Study, Focus Group Report,* April 1998 (a study commissioned by the Georgian government and the World Bank and carried out by the Georgian Opinion Research Business International) at iv (hereinafter *Legal Focus Group Report*).
72. *Ibid.*, 8-9.
73. *Ibid.*, 9. The respondents who spoke of this awakening were "members of the NGO, business and media sectors and some younger participants". *Ibid.*

in 2000 the figure had risen to 51.2%.[74] Certainly with respect to university students, I have witnessed increased interest in and awareness of human rights standards between 1998 and 2001. This increased knowledge, attributable in part to the cumulative effect of school activities and public awareness campaigns,[75] may ultimately be a source of challenge to corruption and inefficiency in all aspects of the legislative, administrative and judicial systems.

Concretely speaking, there has been an apparent increase in citizens' knowledge of their right to counsel, and, specifically the right to counsel of choice. Indeed some participants in the 1998 survey indicated that they considered this right to be a particularly important one.[76] While it is difficult to definitively say that knowledge about the right to counsel has come from public awareness campaigns, it seems a fair assumption that they have had an impact. The Article 42 pamphlet states that "if you are arrested":[77]

> —You have the right to be provided with the services of a defender after having negotiated with him or her.
> —You have the right to refuse the services of the appointed defender. It is your right to remain silent at the interrogation session before and after the arrival of a defender.
> —You have the right to refuse the services offered by an appointed defender. The law gives you or your relatives enough time to find an appropriate defender. If the chosen lawyer has not arrived for three hours after your apprehension, the investigator is obliged to appoint a lawyer.
> —You have the right to refuse the services offered by the appointed defender and defend yourself before the arrival of your chosen defender.

The effect of citizen awareness of these points has several effects on the profession. First it increases demand for legal services; citizens are more likely to think that lawyers may find a solution to their problems short of paying bribes. Second, knowledge of the right to counsel of choice has loosened up the market for legal services. Specifically, there is increased understanding about the ability to refuse an appointed defender. Defenders appointed by investigators to accused persons, who are members of the Collegium of Advocates, may well be expected to act as nothing more than a go-between in bribery negotiations. They certainly are unlikely to mount a vigorous defence of their clients. Clients' knowledge that they need not accept appointed defenders is also one of the contributing causes of the erosion of the Collegium's power. A related point is that when counsel of choice is retained, more sophisticated clients are able to critically appraise lawyers' work than in the past. Finally, citizens' newfound awareness of what lawyers can do for them has led to an increase in the overall prestige of the profession, a topic returned to in Chapter 6.

74. GORBI, *op. cit.* chap. 3, note 40 at 4.
75. Other sources may be contact with foreigners, travel abroad and Western media.
76. *Legal Focus Group Report*, *op. cit.* note 71 at 3.
77. *Op. cit.* note 65.

Chapter 5
The Politics of Regulation and Self-Regulation

For the first ten years of independence there were few restrictions on who could act as a lawyer (an interesting parallel to the situation just following the Bolshevik revolution in Russia).[1] None of the usual measures limiting the number of "producers"—quotas or formal exclusions, legal education requirements, mandatory apprenticeship, professional examination, mandatory bar membership—were in place.[2] At least formally Georgian lawyering was a "free for all". Two things are striking about this period. The first is that many lawyers actively opposed a state-mandated monopoly over lawyering. This fact seems to defy many of the comparative and theoretical assumptions about the "professional project" of market control and status enhancement. The second is the degree to which lawyers self-regulated, albeit in a splintered way, in the absence of state regulation or roots in civil society. In June 2001, roughly ten years after independence, the Georgian Parliament finally passed a law on the bar establishing a mandatory association and prescribing examinations.[3] However, it is likely that the law—which came about as a result of prompting more from the Council of Europe than from lawyers—will be somewhat of a "sideshow" in lawyer governance. At least for the foreseeable future, the main story will continue to be how lawyers self-govern.

The first part of this chapter explores the politics of regulation—how the competing interests of lawyers' groups and the government clashed and why a law on the bar was so long in coming. The second part of this chapter examines the question of self-regulation and speculates on how the ten-year experience with self-regulation will interact with the recent legislative attempt at lawyer governance. In addressing both regulation and self-regulation, this chapter initially poses the Weberian questions regarding supply control. This theoretical orientation goes far in providing a comparative framework to understand the motivations of various actors. Ultimately, however, this theoretical perspective has its limitations, at least as classically stated. This is in part a consequence of the nature of comparative studies carried out to date, which have generally ignored socialist and post-socialist countries (and, to a lesser extent, developing countries). More fundamentally, the theories have been built on legal professions that are either deeply rooted in civil society and/or regulated by functioning states. By contrast, the Georgian legal profession has few independent roots in civil society and exists in the context of a partially failed state which has only weakly regulated lawyers. The regulatory vacuum is not filled

1. Although a 1980 law on the bar formally remained in effect for the first post-independence years, its terms were generally ignored in practice.
2. These methods of restricting supply are noted by Abel in "Comparative Sociology of Legal Professions", *op. cit.* chap. 1, note 10. He adds an additional restriction, starting practice, which is dealt with later in this chapter.
3. Law on the Bar, *op. cit.* chap. 4, note 49.

by professional customs or norms of mature market capitalism. Furthermore, while most legal professions are divided by occupation (barristers/solicitors, employed/entrepreneurs) or by clients, prestige and wealth (corporate/"personal plight"), few are fractured in the same way that Georgian lawyers are with deep generational and political cleavage. Accordingly, while this chapter relies on a theoretical perspective, this reliance is tempered by post-Soviet and Transcaucasian realities, and supplemented by a pluralist perspective to examine how the various clusters of lawyers have responded to the regulatory vacuum.

State Regulation

As a condition of accession to the Council of Europe in 1999, Georgia was expected to undertake a number of legal reforms, including "adopt[ing] a law on attorneys within a year after its accession".[4] It took over two years and several failed legislative initiatives before such a law was passed. In part this delay is due to the heavy legislative plate facing Parliament, questions of priorities and the series of crises which the government continuously seems to face.[5] But passage of a law was also delayed due to bitter divisions in the legal profession over what kind of law was needed, or whether a law was needed at all. In the end, the legislation passed more at the insistence of the Council of Europe than at the behest of lawyers who had captured the legislative agenda.

The Players

The key players in the debate over regulation of the profession are the Collegium of Advocates, the Georgian Young Lawyers' Association, parliamentarians, the Ministry of Justice and several academic and other interested individuals and organizations, including the American Bar Association.

The Collegium's position on a law on the bar is simply stated: its legal monopoly on the admission and discipline of advocates should be restored.[6] The Head of the Collegium argues that its members are the most experienced advocates in Georgia and that it has a large membership (over one thousand) spread across the entire territory. He also points out that a structure is already in place, including an elected Presidium which deals with discipline and other matters and a network of Legal Consultation Bureaus staffed with Collegium members.

Detractors argue that the Collegium is a corrupt "old man's club" (US$ 500 is reportedly the going rate for an entry bribe),[7] whose mostly incom-

4. Council of Europe Parliamentary Assembly Opinion 209 (1999) ("Georgia's Application for Membership to the Council of Europe"), para. 10(ii)(d).
5. Among the crises which the government faced during the weeks the bill was being considered were an army mutiny and the kidnapping of a Member of Parliament.
6. Interview with Y on 3 September 1999.
7. Interview with H, *op. cit.* chap. 2, note 126.

petent members are mired in their Soviet mentalities.[8] In fact the vehemence with which many younger lawyers attacked the Collegium during interviews was surprising. A member of the Executive of the Georgian Young Lawyers' Association described the situation to me as follows: "Since 1990 there are two completely different groups of lawyers working in this country. There are those who are relatively young and obtained an education outside the Soviet Union and simply know about ethics. The others are those who have been members of the Collegium of Advocates and simply do not why they should follow any rules."[9] She then went on to dismiss Collegium members out of hand as "doing nothing".[10] Another GYLA member, one of the organization's founders, described the Collegium as a "disaster" which "should be forgotten".[11] Not all Collegium members themselves are content with their organization. For example, a well-respected head of an LCB in Tbilisi complained that while his office paid a portion of all earnings to the Presidium as required, the Presidium never channeled funds back into the LCB for repairs or bookkeeping services, as was the formal policy.[12] Advocates at another LCB in Tbilisi reported that despite paying the Collegium a portion of their fees, they receive no legal information from the Collegium and rely instead on clippings from newspapers to learn about legal developments.[13] Nonetheless, few Collegium members I spoke with suggested that the organization should be disbanded. Rather they suggested that, despite its faults, the Collegium at least ensured some lawyering standards were in place; as the Chairman of one LCB put it, the Collegium was important since there must be "someone above, someone in charge" in order to accept new members and discipline members when necessary.[14] But this is an inadequate explanation for why Collegium members "stick with" the organization—the Collegium manifestly does not govern the behaviour of lawyers. To take ethics and discipline, for example, according to the Head of the Collegium only one advocate was expelled since he became head in 1994, apparently for abandoning a client in the middle of a long trial. As no member has been expelled in this period for corruption, it is difficult to take seriously the notion that the Collegium exercises any real ethical control over its members. Furthermore, it does not *appear* that the Collegium is serious with respect to ethics. The question remains then, of why its lawyers stay.

8. A popular stereotype—repeated to me numerous times—is of the Collegium member as "an old man who shows up at the office everyday only to spend most of his time playing chess". On the Collegium's demographics, see *infra* chap. 6.
9. Interview with PP, *op. cit.* chap. 4, note 58.
10. *Ibid.*
11. Interview with H, *op. cit.* chap. 2, note 126.
12. Interview with B, *op. cit.* chap. 2, note 138.
13. Discussions with D and other advocates at Vake LCB on 21 May 1999.
14. Interview with B, *op. cit.* chap. 2, note 138.

Despite the insistence of young reformers that the Collegium is near-death (a fine example of myth-making used to promote social closure),[15] the majority of criminal cases in the country—and large numbers of civil cases particularly in the area of family and property law—are handled by members of the Collegium.[16] Many members have access to these criminal and civil clients because of their membership. To a limited extent this happens directly through "walk-ins" to the LCBs and through court-appointed "legal aid" cases, but, more lucratively, through client referrals from police, investigators and prosecutors. Most investigators and police have their favourite advocates whom they can call after an arrest, though LCBs also provide their duty rosters to police. Physical access to clients and information (especially at the Preliminary Inquiry stage) is also much more readily given to Collegium members than non-Collegium members, making practice easier. At one point, a letter from the Interior Ministry was reportedly circulated among its employees to the effect that only Collegium members were to be afforded "privileges", which was taken to mean access to clients and files.[17] In short, members stay in the Collegium (or join as new members) because they see membership as good for business. Finally, it should be noted that the Collegium is stronger in the regions than in Tbilisi. The reasons for this include the facts that in the capital there is competition (there are more legal clinics and more lawyers operating outside of the Collegium), there are better informed clients, and there are business clients with complex legal needs which most Collegium members do not have the capacity to handle.

However, the Collegium has not passively watched its monopoly eroded. It has learned to counter-attack using reform language, as the following example illustrates. A brief experiment with placing lawyers inside Tbilisi police stations was launched in 1999. The project was sponsored by the City of Tbilisi and promoted by several NGOs which recognized that most beatings and illegal detentions were occurring at police stations when suspects were first arrested. The Collegium was strongly opposed and allied with police to force an end to the project. It was apparent to most that the Collegium's concern was self-interest: when the city's duty counsel approached detainees directly, Collegium members lost referrals from police and investigators. These referrals would often lead to a "negotiated" settlement of a charge, or at least a less than

15. A good account of lawyerly myth-making is Wesley Pue's "In pursuit of a better myth: lawyers' histories and the histories of lawyers", XXXIII *Manitoba Law Review* 1995 No. 4, 730-767.

16. With respect to criminal law the situation is similar in Russia, where advocates of the Soviet-era Colleges (the "original" or "traditional" colleges) handle 90% of criminal cases. By contrast it was reported that advocates of the newer "parallel" colleges only handle 2.5 % of civil cases in Russia. While there are no available statistics, the number of civil cases handled by Collegium members in Georgia appears to be higher. ("The Russian Advokatura", *op. cit.* chap. 1, note 54, 771).

17. Interview with H, *op. cit.* chap. 2, note 126.

vigorous defence of the client. The Collegium Head, however, publicly argued that the City Hall project had to be discontinued because lawyers would lose their "professional independence" if salaried.[18]

The lobbying activities of the Collegium with respect to its official reinstatement (or at least mitigation of government "reforms") have typically been behind the scenes attempts to influence government officials and Parliamentarians. Only more recently has it resorted to the media to deliver its message. Physically speaking, the Collegium has a geographical advantage for its lobbying activities—as in Soviet times its offices are located in the main building of the Ministry of Justice.

The Georgian Young Lawyers' Association is the second major player in the debate over the bar. The organization, formally founded in 1994, traces its roots to moderate dissenters at the Law Faculty in the late 1980s and young law students and lawyers who found themselves in important positions in the first years of the 1990s. The spur to draw together these loose associations came when attempts to draft an acceptable Constitution seemed to be faltering in 1993. Eighty people attended the founding meeting, although one of the "founding fathers" reports that "only 15 out of the 80 knew what needed to be done" in the sense of creating an independent NGO to promote legal reform and adherence to legal ethics.[19] The organization is the largest NGO in Georgia, with roughly 700 members, both students and lawyers. The organization is formally open to those under the age of 40 who have a recommendation from two GYLA members, though as will be explored below, the organization retains club-like attributes. GYLA has in many ways been the "poster child" of Western aid agencies.[20] Although in its first year members agreed to refuse any outside funding in order to remain independent (members continue to pay nominal fees), that has changed. The organization now has numerous grants from aid agencies and foreign governments. It has embarked on ambitious projects (including a phone-in legal clinic and legal education in public schools) and has carried out many legislative drafting projects on its own initiative as well as at the behest of the government.[21] The organization also has a code of ethics and a disciplinary process. Its members occupy key positions in government, and it has acted as a sort of recruitment agency for Parliamentary lawyers.[22] In the seven years since its founding, members have also gone on to hold judicial

18. Interview with Y, *op. cit.* note 6.
19. Interview with H, *op. cit.* chap. 2, note 126.
20. For example, GYLA has been billed a "Eurasia Foundation Success Story": A. Williamson, "Building a Professional Legal Corps for Georgia: The Georgian Young Lawyers Association Raises the Bar for Legal Services" (promotional literature of the Tbilisi office of the Eurasia Foundation, January 2001).
21. And even foreign organizations wishing to influence the policy process.
22. In 1995 Zurab Zhvania, current Parliamentary speaker, wrote to the organization requesting 57 lawyers to work for various committees and departments. GYLA supplied 54 of those lawyers. (Interview with PP, *op. cit.* chap. 4, note 58.)

posts (including on the Supreme Court) and high positions in banks, foreign organizations and private practice. Some members are also employed by the organization itself, including the executive, the telephone clinic's lawyers and lawyers working on funded projects. The lawyers in private practice tend to be largely involved in Georgia's "new economy" of commerce and international trade; they are not the primary deliverers of criminal legal services.

The organization is, however, not without its critics. As to be expected the chief critics are from the ranks of the Collegium. For many Collegium members GYLA lawyers are too young and too inexperienced to be taken seriously. Even the young lawyers' education is suspect. As one advocate put it: "At least when we were in school we studied—we knew something. What we knew is a different matter, but at least we knew something. Now, they know nothing, they don't learn!"[23] But criticisms do not only come from the old guard. Some of GYLA's own early leaders warn that there must be vigilance in ensuring professional distance between the organization and its members who now occupy powerful posts. There are also some young reformers outside of the organization as well as Western observers who criticize it, albeit softly and "off the record," as having some unethical members, being grant-driven, and acting in a self-serving way. With respect to the latter criticism, it has been suggested that the telephone legal consultation service that GYLA offers is sometimes used more as a referral service, to channel clients towards practicing GYLA lawyers, than as a source of legal advice for the poor.[24] This allegation has not been independently verified. As will be discussed below, GYLA's position on a law on the bar has shifted over the last several years from an initial rejection of any law on the bar to support for a law which mandates examinations for all lawyers and the creation of a new bar.

In addition to the Collegium and GYLA there are several other actors in the debate. Obviously Parliamentarians (particularly those on the Legal Affairs Committee) and the Ministry of Justice are key. With respect to Parliamentarians, the first thing to note is that jurists are not over-represented. In the 1995 Parliamentary elections, only 16 out of 230 MPs were jurists.[25] While this number more than doubled in the 1999 elections, the percentage of lawyers is still not comparatively high.[26] Furthermore lawyers are spread throughout the

23. Interview with HH on 21 May 1999.
24. In fact, there is often a close connection between free legal advice and lawyer marketing. For example, the Lawyer Referral Service of the Ontario Bar offers potential clients one half-hour free legal consultation.
25. Biographies of MPs from both the 1995 and 1999 elections can be found at the Georgian Parliament's web site: www.parliament.ge.
26. *Ibid.* For some figures on lawyers in politics see "Comparative Sociology of Legal Professions", *op. cit.* chap. 1, note 10, 104-105. For a more qualitative assessments of the role of lawyers in public life see T.C. Halliday and L. Karpik, *Lawyers and the Rise of Western Liberalism*, Oxford 1997.

political spectrum and do not appear to have common positions on whether or not advocacy should be regulated or how it should be regulated. Rather lawyers, like most of their counterparts from other occupational backgrounds, are divided along party lines and between those who favour "the young lawyers", as GYLA members are called, and those who favour the position of the Collegium. The latter tend to be the same who, on justice matters, support the *status quo* in the Procuracy and Interior Ministry, while those who favour GYLA's position tend to vote for reformist positions. This split is also reflected in the key Legal Affairs Committee whose membership of 19 included 14 jurists at the time when the 2001 Law on the Bar was passed. Despite the high proportion of lawyers on the Committee there has been no consensus on if or how to legislate on lawyers' activities. This lack of consensus—or even interest—with respect to a law on advocacy among jurists in Parliament is reflected in the Russian experience and reveals a low corporate identity.[27]

In the latter stages of debate over the form of the legal profession, the Justice Minister was Mikhail Saakashvili, an unabashedly pro-Western reformer, who was recruited at Shevardnadze's behest from his New York law practice in 1995 to enter politics.[28] At age 26 when recruited, the Columbia-trained lawyer is known to have close ties to GYLA. Nonetheless, having reformers in positions of power over justice matters in Parliament or the government has not guaranteed passage of reform legislation or implementation of that legislation.[29] This is due in part to the number of political compromises which reformers have had to make within the governing party's coalition of old-guard and reformers, with entrenched bureaucracies, and with Shevardnadze himself (who often "clips the wings" of the young reformers). Indeed, shortly after the Law on the Bar was passed, Saakashvili resigned over what he saw as Shevardnadze's unwillingness to combat corruption.[30]

The American Bar Association's Central and East European Law Initiative is also closely connected to GYLA. Operating in Georgia since the mid-1990s, its efforts have been spearheaded by a number of American lawyers called "liaison officers" who typically spend 6-12 months in Georgia. The stance of ABA liaison officers to a law on the bar changed over time, though the organization's position eventually settled in support of passing such legislation. At times, ABA advice has been to recreate the American system with respect

27. "The Russian Advokatura", *op. cit.* chap. 1, note 54, 777.
28. S. Kinzer, "The 'Man of the Year', Just 29 and Via Manhattan", *New York Times* 4 June 1998, A4.
29. Saakashvili was former head of Parliament's Justice Committee. Another key young reformer, Lado Chanturia, also held the post of Justice Minister and was later named Chief Justice of the Supreme Court.
30. L. Fuller, "Georgia's Robin Hood Stakes His Political Future", *RFE/RL*, Vol. 4(33), 8 October 2001.

to lawyers' governance. For example, in a commentary on two draft laws on the Bar, an ABA report suggested:[31]

> The compromise position utilized in the United States may be worthy of consideration by the drafters. In the United States, licensing, discipline and removal of attorneys is largely under control of the judiciary, while bar associations are mostly unofficial, private organizations. While the bars may be consulted on discipline matters, it is the courts that decide. By placing the powers in the judiciary, the bar as such does not control who will be or who will remain to be, an attorney. However, because the judiciary is free from day-to-day political pressure, these decisions are rarely seen as political ones.

For anyone remotely familiar with the fragile state of the Georgian judiciary, this proposal seems at worst dangerous and at best unhelpful. ABA's attempts to facilitate compromises between various reformist positions have been more helpful.

One other interested group is the Independent Lawyers Association under the leadership of a former Presidential candidate and high profile advocate Kartlos Garibashvili. The group is small but vocal and has demonstrated in front of Parliament to oppose examinations for senior lawyers.[32] It has been suggested that Garibashvili's leadership of this association is primarily a vehicle for him to return to public life.[33]

The Process

The failure to regulate lawyers earlier is not a product of a lack of drafts. There are perhaps a dozen in circulation. The numerous drafts, however, have not followed one from the other in a series of improvements or renegotiations. Most bear little resemblance to each other and reflect not only radically different conceptions but, in many cases, muddled and self-contradictory conceptions. A convenient way to approach the legislative process is to divide efforts into three periods. The first can be termed the "period of confusion". Running from the first serious drafting efforts in 1996 to 1999, this period is marked by loosely drawn battle-lines between interest groups, lack of consensus among the reformers and confusing and incoherent drafting attempts. The second period can be termed the "Gudauri process", named for the mountainous resort town where reformers met to discuss legislative options in Winter 1999. Running from the Gudauri meeting to the defeat of a reformist draft in the Spring of 2000, this period reflected emerging consensus among reformers

31. "Analysis of the Draft Law on the Bar and the Draft Law on Barristers' Activity", 19 August 1996 (the report is available from ABA-CEELI's Legal Assessments Department in Washington, DC). It should be noted that ABA assessment reports are written based on comments by panels of experts, not in-country liaison officers.
32. See "Kartlos Garibashvili Urges to Discuss the Draft of the Bill on Legal Profession", *Caucasus Press* 10 May 2001 and Z. Tarkashvili, "Lawyers Will Have to Learn", *Resonance* 19 January 2000 (cited in *South Caucasian Human Rights Monitor*, January 2000).
33. "The Bar Wants Not to Be Examined", *Caucasus Press* 10 May 2001.

and corresponding sharp opposition from "reactionary" forces. The final period is that leading to the passage of a law in June 2001, a generally pro-reform compromise brokered by the governing party but containing some concessions to the opposition inside and outside of Parliament.

During the "period of confusion" only the Collegium and its supporters had a clear position; that is, restoration of its monopoly. Some of the pro-Collegium drafts did not specifically name the Collegium, but *de facto* would have restored the monopoly of Collegium members. For example a 1998 draft provided that a lawyer was one who: a) had graduated from a law school, b) had at least five years working experience, or c) passed a one-year internship.[34] The lack of access to the profession through an examination meant that the older generation of lawyers would have retained all the power (in voting for an executive, deciding who to accept as interns). Furthermore this draft blurred the distinction (at least formally maintained in the West) between a lawyers' guild and a body established for the protection of the public. One article states the "Principal Goals of the Bar" as follows:[35]

> The perfection of lawyers' activities in the process of protecting the interests of real and legal bodies, protection of professional and social rights of lawyers and defence of their dignity and authority, creation of a strong and objective bar as a guarantee for a strong and legitimate state, to raise the role of lawyers in public relations, the unification of lawyers and creation of a united bar, development of international relations between lawyers.

The same draft provides for criminal prosecutions to be launched against lawyers only with the permission of the bar.[36] Other drafts put forward by academics, the Ministry of Justice, and the Parliamentary Legal Affairs Committee, can only be characterized as incoherent and vague. For example, a 1996 draft stated that "the legal profession is not entrepreneurship or a source of gaining profit" yet permitted the creation of private law firms.[37] The same draft required a degree in law, but did not specify any procedure for accreditation of the law school or even that the school be licensed.[38] Few of the drafts made reference at all to ethical precepts and the ones that did, did so in a cursory manner. Despite the fact that none of the drafts reviewed proposed establishing a Western-style bar, on either a common law or civil law model, it is noteworthy that they all provided for private practice; there was a seeming *de facto* recognition during

34. Draft put forward in 1998 entitled "Law of Georgia on the Bar" (authored by an unnamed Parliamentary lawyer), Art. 22 (unofficial translation on file with author).
35. *Ibid.*, Art. 4.
36. *Ibid.*, Art. 47.
37. Draft put forward in 1996 entitled "Law of Georgia on the Bar" by the State Committee for Reform of Juridical and Legal Organization of the Ministry of Justice, article 2(1) (unofficial translation on file with author). The non-profit disclaimer is likely intended to exclude lawyers from certain tax obligations.
38. *Ibid.*, Art. 17(1).

this period that law firms were "here to stay" and that all legal needs could not be met solely through LCBs.

Among the early drafts there were surprisingly few from young reformers. I had assumed that GYLA would actively seek a law creating a self-governing profession. At a simplistic level, this hypothesis was formed in light of the fact that GYLA was promoting various judicial reforms along Western lines; that this reform agenda would be extended to lawyers seemed obvious. Furthermore, from a theoretical perspective, it is axiomatic that lawyers and other professionals seek state-backed "self-governance." For structural-functionalists self-regulation is necessary to protect the public, since only professionals have the expertise to adequately regulate other professionals. Furthermore, the profession must be independent from the state in order to stand up to the state if necessary and protect the public. In the Weberian view, self-governing professions are used by lawyers as monopolistic "associations of producers".[39] Finally, although a comparative view reveals that the state has played a significantly greater role in constructing professional monopoly and identity in the civil law world than in the common law world, the Russian experience seemed especially à *propos* to Georgia given the shared Soviet past.[40] In the 1990s, Russian advocates from both the Soviet-era colleges (called the "traditional" or "original" colleges) and the newer "parallel" colleges allowed to open in the early 1990s, attempted to safeguard their independence from the state. For example, advocates successfully managed to kill a draft brought out of the Russian Ministry of Justice in 1996 which "attempted to return state-bar relations to their pre-Gorbachev status" by restoring the Ministry's supervisory power over the *advokatura*.[41] While Russian advocates have compromised with the state and even seen the state as their patron (to protect them against unfavourable taxation, to maintain the monopoly of advocates over legal services, etc.) advocates of all stripes in that country appeared to want professional autonomy for their colleges and organizations.[42]

In light of the theory and the Russian experience, I anticipated that GYLA would seek a law creating a bar with maximum independence from

39. See R.L. Abel, *American Lawyers*, New York 1989.
40. The Weberian approach also recognizes that independence from the state—much vaunted by structural-functionalists and by professions themselves—is somewhat of a fiction in that the state is used to construct and maintain the profession's regulatory power. See D. Rueschemeyer, "Comparing Legal Professions: A State Centred Approach" in Abel and Lewis (vol. 3), *op. cit.* chap. 1, note 10, and see R.L. Abel, "Lawyers in the Civil Law World" in *Lawyers in Society* (vol. 2), *op. cit.* chap. 4, note 47.
41. "The Russian Advokatura", *op. cit.* chap. 1, note 54, 777.
42. As Jordan has put it, the Russian *advokatura* was "compromising some of its autonomy in order to gain material resources, protection and validation from state agencies." *Ibid.*, 774.

the state (although relying on the state to protect the monopoly of lawyers). The 1996 GYLA draft prepared for Parliament's Legal Committee proposed the opposite. The draft stated:[43]

> The powers of the state to regulate the practice of law are exercised by the Ministry of Justice which creates a committee to issue licenses to practice law.
>
> The chairman and members of the Committee are appointed by the Minister of Justice. The organizational structure and procedures for work of the Committee are determined by the bylaws which are to be approved by the Minister of Justice after submission to him by the Committee.

Among other things the Ministry of Justice (through the Parliamentary Committee) would have had the power to set professional examinations and revoke licenses to practice. Given the Soviet legacy of interference and control by the Ministry of Justice over the governance of lawyers, and the recent Russian experience, this position seemed extraordinary. Ironically, it was the "old guard" who wanted a completely independent self-governing profession while the young reformers did not want to create a "classic" profession.

In fact, many young reformers were opposed to any law on the bar at all. In September 1998, for example, GYLA struck a committee to prepare a draft law on the bar at the behest of the Minister of Justice. At the initial committee meetings which I observed, there was real ambivalence to the very idea of a law on the bar.[44] To the extent that a law had to be drafted, many committee members were only in favour of licensing lawyers through a simple procedure. Specifically, while they were willing to see examinations put in place by some neutral body, they were unwilling to see a mandatory bar. Others suggested a law permitting multiple bar associations which could admit and discipline members. This, it was suggested, would create reputational competition among the associations, and ultimately improve the profession. Members clearly anticipated GYLA's success in this competition. Some suggested that the certification of knowledge could be a first step along the way to more complete regulation. One of the underlying themes among the proposals was distrust of a mandatory bar with governance powers. For some, the idea of a mandatory bar reflected a Soviet "collectivist" mentality. The greatest fear, however, was rarely expressed at meetings at all, and only became clear in subsequent interviews and observations: young lawyers were fearful that they would be "squeezed out" of power in any new bar by the majority of older lawyers reasserting control. The following statement by one GYLA member accurately summed up the prevalent attitude of GYLA members towards a mandatory bar:[45]

43. "Draft Law of Georgia on Barrister's Activity", 9 June 1996 (unofficial translation on file with author).
44. Attendance at GYLA meetings on the Bar, 15 and 22 September 1998, Tbilisi.
45. D. Pataria, "Personal Thesis regarding the draft law on legal practice" (undated, distributed at a GYLA meeing on 22 September 1998).

> I do not consider creating a united (compulsory) collegium of advocates expedient because of several reasons:
>
> 1) Advocates' rights to make an independent choice of whether or not to affiliate or be united with any organization or union must be respected.
> 2) The collegium will accommodate shifting power back to the older generation of lawyers. Of course, there are many moral and incorruptible individuals among them, but the majority of old-styled lawyers do not live up to the needs and standards of modern society.
> 3) The collegium will weaken competition among lawyers and will prompt an upswing in careerist views and values.
> 4) The collegium will cause inequality between today's advocates and future advocates.
> 5) Considering people who will be privileged in the collegium, it is clear that the collegium will become corrupt and unethical.
> 6) On account of the collegium, being an advocate will no longer be a free profession, it will be more like government service.

The attitude expressed by young "progressives" to a law on the bar was reflected by American rule-of-law reformers as well. One early ABA liaison officer reported that he "counted as one of his successes" the fact that since he had been in Georgia no law on the bar had passed:[46]

> The reason is that all the drafts, especially those coming out of the Ministry of Justice, were the old style Collegiums "plus". And the "plus" is a Collegium completely unregulated by the political body. When I first got here I rather naively began to have discussions with the powers drafting those laws. I would mention the purpose of an independent body of lawyers and they were eating it up and I felt, "oh it is going to be so easy". I'd say the word independence and they loved it. Then I read the drafts and it occurred to me that when I said independent and they thought independence, we were thinking of two different things. Independence for them was: "I finally don't have to kick any money higher than me."

In fact the question of foreign legislative models and the input of foreign lawyers proved a divisive one for GYLA members. As one drafting committee member put it, "foreign laws are not applicable to what's going on in Georgia".[47] Others were quite insistent that a foreign model should be adopted—"they have already figured it out".[48] To the extent there was interest in foreign models, the German and American models were the ones most frequently put forward for discussion, often reflecting where the committee members had studied. At one meeting it was requested that foreign lawyers not attend further drafting meetings because their presence was distracting to the goal of creating workable legislation for Georgia. The internal disagreement over whether Western models were relevant appeared to follow the split over whether a law on the bar was necessary at all. Those who rejected the applicability of the Western experience were the least likely to support a law on the bar.

46. Interview with NN on 16 September 1998.
47. Attendance at GYLA meeting on 15 September 1998, Tbilisi.
48. Attendance at GYLA meeting on 22 September 1998, Tbilsi.

The weak desire on the part of many lawyers during this period for state regulation is linked to the question of numbers. Curiously few lawyers complained that there were too many of them or that a *numerus clausus* was in order. One reason for this lack of complaint is that in a state of uncertainty as to the rules (with nobody sure that they are *in*), any quota might have had unforeseen impact. And complaints about numbers undoubtedly came in shorthand; for example, many complained that there were too many unqualified or unethical lawyers in practice. Nonetheless there was a genuine sentiment among some lawyers and outside observers that there were not enough lawyers or, at least, not enough lawyers actively practicing.[49] Thus when positions for lawyers to be placed in Tbilisi's police stations were advertised, only 40 applications were submitted for the 110 vacancies by the first application deadline.[50] While this is due in part to the mediocre salary (200 Laris/month) and the uncertainty and even danger associated with the job in the face of police resistance, this lack of interest remains striking. This shortage of lawyers appeared to be backed up by public opinion polling as well.[51] There was also near-consensus that there were insufficient numbers of lawyers outside of the capital. While Georgia in the late Soviet period had a higher percentage of advocates than the Union average (one advocate for 6,000 people in Georgia compared to the USSR average of one in 13,000)[52] many of the Soviet-era lawyers were no longer practicing or did not deal with new "bourgeois" areas of law. And, while thousands were enrolled in expanded state and new private law faculties, they did not all graduate during this period and those that did were faced with informal exclusionary measures, outlined below. But the competitive pressures from new law graduates (as well as non-jurists who were essentially practicing law) began to heighten by the late 1990s and may in part account for the decrease in anti-regulatory sentiment in 1999–2001.[53]

The second phase, the "Gudauri process", was spurred by the Council of Europe's accession condition and subsequent requests from government to GYLA for a draft. With these pressures, GYLA members and other reformers renewed their efforts. Working sessions were held in the Winter of 1999-2000

49. Human rights observers have suggested that a general shortage of lawyers exacerbates the difficulty victims of human rights abuses face in finding counsel. (Interview with II on 20 September 1999.)
50. "The time for applications expired", *Svobodnaia Gruziia* 20 August 1999, 7 (cited in *CIPDD Press Digest*, 20 August 1999).
51. A poll conducted in 2000 asked respondents if they agreed that there was "adequate legal counsel available". Only 17% agreed. The question is ambiguous, but presumably "adequate" includes the availability as well as quality of counsel (GORBI, *op. cit.* chap. 3, note 40, 21).
52. *Op. cit.* chap. 2, note 99.
53. On the effects of the "numbers explosion" in other jurisdictions, see R.L. Abel, "Lawyers in the Civil Law World" in *Lawyers in Society* (vol. 2), *op. cit.* chap. 4, note 47, 31-35.

culminating in an ABA-sponsored conference held in the isolated Gudauri resort. The compromise draft which emerged was described by an ABA liaison officer as based on "what's politically possible, what has already been rejected and what was learned from judicial exams".[54] Despite the many compromises which apparently went into the draft, it was a remarkably coherent and well-structured document in contrast to clumsier early efforts.

The compromise, however, was only between various reform positions, and did not involve compromise with the Collegium or power ministries. Legal practice was widely defined to include giving legal advice (some of the earlier drafts dealt only with court representation) and would have included prosecutorial activities after a transition period. The inclusion of prosecutors in the draft, it should be noted, represented less a desire to fuse legal occupations along North American lines (although the attraction of this model for some cannot be ruled out given pervasive American influence) than a way of circumventing the stalled reform of the procuracy launched in the late 1990s. The draft also specifically countered previous attempts by police to hamper lawyers' activities. In a clear reference to the failed initiative of the City of Tbilisi to place duty counsel in police stations, the draft provided that advocates had the right "to provide legal advice to persons detained in any police station or police sub-station if acting under the terms of an agreement with the municipality".[55] In a similar vein, the draft would have prevented investigators from depriving accused persons of legal representation, by naming defence counsel as witnesses in the case. The Gudauri draft provided that no advocate shall be a witness in a case "in which he is giving legal advice".[56] And, unlike most previous drafts, legal ethics were spelled out in a summary (one page) but clear manner.

Where the law compromised between reformers was over the question of licensing or creation of a mandatory bar. A mandatory bar was to be formed, but was to be given little discretion in controlling access to the profession. The key point of access to the bar was to be an examination, which all those who wished to practice law—including those already practicing—would have to write. Anyone with a law degree and no criminal record could take the exam. If the applicant passed, s/he would be entitled to practice law in Georgia. There were no provisions for character screening and no restrictions on numbers of exam writers (or passes); in other words, there was no room for discretion over who could become a lawyer. In fact, the way in which this exam was to be carried out was carefully specified in the draft, down to matters such as the

54. "Revised Draft Law on the Bar", 1 March 2000 (the "Gudauri Draft", unofficial translation on file with author).
55. *Ibid.* (unnumbered article in chapter entitled "Rights of Advocate").
56. *Ibid.*

number and size of colour photographs applicants were to include in their request to take the exam. Content of the exam was also prescribed:[57]

> Part One of the Examination shall consist of 50 questions equally chosen from the fields of Civil Law and Procedure, Criminal Law and Procedure, Constitutional (State) Law, Administrative Law and Procedure, and Human Rights Law. The task is to answer each question by choosing one of four possible answers and circling the letter of that answer. No normative acts, commentaries, texts or other material may be used by the Applicant to assist in answering these questions.

Detailed provisions were also used for the articles establishing a Bar Association. Power was to be distributed between several officials and committees (Examinations, Ethics, Finance, By-Laws and Education), and the General Assembly (consisting of all those who passed the exam) was to retain significant power. Executive members, who were to be elected by secret ballot by those who passed the exam, were limited in their terms of office. The purpose of the detail—matters which would normally be contained in regulations or delegated to the institution itself—was to prevent another site for corruption or one where access could be controlled by "old guard" leadership. In fact, the detailed draft reflects a profound distrust on the part of the reformers of establishing a body in the justice sphere empowered with discretion.

Despite intense lobbying on the part of reformers and the ABA in the Spring of 2000, no consensus emerged in Parliament, where the draft was seen as anti-Collegium and anti-Procuracy. Ultimately the draft died in the Legal Affairs Committee before Parliament recessed at the end of June 2000. With the failure of the draft, reformers seemed to lose momentum. Only a few weeks later, the President presented a draft which differed substantially from the Gudauri draft. In contrast to the Gudauri draft, which would have allowed anyone who passed the exam to practice, and to practice in a manner in which they saw fit (subject only to other applicable laws and a detailed disciplinary procedure and ethics code), the President's draft established supervisory "chambers". The chambers in Georgia-main were to be in Tbilisi and Kutaisi, an interesting revival of the Tsarist split of Georgia into two judicial districts, East and West. In a nod to political realities, the autonomous republics of Ajara and Abkhazia were also to have their own chambers, though South Ossetia was not, reflecting a long-standing Georgian claim that the region is an integral part of historic Georgia.

It is unclear who lobbied for the East-West split, although one can speculate that the government was uncomfortable with the notion of a centralized powerful bar—dominated by Collegium or reformist members—which could potentially represent a site of opposition to its authority. Certainly a unified bar has been a real or perceived threat to the state in post-Soviet Russia and

57. *Ibid.* (unnumbered article in chapter entitled "National Bar Examination").

elsewhere.[58] Of course the idea that lawyers can only practice in certain provinces or judicial districts is common in other jurisdictions; in these jurisdictions the restrictions serve the profession's purpose of limiting competition among domestic lawyers.[59] By contrast in Georgia it does not appear that geographical restrictions on competition were a part of the profession's aims (either as manifested by the Collegium or reformers). Furthermore the laws do not differ between East and West Georgia and therefore the North American justification (flimsy according to some) for limiting the right to practice to specific provinces or states is inapplicable.[60] These facts lend credence to the possibility that the government wished to avoid the creation of a strong, national bar.

Although the President's draft maintained examinations (with some modifications), it was feared by reformers that the draft left room for chambers to refuse access to applicants who successfully passed the exams.[61] Chambers would also have had discretion in creating codes of ethics and in disciplining members. Reformers rejected the President's draft as one which would not give enough independence to individual advocates and debate on legislation for advocates was deferred.

The final phase in the legislative process took place in the Spring of 2001, when lawyers again became a focus of Parliament's Legal Affairs Committee with the reintroduction of an altered version of the President's draft. The most significant change was the replacement of the unpopular Chambers concept with a single Georgian Bar Association (and subsidiary Bar Associations in Ajara and Abkhazia). The entire draft, however, reflected a careful compromise between reformers and old guard and the advice provided by Council of Europe and other international experts.[62] Exams were to be retained though this was softened by providing for civil-specialized or criminal-specialized exams and by giving practicing lawyers until June 2003 to pass the exam. An internship requirement was added but was to be only for a one-year duration and there was no requirement that the intern's principal have a minimum number of years of practice. Prosecution activities were not included in the definition of legal practice but legal representation for those in places of preliminary detention was specifically included. The question as to what degree "solicitors' work" is covered by the law is also left ambiguous. Basic rules of confidentiality and

58. Jordan, for example, has documented how the Russian experience in reforming advocacy has been coloured by the Ministry of Justice's desire to prevent the *advokatura* from becoming an effective, unified interest group ("The Russian Advokatura", *op. cit.* chap. 1, note 54, 773). On the opposition of the bar to state authority in different geographical and historical contexts, see the essays in Halliday and Karpik, *op. cit.* note 26.

59. See "Lawyers in the Civil Law World", *op. cit.* note 53, 25-26.

60. *Ibid.* at 25.

61. Communication with A on 14 August 2000.

62. Interview with CC on 3 August 2000.

conflicts of interest were established by the draft, but all other ethical standards were to be defined by the Association and applied by an Ethics Committee. In general more discretion was given to the bar's executive than in the Gudauri draft, but the draft likely contains sufficient details and protections (the right to a hearing for an advocate accused of unethical behaviour, for example) to preclude a faction who has captured the executive from fundamentally "changing the rules". Although there are no limits on the numbers of advocates, this law goes further than any other law in controlling suppliers. Legal education is required (although there is no mention of accreditation), an examination must be written (in the "state language", effectively excluding large numbers of ethnic minorities whose schooling is in Russian) and an internship must be found (opening the door for discriminatory hiring practices). The greater controls on suppliers possibly represent a final recognition of the "unsustainability", as the World Bank put it, of the burgeoning number of lawyers.[63]

Despite the compromises the draft encountered heavy opposition from several Parliamentarians. The Parliamentary bloc "Revival" led the opposition to the bill, claiming that it was flawed in many respects and needed further rewriting in the Legal Affairs Committee. In particular the opposition's point-man on legal affairs charged that the examinations were unnecessary for older advocates and—in another example of "old guard" using reform language—indicated that the bill's proposed regulation of lawyers "reminded him of Soviet times" in its degree of control over lawyers.[64] Complaints were also made that if lawyers in the regions failed the exams then those areas would be left with no lawyers at all. In the face of the opposition, the government made further concessions, including agreeing to have the test questions publicly released beforehand (to be mixed in with questions which would not ultimately appear on the examination).[65] Despite the concessions, the bill was further stalled due to opposition objections and filibustering.[66] Ultimately, it was passed despite opposition objections on 20 June 2001.[67] The potential efficacy of the bill in light of the divided and hitherto unregulated profession are addressed below.

63. "Georgia Judicial Assessment", *op. cit.* chap. 1, note 53, 25.
64. "MPs have different opinions of Bill on Advocacy", *Sarke News Agency* 22 May 2001.
65. "Consent on Bill on Advocacy Reached", *Sarke News Agency* 24 May 2001.
66. "Today's Session of the Parliament Has Actually Been Interrupted", *Sarke News Agency* 6 June 2001.
67. Law on the Bar, *op. cit.* chap. 4, note 49. See C. Waters, "Georgian Lawyers Get in Line", *Eurasia Insight* 23 August 2001. On the opposition protest see "Law on Advocacy Passed Without Considering Alternative Version", *Sarke News Agency* 22 June 2001.

Self-Regulation

The previous section established that there were no state-sanctioned or uniform restrictions on entry to the profession or control of practicing lawyers. By itself this is not without historical parallel. For example, an independent bar existed in England before the emergence of the modern state, rooted in what ahistorically can be called "civil society". And the English Bar remains jealous of its independence, privileges and customs.[68] By contrast the Georgian Bar has few roots in civil society; to recall from Chapter 2, Georgian lawyers had few pre-Tsarist precedents and the Tsarist and Soviet professions were essentially imposed. In the absence of state regulation over the last decade, Georgian lawyers had no long-standing privileges, customs or even history to fall back on. This presented an extraordinary opportunity to examine how one country's lawyers, individually and in clusters, attempted to create or recreate professional identity and control over their markets.

Restricting Supply

In describing supply restrictions on lawyers, Abel writes:[69]

> The last step in entering the profession is finding an initial position. At first sight this barrier appears to represent control of the profession *by* the market rather than professional control *of* the market. Yet, here, too, the profession has imposed rules than hinder the free play of market forces.

In support of this proposition he points to the fact that even in the absence of formal restrictions, "it may be difficult or impossible to start practice except as an employee".[70] By itself this hardly proves his point about market control. It is difficult to think of an occupation where most people start off self-employed; they may not have sufficient capital, know-how, exposure to potential clients and even self-confidence to immediately open their own business upon entering the work-world. Similarly potential clients may not trust young, inexperienced business owners. However, to the extent that difficulties in finding employment are related to discrimination, Abel's point is well taken. The usefulness for job seekers in Georgia of having attended an elite law school has already been noted. Social connections are also extremely important, and there is discrimination in some quarters against non-ethnic Georgians. Similarly, as will be explored below, membership in a voluntary bar association is a vital element in getting work and each of the associations has its own controls on entry. Ultimately, however, the market does dictate the fact that thousands of law graduates will not find employment in law.

68. Even in the face of state attack; see M. Burrage, "Mrs. Thatcher Against the 'Little Republics': Ideology, Precedents and Reactions" in Halliday and Karpik, *op. cit.* note 26.
69. Abel, "Comparative Sociology of Legal Professions", *op. cit.* chap. 1, note 10, 94.
70. *Ibid.*

Controlling Practice

There are various ways of enforcing ethical norms or standards of practice in the legal profession. In the American context David Wilkins has identified three broad methods, each involving the state: disciplinary/legislative controls (criminal law-like procedures carried out by independent decision-makers under the supervision of courts or independent state agencies), liability controls (malpractice suits) and institutional controls (sanctions imposed by judges or administrative tribunals for improper conduct).[71] In Georgia, disciplinary controls did not exist in the 1990s because the legislation to establish them did not exist. While legislation has recently been put in place, its efficacy—like all other legislative regimes put in place since independence—will be questionable. Liability controls are reportedly not exercised, despite their theoretical availability, and institutional controls are exercised only sparingly and at any rate can be used only for in-court activities. But despite the absence of state-mandated professional regulation for most of the last decade, Georgian lawyering is not and was not a "free for all". There is order and there are standards of practice, although the order may be pluralistic and uneven and the standards often unethical according to most Western codes. This order is imposed by several informal sources considered in this section, including ties of kinship and friendship, clientelism, reputation and associations.

It would be unthinkable for a Georgian lawyer to betray a client with whom he was connected by ties of kinship or friendship, or involved with in a patron-client relationship. In an "honour and shame" society such as Georgia, such betrayal would damage the lawyer's reputation and be met with social sanction. Even where lawyers and clients are not connected through personal ties, reputation plays a great role in determining a lawyer's prestige and even financial success. That is not to say that reputation guarantees ethical behaviour, in the sense of adherence to a code of ethics recognizing duties to the public or the justice system. However, it does provide some guarantee of loyalty to the client's interest. This point can be illustrated through the corruption label usually applied to Georgian lawyers. For many individual clients, who wish positive results in their cases (an acquittal, a speedy divorce), the lawyer is judged by his or her success, not allegiance to abstract ethics. In fact many of the "best", in-demand lawyers in Georgia are known to pass bribes to judges, prosecutors or investigators. Others who refuse to taint themselves directly reportedly "turn a blind eye" to the passing of bribes by clients.[72] One lawyer summed up the ethics situation this way: "In Georgia there are bad famous lawyers and unemployed good ones."[73] This is an exaggeration, and increasingly less true.

71. D.B. Wilkins, "Who Should Regulate Lawyers?", 105 *Harvard Law Review* 1992 No. 4, 799-887. In his article, Wilkins separates disciplinary and legislative controls.
72. Interview with T on 3 November 1998.
73. Observation of GYLA meeting, *op. cit.* note 47.

As another respondent, a successful young lawyer with foreign contacts, put it: "People trust that I am working honestly. And they also see you as a kind of example, that even if you are not corrupt you can earn good money. When I started it was impossible or unimaginable that without corruption you can make good money and be a good person and have a good name."[74] Nonetheless the fact remains that lawyers are frequently unethical in their tactics yet loyal to their clients.

At the beginning of this section I noted that liability controls are used infrequently. Reasons for this include distrust of the legal system (doubly so when a member of the legal apparatus is threatened) and expense. But at least part of the explanation for the absence of malpractice suits lies with the fact that many lawyers are loyal, seek successful outcomes for their clients and build upon this reputation. That reputation is a key factor in gaining and keeping clients was universally reflected in interviews. As one observer noted, reputation guarantees a certain amount of consumer protection:[75]

> Georgia is such a small community, people ask around to find out who is a good lawyer and who is not. People who have had successful cases become well-known and people start coming to them. So protecting the consumer in a society like Georgia is not nearly the issue it would be in New York; there, any charlatan can call themselves lawyers and people would have no way to check it out.

The major exceptions to this principle of loyalty are lawyers who serve the poor—their clients cannot afford the services of lawyers with good reputations—or the unconnected—they do not know of lawyers' reputations. The people in these categories may have counsel forced upon them by courts, police or investigators in a manner described earlier; these lawyers will often show disloyalty as well as other forms of unethical behaviour common to even the "good" Georgian lawyers.

The importance of reputation was particularly stressed by those working with foreign organizations and investors. There are only a handful of law firms which handle the bulk of this work. They frequently make referrals to each other (when "conflicted out" for example) and report feeling comfortable when another lawyer from one of these firms is opposing counsel.[76] The members of this "club", who tend to have some foreign training, report that they avoid dealing with lawyers outside of this group where possible.

74. Interview with AA on 19 September 1998.
75. Interview with KK on 15 September 1998. Another lawyer described the situation as follows: "[I]f you make a mistake you are done for. Your reputation is at stake and there is an unwritten code of morals here...more powerful than written laws." (Interview with X on 14 May 1999.) On the failures of "word-of-mouth" referrals in the US, see S.K. Berenson, "Is It Time for Lawyer Profiles?", 70 *Fordham Law Review* 2001 No. 3, 645-690.
76. Interviews with OO and GG on 14 May 1999.
77. According to the Collegium head there are 3-4 disciplinary cases a year: interview with Y, *op. cit.* note 6.

Membership in an association or a law firm also acts as a potential source of standard enforcement. Now a voluntary association of lawyers, the Collegium's ability or willingness to govern lawyers is suspect. By most reports the Collegium as a whole appears to be largely inactive in discipline matters, despite the existence of a central discipline committee.[77] Certainly there seems to be no will to tackle the corruption problem in the Collegium's ranks; the Collegium head went so far as to assert that *no* Collegium members were corrupt.[78] There is also a second level of management in the Collegium's structure, namely, the LCB level. Well-run LCBs have internal review committees which review advocates' work and discipline advocates where necessary. However, the effectiveness of these committees appears to be limited.

Membership in a reformist organization appears to act as somewhat more of a mark of adherence to ethical standards of practice than membership in the Collegium. GYLA members frequently made allusions to the fact that GYLA's offices are contacted by clients looking for a "good lawyer". They claim that potential clients know they can find ethical, competent lawyers through the office; this makes membership good for business since members appear to be the only lawyers who receive referrals from the office.[79] Membership is also a source of prestige and makes practice easier. As one lawyer put it: "We are insured to some extent against corruption and ignorance when a GYLA member is on the other side."[80] In a similar vein, it was reported that judges sometimes ask lawyers at the beginning of a case if they are GYLA members (although often they know who is by reputation).[81] A positive response may put the judge somewhat on guard and lead to responsible decision-making. Similarly, police, investigators and prosecutors take fewer liberties with members of reformist organizations (although as outlined above they also afford them fewer privileges). One amusing case was reported by an Article 42 lawyer who was arbitrarily stopped by the police, likely looking for a bribe.[82] When he showed his Article 42 identity card, the policeman immediately waved him on. As the lawyer was driving away, he heard the policeman's colleague ask, "Who was he?" The first policeman simply replied: "He is against us." But as a result of official antipathy—or realization that no bribe will be forthcoming—membership in one of the young reformers' associations can also impede speedy resolution of clients' cases. One GYLA member described a judge's response to her request that he register an NGO client as follows:[83]

78. *Ibid.*
79. Interview with PP *op. cit.* chap. 4, note 58.
80. Interview with GG, *op. cit.* note 76.
81. Interview with PP, *op. cit.* chap. 4, note 58. Not all judges believe, however, that being a member of GYLA guarantees competency or integrity: interview with ND on 21 May 1999.
82. Interview with AA on 9 June 2000.
83. Interview with PP, *op. cit.* chap. 4, note 58.

> Two days ago I had a case in one of the District Courts of Tbilisi. When I came there the first time, the [judge] told me: "you know, according to the law I have up to one month to respond to a registration request but I can do it in five minutes if..." Then he stopped and asked: "Oh, wait a minute where are you from?" After I told him I am from the Young Lawyers' Association, he said, "Ok, wait for a month."

As noted earlier, some young reformers in the 1990s argued a law on the bar was not needed. According to them the Georgian legal profession was not "mature" enough for a mandatory bar association and that voluntary bar associations were more suitable for Georgia's development. Voluntary bar associations such as GYLA could compete on the basis of reputation with other lawyers. Clients would know what kind of a lawyer they would be getting from an organization like GYLA whereas membership in a mandatory bar association—which might be tainted by corruption or dominated by reactionary leaders—would provide people with no guarantee. Even if the mandatory bar association could guarantee lawyers' knowledge through testing, there would be no testing of integrity. They felt that over time organizations such as GYLA would be the sole source of lawyers for people, as lawyers who remained in the Collegium, or outside of any organization, would lose credibility and business. In much the same way that the existence of law firms simply overtook legal developments (none of the draft laws on the bar would have outlawed law firms), some preferred a "ground-up approach": associations such as GYLA would develop internal standards and eventually the quality of the bar as a whole would be raised.[84] Before a law on the bar appeared inevitable by 1999/2000, GYLA was actively considering setting examinations for its members. Although lawyers who passed the exam would not be state sanctioned, a publicized list of passing lawyers would provide some guarantee of competence to the public. GYLA has also addressed legal ethics from its early days. As one member of the executive put it: "From the day we began we had a big empty list on the wall and we started putting down rules, one by one. And members could sign under the rules [with which they agreed]."[85] Article 42 has also stressed ethics in its legal clinic, the Fundamental Human Rights Centre. It drafted an ethics code and established a disciplinary procedure for lawyers and law students working at the Centre. A three-member ethics committee hears complaints against lawyers, and with "due process rights" for the accused jurist, makes a decision and must provide reasons for the decision.

Yet despite the stated concern for maintaining ethics and practice standards, the extent to which membership in GYLA and likeminded organizations acts as an ethical filter is debatable. Gaining admission to GYLA does provide some guarantees: that the member has a law degree (or is a law student), generational

84. Interview with H, *op. cit.* chap. 2, note 126.
85. Interview with PP *op. cit.* chap. 4, note 58.

"qualifications", and recommendations from two GYLA members. However, the admission procedure does not include an assessment of the applicant's legal education or a systematic screening for moral fitness. Continued membership in the organization also provides only a limited guarantee as to the quality of the lawyer. Between its founding in 1994 and the major court reforms of 1998, only two members were expelled from the organization during what was a particularly corrupt period in post-Soviet Georgian justice. In neither case did the expulsion have anything to do with corruption or even the practice of law.[86] Rather they both were concerned with maintaining the organization's institutional strength. One member was expelled after abandoning his team-mates on a GYLA-sponsored trip to Washington to compete in the Jessup Moot Court Competition. The second member was expelled because he lied to a potential funder by saying that he was not a GYLA member, in order to obtain separate funding for his project.

Part of the weakness of disciplinary control in these organizations comes from a lack of development in the concept of legal ethics. Article 42's code of ethics is fairly "roughly cut" and does not appear to cover any number of situations. Set out in full, the code states:

i) A lawyer should not provide services to a person unless that person is unrepresented;
ii) A lawyer should not represent a client who does not meet the criteria of the Centre;
iii) A lawyer cannot take money from a client;
iv) Confidentiality of case materials must be defended;
v) A lawyer cannot breach confidentiality in any way;
vi) A lawyer cannot give any case material to a third party;
vii) The client must have signed a contract with the Centre.

Since its founding, Article 42 has only expelled one member, a lawyer who was representing a client at court without authorization from the organization. Article 42's code would not appear to cover this behaviour. As was the case with GYLA, Article 42's sole expulsion served to safeguard institutional goals. Perhaps the fact that the Georgian legal profession does a poor job of disciplining itself is not surprising. As Abel has noted, some legal professions have no codes of ethics, most codes are vague and that there is a disconnect between client complaints (the bulk of which involve matters of discourtesy, negligence and high fees) and the matters which disciplinary tribunals typically pursue (offences against the profession).[87]

The character and early policy positions of GYLA are not without historic parallels, albeit in a very different context. For example, certain aspects

86. *Ibid.*

87. "Comparative Sociology of Legal Professions", *op. cit.* chap. 1, note 10, 133-135. For a somewhat more sympathetic treatment of ethics codes and enforcement in the American context, see Q. Johnstone, "Bar Associations: Policies and Performances", 15 *Yale Law & Policy Review* 1996 No. 1, 193-243, 217-218.

of Michael Powell's account of the early years of the Association of the Bar of the City of New York (ABCNY) resonate with the experience of GYLA's first five or six years. ABCNY was formed in 1870 in response to the mid-century democratic leveling of the legal profession; as Powell writes: "While the patrician leaders of the New York bar no longer controlled admission to the profession, by forming an exclusive association in which membership was restricted to those deemed worthy they could distance themselves from the mass of lawyers 'seen in almost all our courts, slovenly in dress, uncouth in manners and habits, ignorant even of the English language, jostling and crowding and vulgarizing the profession.'"[88] ABCNY members were keen to distinguish themselves from the corrupt, heterogeneous masses and did this by restricting membership through club-like means (sponsorship of prospective members was required followed by a screening process). Although not as stringent as ABCNY's standards for admission, GYLA members are as contemptuous of non-members, dismissing them as old, incompetent, corrupt, former-communists. Similarly GYLA membership is not open to all—applicants must be sponsored by current members. There is also the age restriction which has been criticized by funders but defended as necessary for the time being to exclude the "old guard" (one suspects that as GYLA's leaders age the bar may be lifted). GYLA membership is heavily dominated—particularly in Tbilisi—by those who have attended elite law schools. While there are several GYLA offices around the country, there are none in areas heavily populated by non-ethnic Georgians, thus promoting further homogeneity. Finally, members tend to come from "good families" and are socially as well as professionally linked. I do not want to stretch the parallels between ABCNY and GYLA too far. For example, men and women are represented in roughly equal numbers in GYLA (both among rank and file members and the executive) and the organization has actively grappled with poverty law issues from its early days. Furthermore GYLA members genuinely have the sense that they are taking on vested interests—the corrupt, Soviet-era patricians. Nonetheless, GYLA does share with ABCNY a club-like nature. Although the numbers of GYLA members seems high (700), it should be recalled that there are over 30,000 law students in Georgia and several thousand graduates of law schools. Looked at in this perspective membership in GYLA is even more rare than was membership in the ABCNY shortly after its founding (in 1871 ABCNY had only 462 members out of a bar of 4,000).[89]

88. M.J. Powell, *From Patrician to Professional Elite*, New York 1988, 14, citing in part J.A. Matzko, "'The Best Men of the Bar': The Founding of the American Bar Association" in G.W. Gawalt, ed., *The New High Priests: Lawyers in Post-Civil War America*, Westport, CN 1984, 78.

89. Powell, *op. cit.*, 15.

There are also parallels between the two organizations in terms of lawyer regulation. Both held views that they were in the best position to discipline their members (while at the same time having largely inactive disciplinary committees),[90] and both groups shared initial opposition to a unified or mandatory bar. Powell describes the ABCNY's opposition to the unified bar movement, which reached New York from its mid-Western roots in the 1920s, as follows:[91]

> [The President of the ABCNY] defended the principle of selectivity and elite control by arguing that the maintenance of the ethical standards of the profession depended upon the leadership of a moral minority, or elite, of the bar. Here was a clear statement of the upper-class model of professionalism: If you could not exclude the masses from the profession, it was necessary at least to limit leadership to the worthy few. Compulsory membership in a state bar association would open up the organized bar to "undesirable" lawyers to whom power would naturally fall.

Eventually ABCNY was able to institutionalize its role as the guardian of ethics and its grievance committee decided on complaints about non-members as well as members. Like ABCNY, GYLA stepped into a regulatory vacuum and institutionalized its governance role, albeit only for members. And despite the weaknesses of these and other voluntary bar associations in disciplining members, it cannot be denied that they have played *some* role in setting practice standards and regulating lawyers' behaviour. The question remains, however, as to what degree GYLA and other organizations will play a role in this sphere following the new law on the bar.

Prognosis for the Law on the Bar

The Bar Association created by Parliament will be hard-pressed to avoid the institutional malaise (underfunding, corruption, cronyism, external interference, lack of public confidence) which has afflicted virtually every state and quasi-state body since independence. These general problems will be exacerbated by the fact that the bar is divided so deeply and on so many different lines. These divisions will undoubtedly manifest themselves in the area of standard setting and discipline. With respect to standard setting, it is difficult to imagine the new bar association promulgating an ethics code which goes beyond the simple precepts of confidentiality and conflict of interest already contained in the legislation. There is little understanding of legal ethics on the part of most law school graduates (as in numerous other jurisdictions, it is a subject only rarely taught to undergraduates)[92] and there is no broad consensus among prac-

90. *Ibid.*, 19. Although the ABCNY also extended its disciplinary purview to non-members, something which—to my knowledge—the GYLA executive has never proposed.
91. *Ibid.*, 41.
92. A recent British text on legal ethics was inspired by the author's belief that "first degrees in law had much to offer in relation to ethics but had hitherto failed to make a real contribution" (R. O'Dair, *Legal Ethics: Text and Materials*, London 2001, 7).

ticing lawyers on the subject.[93] Furthermore, developing a code of ethics will be highly politicized—it will not be the technocratic task it is often portrayed to be by North American bar associations. It is also likely that the bar will not exercise its disciplinary powers far from the lowest common denominator; in a system where corruption is pervasive the bar cannot prosecute all offenders. The question of who is disciplined will be politicized by some, and the option of appeal to courts may undermine the bar's authority. At the same time the bar will be faced with competing sites of authority. GYLA and organizations such as Article 42 will seek to preserve their distinctiveness and status of members by continuing in a standard setting and disciplinary role. The Collegium and its LCBs will also likely maintain their corporate identity, property and connections with the investigatory branches of the state. In sum, the law will likely be only modestly successful in terms of governance and discipline of lawyers.

Similarly, the effect of the examinations may be muted. If the experience with the judges' examinations is any indication (large numbers of sitting judges failed), many lawyers currently practicing will fail a difficult exam. This possibility has led to government assurances that test questions will be released beforehand, and the provision in the law that lawyers—including those who failed—can practice until 2003. The fears expressed by some opposition parliamentarians that the regions will be left with insufficient numbers of lawyers will also have to be taken seriously; the test standards cannot be so high so as to leave sections of the country without lawyers. The end result will be an examination which only "guarantees" potential clients that their lawyer has minimal knowledge. In sum, the mandatory bar will likely have only limited success in either serving the interests of the profession or the public and self-regulation—through associations and reputation—will continue to play a large part in lawyer governance.

93. I base this conclusion on the ethics activities carried out by lawyers' associations (discussed above) and my discussions with lawyers at a CLE seminar on legal ethics which I presented in Tbilisi in October 2000.

Chapter 6
Stratification and Professional Badges

The idea that legal professions are internally divided and stratified is commonplace in the scholarly literature.[1] That Georgian lawyers are stratified should already be clear. The previous two chapters outlined some of the divisions within the profession based on education and the politics of the bar. And a distinction was drawn between "reformers" and the "old guard", with their associational (GYLA/Collegium) and generational differences. The first part of this chapter examines how those divisions are reflected in the practice of law, by focussing on where lawyers work. As a preliminary point, however, it should be noted the distinctions between the "young reformers" and "old guard" are partly evocative and should not be overdrawn. There are many young lawyers who behave as their older colleagues and *vice versa*. Furthermore the terms are loaded in favour of the young reformers themselves who portray this split (young=reformer, old=reactionary). Alternatively, and to adopt the semantics of older lawyers, the profession could be divided into experienced and inexperienced lawyers!

Lawyers' workplaces can be crudely divided into two main categories, namely, Soviet-style LCBs and Western-style business law firms. While there are numerous axes on which to compare lawyers,[2] the place of practice in Georgia reflects many of the other variants such as management, clients, forms of practice (court or transaction work), lawyers' backgrounds and physical conditions of work.

The second part of this chapter discusses whether the various fracture lines mean that Georgian lawyers are not professionalizing (or even that deprofessionalization is taking place). Certainly stratification hinders professionalization as traced along Western lines. For example, it has been suggested that the American legal profession was so successful in its ambitions partly because its ranks were homogenous in terms of professional identity (lawyers were mostly practitioners until after the Second World War).[3] Conversely, when internal differentiation increased among American lawyers after the War, the "professional project" of market control and status elevation began to falter. Despite

1. For some observers these divisions are even evidence that "the age of professionalism" is ending: if lawyers are divided, and competing among themselves, they cannot act with one voice to assert market control or raise their collective status: R.L. Abel, "England and Wales" in *Lawyers in Society*, vol. 1, *op. cit.* chap. 1, note 11, 66.
2. Lawyers themselves often distinguish private practice from employment, and litigation from transaction work. Researchers have also classified lawyers by their clients (J.P. Heinz and E.O. Laumann, *Chicago Lawyers: The Social Structure of the Bar*, New York 1982), by degrees of autonomy (J. Hagan and F. Kay, *Gender in Practice: A Study of Lawyers' Lives*, New York 1995) or by their degree of risk-taking (C. Seron, *The Business of Practicing Law: The Work Lives of Solo and Small-Firm Attorneys*, Philadelphia 1996).
3. See R.L. Abel, "United States. Contradictions of Professionalism" in *Lawyers in Society*, vol. 1, *op. cit.* chap. 1, note 11, 188 (hereinafter "Contradictions of Professionalism").

the fractures among Georgian lawyers, however, I suggest that for the first time in the country's history an indigenously created legal profession is emerging. This process of professionalization is staggered and uneven, and owes little to the state, but is occurring nonetheless.

Stratification

In their groundbreaking study of Chicago lawyers in the 1970s, Heinz and Laumann attacked the myth of a unified urban bar and popularized the notion of practice "hemispheres":[4]

> [W]e have advanced the thesis that much of the differentiation within the legal profession is secondary to one fundamental distinction—the distinction between lawyers who represent large organizations and those who represent individuals. The two kinds of law practice are the two hemispheres of the profession. Most lawyers reside exclusively in one hemisphere or the other and seldom, if ever, cross the equator.

They went on to point out that the lawyers who resided in the different hemispheres were also drawn from different quarters:[5]

> The two sectors of the legal profession thus include different lawyers, with different social origins, who were trained at different law schools, serve different sorts of clients, practice in different office environments, are differentially likely to engage in litigation, litigate (when and if they litigate) in different forums, have somewhat different values, associate with different circles of acquaintances, and rest their claims to professionalism on different sorts of social power... Only in the most formal of senses, then, do the two types of lawyers constitute one profession.

This section describes the Georgian equivalent of Heinz and Laumann's hemispheres by using two short case studies to show where lawyers work. In doing so, however, it is helpful to bear in mind the commonly forgotten caveats that Heinz and Laumann attached to their thesis; namely, that the dichotomy should not be overdrawn, that there is overlap between the hemispheres and that there are significant differences within each hemisphere.[6]

Indeed there are major differences among LCBs and among firms, and a note is in order as to how representative the selected case studies are. Neither are "average". Opened in 1959, the Mtatsminda LCB in Tbilisi is one of the longest-standing Bureaus in the country. Its central location, steps away from Parliament in an elite district, influences the character of both its advocates and clients. Furthermore it was considered one of the best Soviet Georgian LCBs (evidenced by numerous awards for service which decorate the Chairman's office), a reputation which persists among advocates. The firm studied here,

4. Heinz and Laumann, *op. cit.* note 2, 319. The basic thesis has been reaffirmed with data collected twenty years after the initial survey. See J.P. Heinz, R.L. Nelson, E.O. Laumann and E. Michelson, "The Changing Character of Lawyers' Work: Chicago in 1975 and 1995", 32 *Law and Society Review* 1998 No. 4, 751-775.
5. Heinz and Laumann, *ibid.*, 384.
6. *Ibid.*, 321.

the Georgia Consulting Group (GCG), is even less average. There are roughly three or four firms in Georgia operating in a Western manner or, as a lawyer working for a USAID "rule of law" contractor put it, there are "three or four firms that are practicing law in a way that would be recognizable in any city of America".[7] These firms, he went on, "are pretending that they are in a normal legal environment".[8] Of the "pretenders", the GCG is by far the most Western on all bases of comparison including, most obviously, the fact that one of the principals of the firm during its formative years was American. There are other firms outside of this small core of three or four "pretenders", but they do not resemble Western firms except for the fact that they are organized as businesses with principals and employees.[9] Like the Mtatsminda LCB then, the GCG is not an "average" site for the delivery of legal services. The selected workplaces are, however, the "models" for other LCBs and firms and therefore can be usefully compared.

One attribute both the selected sites share, location in Tbilisi, is also relevant to their representativeness. Tbilisi lawyers have always had a reputation for being the best in the country and there is a higher percentage of lawyers in the capital than in the regions. They also handle a wider range of work than their counterparts in other cities. According to the Mayor of Gori, Georgia's sixth largest city, there were fewer than 140 jurists to serve his region's population of over 70,000.[10] Of the roughly 140, many were former jurisconsults whose Soviet-era enterprises had closed leaving them unemployed. In his estimation there were only ten good, active lawyers in the city and none worked in the area of business law. He complained that in light of the growing legal needs of businesses in the area and the legal work created as a result of municipal reforms, occasionally Tbilisi lawyers had to be "imported". Obviously then the urban-rural split should be kept in mind in assessing how representative a Tbilisi LCB is of LCBs across the country.

Further, while I suggest that the workplace distinction is the most relevant, there are some legal occupations, including notaries, which are not covered by it. These occupations will be lightly treated below.

Mtatsminda Legal Consultation Bureau (LCB)[11]

Management and Structure—The 60-member LCB is formally structured along Soviet lines, in which lawyers are supervised by the Bureau's administration and

7. Interview with KK, *op. cit.* chap. 5, note 75.
8. *Ibid.*
9. While reliable figures are unavailable it has been estimated that only 30% of Georgian lawyers are practicing in firms (see www.freedomhouse.org/research/nitransit/2000/georgia/georgia_rol.htm).
10. Interview with G on 17 April 1999.
11. The details in this section are based on interviews with the Head of the LCB (B) and other advocates of the Bureau on 22 September 1999 as well as my physical observation of the LCB.

the Bureau Head is answerable to the Presidium of the Collegium. In theory the Chairman of the LCB manages the day-to-day activities of the Bureau, monitors the work of advocates and does long-range planning. Not atypical of LCB heads appointed during the Soviet era, the Chairman came from outside the ranks of advocates; in this case he was transferred to the position from his job in the Ministry of Justice. The Head of the LCB proudly shows visitors four-month and one-year plans for the office on neat, hand-written charts. Among other things the charts contain dates for the meetings of committees sharing the administrative tasks of the Chairman. The most important committee is the Management Committee which meets every four months to review the LCB's finances and the operation of the LCB as a whole. Other committees are the Internal Review Committee (which periodically assesses the work of individual advocates) and the Discipline Committee. The Chairman and lawyers are supported by one secretary.

Fees are directly negotiable between the advocate and client, although they are to be made taking into account the fee schedules put out by the Collegium and an assessment of the client's means. The LCB uses standard forms from the Collegium on which the negotiated fees are set out and the legal service requested is specified. These agreements require the signature of the LCB head as well as the advocate and the client. Another form sets out the nature of the advice or representation given.

In reality, the advocates working in the LCBs are more autonomous than the formal management structures and procedures suggest. Advocates do not meet with all of their clients at the LCB, thus removing the potential for strict, day-to-day physical surveillance by management in many cases. Without self-reporting, management has no way of knowing who these clients are and what fee arrangements have been made. Direct supervision of advocates by management is only possible for those advocates dealing with "walk-ins", and those on the duty rosters for appointment by courts or investigators. Some advocates rely heavily on these cases, and they are therefore subject to more degrees of control, including the obligation to pass a small percentage of the fee on to the LCB. During business hours it is usual to find three or four advocates in the LCB.

Some entrepreneurial advocates work almost as sole practitioners; they are required to belong to an LCB to be a member of the Collegium but they have little day-to-day contact with it. These advocates also make payments to the LCB but the payments are based on what is considered "appropriate" (informally negotiated between the advocate and the LCB) rather than a strict percentage of earnings. Finally, as pointed out in the previous chapter, unethical behaviour is rarely punished.

Just as individual advocates are more autonomous from the LCB than in Soviet times, so to the LCB as a whole is also more autonomous from the Presidium than it was in the past. Although theoretically required to pass 5% of all earnings to the Collegium, the Bureau transfers only a fraction of that sum. In turn the Collegium provides no money for bookkeeping, repairs or legal materials as in the past. The lack of material exchange is reflected in the absence of Collegium interference in the day-to-day operations of the Bureau.

Clients—There are two types of clients, "collective" clients and "personal clients". The collective clients are "walk-ins" and clients appointed by courts or investigators to an advocate on the duty roster. The majority of walk-ins are poor. They do not have social connections to a lawyer and an LCB is the cheapest place to find one. Their legal issues are of the "personal plight" sort—criminal, family and housing problems. Similarly, accused persons who are appointed advocates by courts or investigators are generally poor. Lawyers who take court-appointed clients receive two Laris per day of work from the state. This is not a living wage for lawyers, and clients are expected to come up with more (for the legal fees and/or the bribe to the investigator/prosecutor/judge) by pressing family and friends for gifts and loans. Those who cannot provide more receive only the most summary of legal services. Not surprisingly, indigent clients are increasingly seeking assistance through legal clinics rather than LCBs. The LCB has roughly 400 criminal and 300 civil collective cases each year, a figure which works out to roughly one per lawyer per month. Some lawyers take more of these cases than others, and some of the older lawyers at the Collegium are almost completely inactive.

The "personal clients", on the other hand, directly contact specific lawyers attached to the LCB. They call the lawyers on the basis of referrals or on the strength of an advocate's reputation. They know they will have to pay and typically they are not poor. Wealthy accused persons and political dissidents will often hire high profile advocates and pay large sums of money for representation. As noted above, most of the "personal clients" are individuals rather than businesses or organizations, although some small businesses will use these advocates. Clients who directly contact lawyers attached to LCBs may never come to the LCB—or will meet the lawyer there by appointment. Both sorts of clients tend to retain lawyers for discrete legal services related to a specific objective; only rarely is there an ongoing relationship.

Forms of Practice—Advocates infrequently engage in transaction work. When they do it is normally of a small-scale nature such as drafting simple contracts between individuals or small businesses. Members of the LCB spend the bulk of their time on advocacy. This advocacy takes place before courts of course, but lawyers are also asked to intercede with police, investigators and prosecutors (at the point of detention and at the preliminary inquiry stages) and government officials (denial of benefits cases are common).[12] This advocacy

12. Often in administrative matters, the lawyer will be asked to write letters putting forward the client's case, with no instructions from the client to commence proceedings if the letter fails to have its desired effect. Lawyers are simply used in these cases to translate client complaints against the state into "official" language.

is not always orthodox by Western standards. In criminal cases, as suggested earlier, some advocates (including high-profile ones) are known to act as go-betweens between accused persons and judicial or prosecutorial authorities in passing bribes. They may also rely on personal connections to advance their clients' causes.

At times rough strategies—including what can only be described as antics—are used by lawyers to pressure judges into making decisions in their client's favour. One of Georgia's best-known advocates and the head of the Independent Lawyers' Association reportedly punched a judge with whom he disagreed (it is noteworthy that four other judges refused to try the advocate after he was charged for this act).[13] One client in a civil suit indicated that her lawyer paid journalists to threaten the opposing party and judge with a "corruption story".[14] In another case, an advocate reportedly ate a court document in front of judge when he disagreed with the contents of the document.[15] These anecdotal accounts abound and are undoubtedly exaggerated. Nonetheless, they reveal the general perception that if you need to engage in legal "trench warfare", you must hire a good advocate. Of course not all advocates are good, even in the results-oriented sense alone. Many collude with police and investigators and others—while not co-conspirators—are formed in the Soviet mould and are unwilling or unable to present a vigorous defence of their clients.[16] Some are simply ignorant of developments in the law. Needless to say, however, there are also a number of advocates who have developed a reputation for straight, competent advocacy.

Lawyers' Backgrounds—To begin with demographics, the stereotype of the LCB lawyer is of an old man who spends his days at the Bureau playing chess and reading newspapers. While this portrayal represents a common sight in most bureaus, it is not entirely representative. First of all, the Soviet-era gender split remains roughly accurate (a quarter to a third are women).[17] Secondly not all advocates are elderly. The Head of the Collegium suggested that two-fifths of all Collegium members are young,[18] while the Chairman of the Mtatsminda LCB stated that half of the lawyers in his bureau were young (roughly defined as under 40 years of age). Collegium figures also reveal that in 1990 there were 800 advocates in Georgia, while in 2000 there were 1,100, suggesting that 37% of its members joined at the cusp of independence or after independence.[19] While these figures may be somewhat suspect, given the Collegium's

13. "Kartlos is saved by friendship", *Svobodnaia Gruziia* 2 July 1999, 1.
14. Interview with R on 18 May 1999.
15. Interview with T, *op. cit.* chap. 5, note 72.
16. Communication from II dated 20 September 1999.
17. Official Soviet statistics are reprinted in "Female Lawyers (Statistical Data)", *op. cit.* chap. 2, note 102.
18. Interview with Y, *op. cit.* chap. 5, note 6.
19. *Ibid.*, and archival research at the Collegium conducted on behalf of the author by Dr. Georgi Glonti of the Institute for Legal Reform in Tbilisi in May 2001.

desire to portray itself as relevant in "transition" Georgia, it is clear that not all LCB members are as elderly as the stereotype suggests. Many of the younger members of the Collegium, however, spend little time in the Bureaus. While their attachment to the LCB is something more than nominal, their activities reflect a sole-practitioner model more than attachment to a lawyers' collective. They tend to be more entrepreneurial than their seniors and have more personal clients.

The bulk of advocates joined LCBs in the Soviet era, when the prestige of advocacy was low and jurists from elite families managed to get positions as investigators, prosecutors or judges. Furthermore a number of the advocates in the LCBs were former investigators or other officials who were essentially demoted to advocacy. In terms of ethnic composition, minorities are under-represented in the LCBs, although it has traditionally been more open to Armenians, Russians and others than the procuracy and judiciary. By education, most studied law at Tbilisi State University (one of the few commonalities LCB lawyers have with firm lawyers, although the latter often supplement their Georgian education with study in the West).

Physical Conditions of Work—Physically the Mtatsminda LCB has changed little since Soviet times. The interior consists of a small waiting room (with an attached photocopying kiosk, a small business offering services to the public at large), one large room with seven desks and the Chairman's office. The desks in the large room are bare. The room itself is tidy, though poorly lit and spartan. Client interviews take place here, in plain view of others. Because of the size of the room, some confidentiality in terms of what was being said is maintained, although this is not the norm for other LCBs (for example, the Vake LCB in Tbilisi is so small that confidential oral communications are impossible). There appeared to be one telephone for the LCB and no computers. There was also no law library, though the Chairman's office contained a few law books as well as a file folder holding copies of laws clipped from newspapers.[20]

The Firm—Georgia Consulting Group (GCG)[21]

Management and Structure—The firm has been managed by several partners including, for a few years, an American, who had stayed on to practice law in Georgia after working for an American NGO on constitutional and electoral issues in Georgia in 1994–1995. The number of employed lawyers at the firm varies between five and seven depending on demand and the availability of lawyers with the requisite education and skills. There are also around six support staff, including legal translators.

20. The lack of legal materials is partly the fault of Parliament, which publishes laws in small quantities.
21. The assessment of the Georgia Consulting Group is based on on-site interviews with two principals of the firm (OO and GG, *op. cit.* chap. 5, note 76), a review of the firm's promotional literature and discussions with others in the legal community on the firm's reputation.

The firm (GCG Law) is part of a multi-disciplinary partnership (MDP) of three companies. The second company (GCG Consulting) consults with foreign businesses and organizations seeking entry to the Georgian market or access to state decision-makers. The third, an accounting firm (GCG Audit), is the largest of the three. The three entities share management and space. The creation of an MDP in Georgia is intriguing, since these partnerships have developed only recently in jurisdictions with more advanced markets. But the presence of an MDP in Georgia is due not only to business logic ("one-stop, Western-style shopping" is naturally attractive for foreign clients seeking to enter a confusing developing market), but to the lack of any opposition to the development. Many state and professional bodies have approached MDPs cautiously in other jurisdictions. For example, in a recent report, the Canadian Bar Association stated that these entities "may threaten some or all of the core values of the legal profession, which include independence of the profession, avoidance of conflicts of interest, preservation of client confidentiality, and preservation of solicitor-client privilege".[22] In Georgia, neither lawyers nor state organs have identified any difficulties with MDPs.

Clients—Most of the firm's clients are foreign businesses, joint ventures and international organizations, although the firm also has some Georgian business clients. Individual clients, except those related to corporate or organizational clients, are rare. Clients are referred to the firm by foreign embassies, international law firms (the firm has "local counsel" arrangements with a number of international firms) and other businesses, as well as GYLA (one of the founding principals of GCG was also a founding member of GYLA). The firm's clients include British Airways, British Petroleum and the European Bank for Reconstruction and Development. Its involvement with larger clients is ongoing and long-term. The firm also gains and refers clients through the three branches of the MDP. This cross-fertilization typically begins after clients approach the consulting branch for advice on entry into the Georgian market or how best to structure technical assistance programmes. If they decide to work in Georgia, they will often bring their legal and accounting needs to the other branches of the partnership.

Forms of Practice—The firm concentrates on transactional work with roughly 40 active files at a time, 10 of them large ones. The larger files are privatization matters or joint ventures in the significant fields of oil and gas and telecommunications. Generally, the joint ventures structured by the firm's lawyers attempt to insulate foreign investments to the extent possible from the application of Georgian justice, by insisting on international arbitration clauses

22. Canadian Bar Association, "Striking a Balance: The Report of the International Practice of Law Committee on Multi-Disciplinary Practices and the Legal Profession" (Report summary), Ottawa, 22 August 1999.

or careful drafting of choice of forum and law clauses. This is certainly the rule in the natural resources field.[23] Smaller files handled by the firm include compliance matters such as registering businesses. The firm rarely takes on litigation cases except for those of existing clients. Litigation briefs number roughly six to eight each year. The reluctance to litigate is evident in some other firms as well and at least one of Georgia's most well-respected lawyers in private practice reported "boycotting" courts for over a year to avoid dealing with the corrupt judicial system.[24] She also had the luxury of turning away court work given her standing and ability to attract transaction work from Western clients.

As noted in the chapter on legal education, the firm's senior lawyers mentor juniors and stress the importance of delivering "Western quality" legal services. The firm also stresses to its junior lawyers that the firm is a business. All lawyers docket to the tenth of an hour and enter the figures into their computers. The computers in the office are networked, and an accounting programme produces invoices along with fax cover sheets to be sent to clients. The firm also has a well thought-out marketing strategy, portraying itself in brochures as "provid[ing] its clients with a combination of local knowledge and Western experience which is unique in Georgia and rare in the Caucasus as a whole".[25] In addition to creating general promotional literature listing practice areas and lawyer biographies, the firm also puts out monthly updates on legal developments in Georgia. Legal developments impacting on the oil and gas sector and other large-scale commercial projects figure prominently in these updates. This promotional literature generally portrays a legal system which is improving and increasingly friendly to foreign investment; examples include: "The Georgian government continues to pursue its course of supporting the creation of a healthy banking sector in the country...";[26] "The government of Georgia is making certain progress in adopting a healthy economic and fiscal policy...";[27] and "...Georgians and foreigners alike expect the new judges to bring two indispensable qualities to the new judicial system—professionalism and honesty".[28] This form of advertising is intended to stimulate foreign investment and, in turn, demand for legal services. GCG is not the only firm which advertises—a handful of other firms have actively marketed their services in the local English-language press and are involved with Chambers of Commerce—but its marketing strategy is the most sophisticated.

Lawyers' Backgrounds—GCG lawyers (most of whom are in their twenties and thirties) are among the most elite in the country. All speak fluent English

23. Interview with SS on 21 September 1999.
24. Interview with AA, *op. cit.* chap. 5, note 74.
25. GCG, "History, Clients and Practice Areas" (undated brochure).
26. GCG, "GCG Georgian Law Update" (February 1999).
27. GCG, "GCG Georgian Law Update" (March 1999).
28. GCG, "GCG Georgian Law Update" (April 1999).

in addition to Georgian and other foreign languages. They have all been legally educated abroad, in addition to their studies at Tbilisi State University's Faculty of Law. They have close connections with government, GYLA and the foreign diplomatic community, as well as their clients in the business or development sectors. In fact, this "well-connectedness" is one of the firm's major assets.

In 2000 the firm had two foreign lawyers, an Israeli as well as the American principal. The American principal came from an elite law background (legislative assistant to a Congressman, student at Cornell Law School, clerk for a federal appellate court, lawyer at a big firm in Atlanta) and spoke enthusiastically about the firm's successful recruitment of the best young lawyers in the country. He also described himself as a "conduit or bridge" from Western clients to Georgian lawyers with local knowledge and language, self-consciously attempting, as far as possible, to transplant a Western firm onto Georgian soil.

Physical Conditions of Work—The firm is located on Rustaveli Avenue, Tbilisi's main street, and (like Mtatsminda LCB) is steps away from Parliament. The building housing the GCG offices is old and in a state of disrepair, and the corridor leading to the offices is non-descript. At the entrance to the firm, there is only a small sign and a bell—one must be buzzed in and met by a security guard. However, once inside the offices and boardrooms are spacious and well appointed. There is modern office furniture throughout and every lawyer, legal translator and member of the support staff has a desk and computer. While the offices are not as plush as those of large North American firms, the contrast with the LCB is immediately evident.

Other Legal Occupations

Thus far it has been suggested that the LCB-firm distinction is key to understanding the functional and social divisions between lawyers. It should be noted, however, that not all jurists are covered by this distinction, particularly jurisconsults, government lawyers, judges' assistants and notaries (as well as judges, who have been treated in Chapter 3). It is difficult to determine the number of jurisconsults in Georgia today since the majority lost their jobs as state enterprises closed during the early 1990s and few appear to have regained their jobs. New businesses, however, are hiring recent graduates whose work tends to involve the use of standard form contracts and litigation for unpaid debt. Not all of these younger recruits are law graduates *per se* (they may have been business students who took some law courses) and most will be directly involved in the business of their companies rather than acting as arms-length in-house counsel.[29] More resembling in-house counsel along the Western model are a number of elite lawyers employed by banks and foreign aid organizations. Some recent graduates from elite law schools find employment as governmental lawyers. They are generally considered dedicated civil servants and competent

29. Interview with MM on 14 May 1999.

lawyers, although the salaries are below a living wage (roughly 40 Laris per month) and lawyers must be from wealthy families and/or work in business on the side (creating numerous potential conflict of interest situations). Of course corruption, particularly for lawyers in the power ministries, remains an element. Notaries are also considered civil servants and are given an important though limited role in many transactions by the Civil Code.[30] Both notaries and judges' assistants are accredited and trained through the Ministry of Justice.[31]

Professional Badges: Collegiality and Prestige

Previous chapters established that Georgian lawyers are divided by education, associations and politics, and that there is little sense of shared professional history. This chapter has shown how the profession is also functionally and socially split. In light of the fractures, it could be expected that some of the more ephemeral "badges" of professionalism, such as collegiality and prestige, would be largely absent. While this expectation is borne out at first blush, the reality is more nuanced. In fact, Georgian lawyers are starting to look professional, albeit unevenly.

There is little sense among lawyers of belonging to a single profession (or professions) unified by common values. Many refer to the majority of their colleagues as incompetent and corrupt, and a lack of "professional courtesy" is said to be commonplace. If, as has been suggested, a sense of collegiality is a necessary ingredient of successful self-governance for a profession, the Georgian Bar Association will face real difficulties.[32] At the very least collegiality is a missing hallmark of professionalism for Georgian jurists as a whole. The "badge" of prestige is also low. In a public opinion poll conducted in 2000, respondents were asked to indicate their level of trust in institutions on a four-point scale (with 1 meaning "no trust" and 4 indicating "very much trust").[33] The average level of trust in lawyers was 2.51, below the private media (2.84) and well below the church (3.45). And, anecdotally, the majority of lawyers are seen as being tainted by corruption. But the situation is not as extreme as it looks.

There is a growing sense of collegiality among lawyers *within* various divisions. GYLA, which is seen by members and much of the public alike as an unofficial bar, has a remarkably cohesive membership given its size. Further-

30. They were regulated earlier than other jurists by the Law of Georgia on the Notariat (3 May 1996).
31. Although called judges' assistants they would be more familiar to Anglo-American jurists as clerks, since they conduct research as well as help manage judges' caseloads: interview with Q on 8 June 2000.
32. "Contradictions of Professionalism", *op. cit.* note 3, 237-238. In the Georgian context, the ability of the Bar Association to fashion rules of procedure and an ethical code acceptable to its members (and then later to decide cases using these rules) is questionable.
33. GORBI, *op. cit.* chap. 3, note 40, 15.

more the organization has drawn members from regional cities into a national organization, perhaps crossing the capital-region divide more effectively than the Collegium did during Soviet times. Cohesive groups have also developed along the lines of legal practice specialties, such as banking law, a phenomenon largely unknown during the Soviet era.

Similarly, despite the low levels of public trust in lawyers in absolute terms, public confidence appears to be rising. According to public opinion polling carried out in 2000, public trust grew by a small margin from two years previous.[34] Equally significant is that lawyers are doing well comparatively. The public opinion research revealed that citizens trust lawyers more than other justice sector occupations such as police (who received a 2 on the four-point scale), prosecutors (2.08) and judges (2.2).[35] Furthermore, the desire to enter the profession, as expressed in applications to law schools, provides another indication of the relatively high prestige with which the legal profession is held.

This rise in prestige is due to various factors, including public legal education (explored in Chapter 4), high incomes for elite lawyers and the increasing media savvy of lawyers who have encouraged and benefited from press coverage. With respect to the latter, Georgia has seen the emergence of "star" lawyers in recent years. They argue their cases in the printed press as frequently as they do in the courts. Sometimes they also litigate on television (cameras are permitted in court at the judge's discretion).[36] But the main reason for the rise in prestige is structural: lawyers can truly *do* something now. In contrast to the Soviet system, where advocates were clearly inferior to prosecutors and judges, lawyers now have a theoretically equal (and practically growing) role to play in criminal justice. Whereas in Soviet times advocates might seek a reduction of charges or sentence for a criminally accused client, they may now seek (and sometimes get) acquittals.[37] Furthermore, as legal reform slowly deepens in Georgia, what lawyers can do increasingly involves the application of abstract knowledge. The characteristics of a successful lawyer in Soviet Georgia included some general knowledge of the law, but, more importantly, the ability to persuade, lobby and act as an intermediary for a client when faced with the prosecuting state. Now when lawyers go into court in complex

34. The level of trust increased by 0.34 points on the four-point scale: *ibid*. The growing prestige of the Bar has also been qualitatively observed: G. Nodia, ed., *Political System in Georgia*, Tbilisi 1998, 27.

35. *Ibid.* at 16.

36. Interview with F on 17 March 1999. One interviewee suggested that lawyers' rise in prestige is tied to exposure to Hollywood's version of lawyering: interview with P on 23 February 2000.

37. The rise of acquittals has also been observed in Russia. One of the most famous acquittals in Russia of the post-Soviet era is that of Alexander Nikitin who was accused of espionage and divulging state secrets. On the implications of this acquittal, many of which are applicable to Georgia, see K. Johnson, "Explaining the Nikitin Acquittal", 9 *East European Constitutional Review* 2000 No. 4, 91 and accompanying articles.

cases, they may be required to educate the judge in a new area of the law such as bankruptcy. The importance of this knowledge should not be exaggerated; as in other jurisdictions the bulk of lawyers' work is not spent researching or presenting the law *per se*. Furthermore, judges are not always receptive to this new role for lawyers and many continue to decide cases using a subjective standard (to recall the discussion from Chapter 3, lawyers have complained that some judges decide cases on the basis of what seems fair without reference to law) or on the basis of which side has paid more. Nonetheless, knowledge of the law is increasingly important for successful lawyers and is reflected in the fact that legal specializations are starting to appear.

The ability of lawyers to *do* something is particularly poignant in the area of human rights. In Tsarist and Soviet Georgia, a few advocates willing to represent dissidents could usually be found, but this was a dangerous prospect and generally involved either a good deal of bravery, self-censorship or "toadyism" with respect to defence strategies. While there are still impediments to finding counsel for dissidents or others wrongfully treated by the state, the situation is much freer than it was in the Soviet and early post-Soviet years. Indeed lawyers are often associated in the public eye now with the role of human rights defenders. Lawyers have taken cutting-edge cases in this area, including on issues of press and religious freedom. This public perception is bound to grow as lawyers begin to take individual cases to Strasbourg under the European Convention for the Protection of Human Rights and Fundamental Freedoms.[38]

A good deal of the human rights work has been carried out by clinic lawyers who provide free legal services or information to the public. Some of these services are provided *pro bono* by unpaid volunteers, although most are made possible by foreign funding which lawyers have successfully sought for their groups' activities. Lawyers have also launched human rights awareness campaigns (detailed in Chapter 4) funded by foreign sources. Some young lawyers are pejoratively called "grant-eaters" for their success in playing to the mandates of international organizations and writing grant proposals. These foreign-funded activities could be considered examples of "demand creation", although the genuine need for human rights clinics and awareness in Georgia is unquestionable.[39] What is certain is that the ability to offer free services to

38. *ETS* No. 5, 11 November 1950 (ratified by Georgia on 20 May 1999).

39. Indeed it might be more appropriate to speak of Georgian lawyers meeting—rather than creating—demand. On "demand creation" see "Comparative Sociology of Legal Professions", *op. cit.* chap. 1, note 10, 110-113; demand creation is described as follows [110, 111]: "The professional project seeks to construct a market in which supply remains constant (or even declines) while demand increases... In some instances lawyers have responded to rising supply and flat or declining demand by actively seeking to stimulate the latter." In general I find Abel more convincing on the supply side; his prime example of demand creation is the advent of legal aid or at least its control by the profession, when in most jurisdictions the state instituted legal aid in the face of the lawyers' opposition.

the public provides employment for lawyers, raises the prestige of lawyers and helps instill in lawyers and the public the idea that lawyers are altruistic (with the latter being another badge of professionalism).

When lawyers act as human rights defenders, they are seen as opposing the state. But it is also important to note that lawyers participate in state-building. Whereas in the first years of the 1990s, Georgian scientists and humanists had the most important role to play in Constitution and legislative drafting, lawyers have largely taken over this role as the rising complexity of legislation requires specialized knowledge. New legislative regimes have been put in place in order to comply with standards imposed by accession to international and European treaties and organizations, such as the World Trade Organization. Furthermore, lawyers are often the ones interacting and negotiating with their counterparts from foreign and international organizations in these matters.

Lawyers' roles have also grown in importance in business matters. Whereas Soviet jurisconsults were facilitators of the command economy, lawyers now have scope to creatively structure business relationships. Market penetration and globalization is frequently said to be a destructive force with respect to professions in the West. In Georgia, however, international market forces rely on the knowledge and skill of lawyers and their colleagues in MDPs to enter the complex Georgian market (even if Georgia is formally "open for business"). In other words, lawyers have finally become "knowledge entrepreneurs".

Of course the growth in the importance of lawyers should not be exaggerated. First of all demand for lawyers is mixed. While the legal needs of businesses have grown dramatically since independence, demand from individual clients seems flat. From public opinion polling done in 1998 and again in 2000, it appears that the percentage of individuals that has ever retained legal counsel remains low (and nearly unchanged between the two years) at roughly 10%.[40] Furthermore, what lawyers can do is limited by the fact that the Georgian state structures have partially failed and that unofficial law effectively excludes lawyers from a wide swathe of potential activity. The weak economy also negatively impacts on lawyers in that many simply cannot afford legal services.

Finally, as has been noted, the extent of professionalization has been uneven. At first glance it appears that large numbers of Collegium lawyers are the "losers" in this regard, while a small elite of young lawyers are the "winners". There is some truth to this. Indeed to some extent Collegium lawyers have *deprofessionalized*; they have lost their Soviet-era monopoly and many of them have failed to adapt to the needs of capitalist Georgia.[41] But this portrayal of winners and losers is too broad. First of all some Collegium lawyers have done

40. GORBI, *op. cit.* chap. 3, note 40, 24.

41. This is particularly true of the LCB lawyers who accept "walk-ins" and court-appointed clients.

very well financially and remain well-known and connected. Moreover, virtually all Collegium lawyers now have increased autonomy from the Presidium and from their own LCBs. This includes more autonomy over the setting of fees than existed during Soviet times, even if competition for clients has increased.[42] As suggested earlier, for the LCB lawyers who have "personal clients", their position is akin to that of sole practitioners. At the same time, professionalizing young lawyers are not a particularly small elite, at least in historical terms. GYLA had roughly as many members ten years after independence as the Collegium did at the time of independence. While not all GYLA members have "professionalized", membership in this organization represents a degree of professionalization.

It is difficult to determine how long this rise of professionalism will last. From a historical perspective "writ large", Georgian lawyers may simply be "behind the times". Perhaps as the Georgian market develops along Western lines, professionalization will reach its peak and then start an inevitable decline; in other words, lawyers will not deprofessionalize until they have professionalized. But for the short to mid-term future there are few signs that the rise of professionalization will stop. The number of university graduates certainly poses the biggest threat to this process and, for reasons stated, the Georgian Bar Association will be of only limited efficacy in controlling these numbers or the behaviour of lawyers. But the importance of reputation (of individuals, firms and educational institutions), together with the continuing role of voluntary associations, appears able to control the extent of competition for some time to come. Thus, while deep divisions will characterize Georgian lawyers for the foreseeable future, this has not stopped (though it may have slowed) the rise of professionalization for comparatively large numbers of lawyers.

42. Although even in Soviet times officially set fees were "topped up" by informal payments from clients.

Chapter 7
Comparisons with Armenia and Azerbaijan

Rounding out the book as a regional study, this chapter looks to the experience of lawyers in Armenia and Azerbaijan. I argue that parallels with the Georgian experience are striking and that a Transcaucasian pattern is discernible. First, shared legal histories, weak legal institutions, and widespread reliance on similar non-state norms equally shape the contours of lawyering in the three countries. Second, law practice is similarly stratified along LCB-firm lines. Third, professionalization has been equally staggered and uneven, with the most professionalized segments engaged with independent lawyers' NGOs, not state-mandated bars. In none of the countries have young reformers sought monopolization of legal services. Finally, there is evidence that links between lawyers in the three countries are growing and that this is the beginning of an informal "Transcaucasian bar". Of course the similarities and linkages between the three countries' legal professions should not obscure their differences (indeed, they can highlight the differences by reducing some of the variables of comparison).[1] Important differences include restricted scope for legal practice in Azerbaijan and three distinct formal models of lawyer governance.

A Regional Legal History?

The three countries have had similar, and, in many respects, shared pasts. Linked by common foreign occupiers (Persian, Ottoman, Russian and Soviet) and ethnic settlement patterns that straddle state borders, there are no neat divisions between the three countries' histories. The similar or shared experiences include the imposition of Tsarist law in the nineteenth century, brief experiments in liberal democracy following the 1917 revolutions, and socialist law and corruption in the Soviet period. Indeed on several occasions in the nineteenth and twentieth centuries Transcaucasia has been governed as a single administrative unit. Finally, the persistence of non-state law focusing on kinship and clientelism is a consistent theme.[2] There are some major differences as well. Two of these, the diasporic nature of the Armenian population and the relatively late statehood of Azerbaijan, will be addressed. The essential point made in this section, however, is that upon the collapse of the Soviet Union each of Georgia, Armenia and Azerbaijan emerged never having had sustained

1. This study is a similar case design. A classic work exploring comparative methodology is A. Lijphart, "The Comparable-Cases Strategy in Comparative Research", 8 *Comparative Political Studies* 1975 No. 2, 158-177.
2. On legal pluralism in Armenia before the First World War, see S.H. Villa and M.K. Matossian, *Armenian Village Life Before 1914*, Detroit 1982. For the Soviet Period see "Breaking the Cake of Custom" in M.K. Matossian, *The Impact of Soviet Policies in Armenia,* Leiden 1962. On the interplay between Islamic and Azeri cultural norms on one hand, and official Soviet secularism on the other, see T. Swietochowski, *Russia and Azerbaijan: A Borderland in Transition*, New York 1995, 116.

periods of indigenous, centralized law-making. A sub-set of that point is that the three countries had never had a "home-grown" legal profession.

Law and the Armenian Diaspora

Unlike Georgians, who have more or less always lived in the lands of historic Georgia, Armenians have long been dispersed. The Armenian population prior to the genocide of 1917 can be divided into three categories: Eastern Armenians (those who lived, roughly speaking, on the territory of what is now the Republic of Armenia), Western Armenians (those who lived on historic Armenian lands in the Ottoman Empire) and diaspora Armenians (who lived and continue to live in various other parts of the world). Together with language and religion, law played an important part in maintaining the cultural identity and coherency of the Armenian communities in the absence of statehood or even shared territory. In fact legal history continues to play a role in Armenian cultural identity as a marker of independent culture and advanced civilization. The legal artifact to which reference is most frequently made is the twelfth century Code of Mkhtar Gosht.[3] It is—in terms of its iconic value at least—the equivalent of Georgia's Code of Vakhtang. Mkhtar's Code has even been cited by legal authorities as a source of principles for the modern Armenian Constitution, an assertion which is untrue in any literal sense.[4]

The extent to which the Code provides a snapshot of Armenian law at the time it was written is unknown, as the Code is both descriptive of customary practices and prescriptive (the author relied heavily on scripture and borrowed from Georgian and Greek sources).[5] It is clear, however, that the Code was written for local circumstances and was not an attempt to systematically expound law in any sort of Napoleonic project. Looked at in that light, the Code reveals a good deal about Armenian legal culture at the time. The focus is on social relations rather than matters of state. Family law, blood price, inheritance and agricultural law are among the matters dealt with. The Code is particularly interesting for its emphasis on legal process. The author insists, for example, that judges be incorruptible and adopt a judicial temperament.[6] Despite this, the author had little use for professional lawyers, whom he viewed as a perversion of the Muslim courts. His introduction to the Code states: "Let

3. See R.W. Thomson, trans., *The Lawcode (Datastanagirk) of Mxit'ar Goš*, Amsterdam 2000 (hereinafter "Mkhtar's Code").
4. See H.M. Khachatryan, *The First Constitution of the Republic of Armenia*, Yerevan 1998, 20.
5. Although canon law had developed steadily from the time of Armenia's early conversion to Christianity, secular legal principles were unwritten and fragmented. This posed a problem following Muslim control of Armenian territory in the eleventh century. While Muslim Emirs allowed Christians to hold their own courts and judge themselves by their own laws, the lack of an identifiable Armenian law meant Christians were being judged by Muslim courts and Muslim laws. Mkhtar's Code filled that gap.
6. *Mkhtar's Code, op. cit.* note 3, 83.

it not at all be allowed to have for a fee some eloquent attorney, whereby they bring the evil [side] to final victory."[7]

Well into the nineteenth-century the substantive and procedural principles contained in the Code remained the central expression of Armenian law in both historic Armenia (Eastern and Western Armenia) and throughout the diaspora. In Poland, for example, where the Code was in use by the fourteenth century, economic, family and inheritance law matters were dealt with on the basis of Armenian law, in many cases by Armenian magistrates.[8] Despite its importance, however, Mkhtar's Code was not the only source of law for Armenian communities. In the first place, public law was typically that of the host state or invader. In addition, the Code was often adapted to local circumstances or mixed with legal imports. For example, Armenian rulers in Cilicia further systematized the Code during the thirteenth century and explicitly incorporated Byzantine and Franco-Norman laws.[9] Others, such as the Armenian community in India, were under the influence of enlightenment concepts of law and combined these with traditional rules. In the mid-nineteenth century, a number of young reformers from Western Armenia—many of whom studied law in European Universities—became enamoured with European notions of constitutionalism and pushed these ideals both within the Armenian community and eventually within the Ottoman Empire as a whole.[10]

The interest in legalism was also apparent during the brief Armenian independence following the Bolshevik and Russian Revolutions when, despite desperate circumstances, legal reform was a real issue for the new republic. Among other things, Armenian was made the official language for court proceedings, a commission was set up to examine Western Armenian customs to be used in the drafting of new laws for the Republic, and jury trials were introduced.[11] The latter reform was hailed by politicians and the press as a particular milestone.[12] While the Code of Mikhtar Gosht was never revived in independent Armenia, the central role of law in scattered Armenian communities was a consistent theme up until the Sovietization of Armenia.

Although during the Soviet era "bourgeois" notions of law were formally set aside in Armenia proper,[13] communities in the diaspora continued to be influenced by notions of law in their host countries in the West and elsewhere. Through migration to the homeland, which was permitted at various points

7. *Ibid.* at 85. See also references to hired lawyers and "deceitful orators", *ibid.*, 86, 101.
8. P. Cowe, "Medieval Armenian and Literary and Cultural Trends" in R.G. Hovannisian, ed., *The Armenian People From Ancient to Modern Times*, New York 1997, 300-301.
9. *Ibid.*, 298.
10. H. Barsoumian, "The Eastern Question and the Tanzimat Era" in Hovanissian, *op. cit.* note 8, 197. Ultimately, of course, these attempts to promote Constitutionalism ended in failure and the genocide of 1917 decimated the Western Armenian population.
11. R.G. Hovannissian, *The Republic of Armenia,* vol. 3, Berkeley 1996.
12. *Ibid.*, 329.

during the Soviet era,[14] one can presume that these Armenians brought non-communist legal memories with them. These memories of non-communist law and civil society may have influenced the more general culture, in much the same way that "parallel cultures" in Hungary and other states of Eastern and Central Europe—nurtured by pre-war memories—kept democratic ideas alive throughout the communist period.[15] More concretely observable is the fact that during the break-up of the Soviet Union, diaspora Armenians played an early and important role in steering Armenia towards a Western orientation, including in terms of law. Since independence, international agencies promoting law reform have employed Armenian lawyers from the diaspora and some diaspora lawyers have started practicing law in the Republic.[16] The establishment of the American University of Armenia (AUA, an affiliate of the University of California), with a law department offering an LL.M. in comparative law, is also due in large measure to the activities of diaspora Armenians. This early exchange of persons and ideas from a diaspora was a uniquely Armenian phenomenon in Transcaucasia and largely unknown in the former Soviet Union outside of the Baltic Republics.

It should also be noted that the Armenian diaspora has had a direct effect on Azerbaijan. Reacting to the war over the disputed area of Nagorno-Karabakh, Armenian-Americans lobbied successfully in the early 1990s for a ban on US state-state co-operation with Azerbaijan.[17] The ban, which was lifted in January 2002 as a reward for Baku's support of US actions in Afghanistan, not only prohibited bilateral large-scale aid but affected smaller-scale ventures as well.[18] To take one example, the ABA was unable to work with Azerbaijan's state universities to develop law clinics. The effect of the aid embargo was muted somewhat, however, through US aid to non-governmental entities.[19]

13. Though perhaps not the idea of legalism. Intriguingly, Armenia was the only Soviet Republic to organize a referendum for independence according to Soviet law (N. Dudwick, "Political transformations in postcommunist Armenia: images and realities" in K. Dawisha & B. Parrot, eds., *Conflict, Cleavage, and Change in Central Asia and the Caucasus,* Cambridge 1997, 69).
14. Although the immigrants, particularly from "bourgeois" countries, were held in suspicion by authorities. On migration to Soviet Armenia see R.H. Dekmejian, "The Armenian Diaspora" in Hovannisian, *op. cit.* note 8.
15. The "parallel cultures" concept was developed by V. Havel, "The Power of the Powerless" in J. Vladislav, ed., *Václav Havel or Living in Truth,* London 1986, 36, 101. On the link between the parallel cultures and the "restoration of trust and fidelity to law" see Janda, *op. cit.* chap. 2, note 7, 267.
16. Interview with O on 9 October 2000.
17. Aid to the Azerbaijani government was prohibited by s. 907 of the Freedom for Russia and Emerging Eurasian Democracies and Open Markets Support Act of 1992 (Freedom Support Act; Public Law 511, 102nd cong., 2nd sess. 24 October 1992).
18. A. Blua, "Azerbaijan: US Lifts Restrictions on Aid", *RFE/RL Feature,* 29 January 2002.
19. Thus for example, the ABA has worked with a private university to establish a legal clinic: interview with L on 6 November 2000.

Azerbaijan's Late Statehood

Upon independence Georgia and Armenia were able to look back at traditions of statehood and indigenous law (however recreated those traditions were). Post-Soviet Azerbaijan did not have this luxury. Azerbaijani law-makers have few legal monuments (a Code of Vakhtang or Mkhtar Gosht) which can be invoked for inspiration or legitimation of current state-building endeavours. Until the downfall of the Soviet Union, Azerbaijan had never been a state, other than during a brief experiment with independence following the 1917 revolutions.[20] Indeed until the twentieth century there was no Azerbaijani nation *per se*. As one scholar puts it: "In 1905 Azerbaijan was still merely a geographical name for a stretch of land inhabited by a people whose group identity consisted of being Muslims."[21] To be clear, there is no question that Azerbaijanis have a rich history and culture, but statehood and national consciousness were not a part of that until the twentieth century.

Besides the lack of independent statehood, there is little that could be labeled Azerbaijani law until the twentieth century. Azerbaijanis prior to the Tsarist occupation lived by local custom, the rule of local princes, and Islamic *Sharia*. And, despite the Russification of administrative and legal apparatus, the use of Islamic and customary law continued into the Tsarist reign. Formally, public law matters were dealt with by the Imperial Codes, while personal law matters such as inheritance and divorce were handled by state-sanctioned Muslim courts.[22] In fact the situation was more complex than that, as is poignantly portrayed in a novel set in Baku just prior to the First World War:[23]

> Citizens seeking justice are supposed to go the Russian judge outside the wall. But hardly anyone goes to the Russian judge, and if he does, wise men despise him, and the children on the street put their tongues out at him. Not because the Russian judges are bad or unjust. On the contrary they are mild and just, but in a manner that our people dislike. A thief is put in jail. There he sits in a clean cell, is given tea, even with sugar in it. But nobody gets anything out of this, least of all the man he stole from. People shrug their shoulders and do justice in their own way. In the afternoon the plaintiffs come to the mosque where

20. Even that experiment was entered into reluctantly and was marked not only by unpreparedness but by a reliance on the Tsarist administrative structures; as one scholar puts it: "The Azerbaijani Republic offered a textbook example of a colonial country unexpectedly catapulted into independence" (Swietochowski, *op. cit.* note 2, 78).
21. T. Swietochowski, "National Consciousness and Political Orientations in Azerbaijan, 1905-1920" in R.G. Suny, ed., *Transcaucasia. Nationalism and Social Change*, Ann Arbor 1983, 209, 231. This observation however is not always recognized by Azerbaijanis. Indeed the Preamble to Azerbaijan's 1995 Constitution begins with "Continuing the centuries old traditions of statehood..."
22. A.L. Altstadt, *The Azerbaijani Turks*, Stanford 1992, 18 and A. Altstadt-Mirhadi, "The Azerbaijani Bourgeoisie and the Cultural-Enlightenment Movement in Baku: First Steps Toward Nationalism" in Suny, *ibid.*, 197, 201.
23. The novel was originally published in German in Vienna in 1937—it has since been rediscovered: K. Said, *Ali and Nino*, New York 2000, 18-19.

> wise old men sit in a circle and pass sentence according to the laws of Sharia, the law of Allah: "An eye for an eye, a tooth for a tooth." Sometimes at night shrouded figures slip through the alleys. A dagger strikes like lightening, a little cry and justice is done.

It should also be noted that the Tsarist state discriminated against the Muslim population in politics and law. Discriminatory measures included limited representation by Muslims in local government and restrictions on non-Christians in the legal profession.[24] Despite the prominence of Islam in Azerbaijan's pre-Tsarist and Tsarist history, however, post-Soviet Azerbaijani legal scholars and lawmakers rarely look to the Islamic legal tradition as a source of inspiration or legitimation. Indeed the Azerbaijani state is avowedly secular—a principle which is enshrined in the Constitution—and fiercely resists any hint of Islamic fundamentalism (as did Soviet Azerbaijan).[25] Ultimately, while it would be untrue to say that Azerbaijani state-building "started from scratch" in 1991, there had been a stunted political and legal evolution before that time.

The Legal Environment

Like Georgia, Armenia and Azerbaijan are partly failed-states. The war between Armenia and Azerbaijan over the disputed Nagorno-Karabakh region is central to this phenomenon.[26] Conflict over the long-disputed territory intensified during the late Soviet period and full-scale war was waged in the early 1990s. The war, which saw both sides breach the laws of armed conflict on numerous occasions, produced tens of thousands of IDPs fleeing to Armenia and Azerbaijan proper. The IDPs remain a destabilizing factor (particularly in Azerbaijan, which lost roughly 20% of its territory during the war), and national security concerns have in many ways dominated the political agenda in both countries since independence. Although most of the fighting ended with a 1994 ceasefire, peace has proved an elusive goal. This continued sense of being on "war footing" partly accounts for the authoritarian streaks in both countries, particularly in Azerbaijan where the military defeat continues to sting and there are calls from veterans groups and others to restart the conflict. The Organization for Security and Co-operation in Europe (OSCE) and other international and foreign intermediaries have so far failed in attempts to broker a lasting peace. Although the leadership in both Armenia and Azerbaijan has seemed poised to compromise on several occasions (under the rubric of shared sovereignty), popular resistance has made concessions politically dangerous.

Partly as a result of the conflict, constitution-making efforts in Armenia and Azerbaijan were delayed (both countries' constitutions were adopted in

24. Kucherov, *op. cit.* chap. 2, note 43, 274.
25. See Principle 4 of the 1995 Constitution's Preamble. Although it would be wrong to discount religion as a factor in popular opinion: A.L. Altstadt, "Azerbaijan's struggle toward democracy", in Dawisha & Parrott, *op. cit.* note 13, 145-146.
26. A clear account of the conflict can be found in Goldenberg, *op. cit.* chap. 2, note 128.

1995) and flawed, technically and democratically. The respective Presidents hold largely unchecked power and the formally enshrined human rights protections—which meet international standards—are effectively muted by the inability of individual citizens to petition the Constitutional Courts.[27] In both countries there have been calls to change the Constitution and a Constitutional Commission in Armenia is actively considering amendments. The proposed changes and the nature of the consultative process appear to reflect a growing constitutional maturity in Armenia.[28] In addition to limiting the President's power and to allowing citizen petitions to the Constitutional Court, the new proposals would strengthen judicial independence from the executive.[29] The need for constitutional reform was underscored by the assassination of the Armenian Prime Minister and several deputies in Parliament in October 1999. Whether true or not, the Armenian President was thought by many to be responsible for the killings—motivated by fears that the Prime Minister was emerging as a threat to his power.[30] The subsequent trial of the accused killers has been dismissed by some opposition groups as a sham and demands have increased for an independent judiciary more capable of checking executive actions.[31]

In Azerbaijan, the issue of constitutional reform is complicated by the question of secession. The current President, Heydar Aliev, is a former Azerbaijani party boss from the Soviet era who has ruled in an authoritarian manner since 1993. The President has created a cult of personality around himself, the signs of which are present throughout the capital; his portraits and sayings are on billboards, the sides of buildings and on the office walls of virtually every state and quasi-state body in the country (including LCBs). While the President is not without numerous supporters—he has brought stability to Azerbaijan and has overseen the development of the country's rich oil reserves—political and legal reform has been slow under his rule and there is widespread concern that the aging President's death will result in political turmoil. The President

27. On presidential powers see Art. 101 of the Armenian Constitution and Art. 109 of the Azerbaijani Constitution. On which bodies can submit cases to the constitutional courts, see Arts. 101 and 130 of the Armenian and Azerbaijani Constitutions respectively.
28. The Constitutional Reform Commission has engaged in what appears to be a genuine exercise in popular consultation and the Head of the Commission speaks frankly in public about flaws in the current constitution. (Attendance at a public consultation held by the Commission Head, Felix Tokhian, at the American University of Armenia, Yerevan on 21 February 2001.)
29. On the proposed changes see H. Khachatrian, "Constitutional Amendments in Armenia: A necessary but difficult task", *Eurasia Insight* 21 August 2001.
30. L. Fuller, "How unified is the new Armenian opposition alignment?", *RFE/RL Caucasus Report*, Vol. 4(32), 24 September 2001.
31. See H. Khachatrian, "Parliament Shooting Trial Poses Challenge for Armenian Political Institutions", *Eurasia Insight* 13 June 2001.

appears to be grooming his son Ilham for the post of President and at one point even suggested that he himself would seek a third term in office in 2003 elections.[32]

Beyond their constitutional peculiarities, the Armenian and Azerbaijani legal systems look quite similar on the ground to Georgia's and need not be described in further detail. Suffice it to say that corruption, lack of material resources and external (often executive) pressure provide some of the context for lawyering in Armenia and Azerbaijan as well as in Georgia. In all three countries, lawyers are regularly denied access to clients in places of detention and human rights abuses committed by security forces are frequent (though it should be noted that torture and ill-treatment appear to be rampant in Azerbaijan).[33] It is hoped that the admission of Armenia and Azerbaijan to the Council of Europe in January 2001—prematurely in the eyes of most human rights observers—will provide additional impetus for the two countries to more solidly entrench human rights norms and democratic values in their legal systems.[34]

Legal Education

There are few distinctions to be drawn in terms of content and teaching methodology between the legal education systems. Static and state-centred teaching still prevails although this has been tempered, at least in the capital cities, by the gradual introduction of Western approaches (through curriculum development workshops and student and faculty exchanges with the West). One exception to this statement, however, is the American University of Armenia. Although touching relatively few students (roughly thirty students are enrolled in the LL.M. programme) the education is Western (and predominantly American) in terms of instructors, content and teaching methodology.[35]

Clinical legal education is a growing trend in all three countries. Yerevan State University's (YSU) is among the most advanced. Opened in September 1999 the clinic involves roughly twenty students a year and takes on eight to ten cases a month. Although the undergraduate students do not receive credit

32. Although Azerbaijan's Constitution permits only two consecutive presidential terms, Aliev's supporters argue that since the Constitution was adopted while he was already President, he is able to run again.
33. In a 2001 report, the UN Special Rapporteur on Torture concluded that Azerbaijani law enforcement officials use torture on a "widespread" basis (UN Doc. E/CN.4/2001/66/Add. 1).
34. See for example, Human Rights Watch, "Council of Europe Cautioned on Early Admission for Armenia, Azerbaijan" (26 January 2001, http://www.hrw.org/press/1999/jan/aze0125.htm).
35. The University also has one of the best law libraries in the region. It should be noted that the Law Department is sometimes criticized as being disengaged from Armenian legal reform efforts.

for the clinic work, they report seeing it as an important way to balance an overly theoretical legal education and put a good deal of effort into it.[36] Skills such as interviewing and oral advocacy are stressed, and a video camera is used to tape students during exercises. The clinic was recently renovated and is well-funded. In addition to the clinic director (who holds an LL.M. from Central European University in Budapest) and her assistant, the clinic employs two part-time lecturers and an advocate who takes criminal cases to court and advises students on their cases. There are also legal clinics in Azerbaijan at the State University and Hazar University, a private institution. The legal clinics in Armenia and Azerbaijan are funded by various international sources although, for reasons described earlier, US government agencies were forbidden from working with the Azerbaijani state universities for some years.

There are more significant differences between the three systems in terms of material conditions. While most state and private universities in the region are underfunded, there are some telling exceptions. For example, the Faculty of Law at Yerevan State University—the most important law faculty in the country—was completely renovated in 1999–2000 with the financial assistance of a diaspora philanthropist. The Faculty also has a well-stocked computer laboratory and library which have been built with US assistance. In Azerbaijan some private universities, catering to the children of the wealthy oil-based elite, also have excellent conditions. Baku's Western University, for example, which offers law courses through its business programme, occupies a well-lit impressive building and has numerous resources—including for English language training—which are simply unavailable in the state universities.[37] Corruption is a concern at all law schools in Armenia and Azerbaijan, with the exception of the American University and possibly some of the Azerbaijani private law schools where instructors' salaries are high.[38]

In terms of differences in legal education, the oppressive political atmosphere on Azerbaijani campuses must be addressed. Signs of this atmosphere are evident in virtually every university official's office—a photograph or bust of the President. Indeed, one university Dean proudly presented a book of the President's sayings to the author of this book. Allegiance to the regime is expected from students as well as professors, and criticism of the regime can result in expulsion from the university.[39] Political dissent is also discouraged

36. Clinic work is also seen as a way to build stature within the faculty (observation based on conversations with students of the clinic in October 2000 and April 2001).

37. Observation and meetings with Western University officials in Baku on 28 April 1999.

38. Instructor salaries at the state universities in Baku are roughly US$ 50 per month. Although higher than Georgian salaries, the level is not sufficient to avoid corruption. See A. Aliyev, "Students Dream of Hitting Books Abroad", *Baku Sun* 3 November 2000, 2.

39. "Azeri students appeal over expulsion from university due to political leaflet", BBC Worldwide Monitoring—Transcaucasus Unit (27 April 2000), citing newspaper *Azadlyg*.

on Georgian and Armenian campuses, but Azerbaijan is clearly in a class apart on this score. This limits discussion and critical dialogue for Azerbaijani law students who eventually will be asked by clients to provide protection from the state.

Turning to the role of legal education in controlling access to the profession, the situation in Armenia and Azerbaijan is similar to that in Georgia. While the number of law schools has proliferated in the last decade, good jobs are only available for graduates of the elite state schools and a very small number of the private schools. In Armenia for example, virtually all judges, prosecutors and law professors are graduates of Yerevan State University's Law Faculty. Admission to the Faculty is for the rich, well-connected and very bright, and is widely seen as a "ticket to success".[40]

Regulation and Self-Regulation

There has been less of a regulatory vacuum in Armenia and Azerbaijan than in Georgia. Azerbaijan in particular has seen the government take an authoritarian approach to advocates. Ultimately, however, many of the same forces are at play in the three countries, including tensions between reformers and the "old-guard". Like their Georgian counterparts, the majority of Armenian and Azerbaijani reformers have opposed monopolistic bar structures; they prefer to rely on self-regulation through independent lawyers' NGOs and competition between individuals and firms for prestige.

Armenia

In principle the 1998 law governing Armenian advocates corresponds closely to the realities of post-Soviet lawyering.[41] Although the law maintains advocates' monopoly over criminal work, advocates are not governed by a single corporate structure such as a collegium. Rather Armenia has compromised between a voluntary and mandatory bar. Those wishing to become advocates must have certain state-mandated qualifications (such as a legal education) and pass a state-administered exam, but they must also be accepted by an advocates' association. The associations can be established with the agreement of fifty qualified persons and—within fairly broad limits—can set their own standards and procedures for admission, ethics, discipline and financial management. Three associations have been formed. The first, the Union of Advocates of the Republic of Armenia (UARA), is the legal successor to the Collegium. UARA has roughly 150 advocates and continues the most traditional forms of practice, often in the LCBs inherited from its predecessor. The two others, the International Bar Union and the International Union of Armenian Advocates, each have about

40. Interview with TT on 8 October 2000.

41. Law of the Republic of Armenia on Advocate Activity (18 June 1998) (unofficial translation on file with author). Prior to this law, advocates were governed by a 1980 Soviet Armenian statute on the *advokatura*; on the provisions of that statute as exercised between 1991 and 1998, see Khachatryan, *op. cit.* note 4, 92.

60 members. The International Union of Armenian Advocates appears to have a younger, more Western-oriented membership than its counterparts.

These advocates' associations act as a second screen on the admission of lawyers to practice, the first being the state qualifications. There are also informal components to both the state and associational admission processes. For example it has been suggested that bribes may be passed at state exams and that candidates for admission to the advocates' associations have sometimes been denied entry on arbitrary grounds. In one case, a candidate with all the proper qualifications was denied admission and reportedly told, "you are too young—come back next year".[42]

When the law was enacted it was hoped that the advocates' associations would compete with each other for reputation and prestige and that this would raise the overall character of the bar.[43] There is some evidence that this competition has taken place (advertising lawyers sometimes indicate the association with which they are affiliated), although personal/firm reputation and affordability (UARA takes on most of the legal aid and walk-in clientele) continue to be more important factors in determining client choice. Nor does it appear likely that many more associations will be formed to give clients greater choice. The primary reason for this is that jurists who are not advocates can conduct civil cases or do solicitor's work without regulation. There is little incentive therefore for the majority of jurists to become advocates and join an advocates' association. Both advocates and non-advocates have, however, joined entirely voluntary organizations such as the Armenian Bar Association.[44] The Bar Association is based at Yerevan State University's Law Faculty (the President and Vice-President are Dean and Vice-Dean respectively) and engages in educational and clinical activities. It also has drafted a model Code of Ethics for Armenian lawyers. Though criticized for its inactivity, the Bar Association's membership is of a fairly elite nature (reinforced by its link with the elite Law Faculty) and represents a badge of status in Yerevan's legal community.

Azerbaijan

The legal regulation of lawyers in Azerbaijan is a murky subject.[45] From independence in 1991 to 1997 the Soviet-era law on the *advokatura* formally

42. Interview with TT, *op. cit.* note 40.
43. Interview with QQ on 31 October 1998.
44. There appears to be no strong equivalent to GYLA: interview with K on 10 October 2000.
45. Much of this discussion on legal regulation relies on two reports from the International League for Human Rights (ILHR): P. LeGendre, *Legislative Regulation of the Legal Profession in Azerbaijan* (2001) and C.A. Fitzpatrick *et al.*, *Restrictions on the Independent Legal Profession in Azerbaijan* (1999) (both reports are online at www.ilhr.org). See also A. Gadzhiev, "Azerbaijan: Imminent Passage of Law on the Legal Profession Cause for Alarm", *Eurasia Insight* 1 February 2000 and E. Dailey, "Before It's Too Late: Adopting the Right Law on Azerbaijan's Legal Profession", *Eurasia Insight* 21 August 2001.

governed and the 500-member Collegium of Advocates' monopoly over court work remained in place. In 1997 this monopoly was threatened by a Presidential decree requiring all those providing legal services (widely defined) to obtain licenses.[46] Licenses were to be granted through the Ministry of Justice to those who had a law degree and two years legal experience and were able to pay the requisite fee (100 million manat or US$ 350). This appeared to put all lawyers, or at least those able to pay the fee (several times the average monthly salary) on an equal footing, by opening up the provision of legal services to the market and removing the Collegium's monopoly. The granting of the licenses was largely a formality, and in less than two years the Ministry granted licenses to 122 individuals and 13 firms. Only two applications were rejected, apparently on the grounds that the applicants did not have sufficient legal education.

Whether the executive intended to break the Collegium's monopoly and require all lawyers, including Collegium members, to pay the fees is not clear, but two months after the Presidential Decree the government backtracked. The Ministry of Justice issued an announcement that the licensing requirements did not apply to Collegium members. One year later, the Ministry retreated further, releasing a letter indicating that only Collegium members—not licensees—could represent clients in criminal cases. While some individual lawyers who were not members of the Collegium successfully petitioned judges to allow them to appear on specific cases, formally at least the Collegium's monopoly had apparently been restored.[47]

The uncertainty following the Presidential Decree was ended on the side of the Collegium with the 2000 Law on Advocates and Advocate Activity.[48] The law confirms that only Collegium members, not licensees, can represent criminal clients in court.[49] And, while the law contains hortatory statements about the importance of an independent advocate's role in promoting the rule of law and protecting human rights,[50] it is clear that the Collegium is true to its Soviet heritage in content. The Presidium and the Disciplinary and Qualification Committees wield a good deal of authority over members, an authority not immune to formal and informal executive pressure. Formally, the Qualification Committee—the profession's gatekeeper—is composed of nine members; three of the members are appointed by the Presidium, three

46. Cabinet of Ministers Decision No. 103 (1 May 1998). See A. Fesenko and V. Shneyer, "Azerbaijan Now Licenses the Practice of Law", 9 *Russia and Commonwealth Business Law Report* 1998.

47. The successful requests from non-members were granted either on the basis of the lawyer's personal reputation or connections to the judge or through the legal argument that the Ministry's policy statements could not alter a Presidential Decree.

48. The law entered into force on 27 January 2000 (unofficial translation on file with author).

49. *Ibid.*, Art. 4(ii).

50. *Ibid.*, Arts. 5 & 6.

are judges appointed by the Supreme Court (which is itself subject to strong executive authority) and three are legal scholars appointed directly by the executive. Informally, there is no doubt that the Collegium is under executive influence. As one human rights observer puts it:[51]

> Although the Ministry of Justice does not micromanage the day-to-day operations, the Collegium leadership knows what is politically acceptable to the presidential apparatus and the Ministry of Justice. The leadership toes the line and ensures that the lawyers it controls stay in line as well. When it does not a phone call from above can quickly energize the Collegium into action.

Similarly, while the Collegium does not micromanage its advocates, pressure is applied through warnings, lack of referrals and potential expulsion. The expulsion of a high-profile media lawyer from the Collegium, essentially for criticizing the government while on a trip to the United States, has drawn condemnation from international human rights groups.[52] Although such direct punishment is not common, his example has unquestionably caused additional pressures for self-censorship. At times the executive bypasses the Collegium altogether to pressure lawyers. Lawyers who have challenged the government—in the sense of taking on opponents of the regime as clients—report intimidation and harassment by both the regular and secret police. The degree to which the political interference has been effective should not be exaggerated, however, as some lawyers do vigorously pursue cases against the government and criticize the government publicly.[53]

As in Georgia and Armenia, the government and the Collegium are not the only actors involved in regulating lawyers. In recent years roughly ten "independent" lawyers' associations have sprung up. Some of these have apparently been created by the government as a show of plurality. Others, such as the Association of Lawyers of Azerbaijan (ALA) and the Azerbaijan Association of Advocates (AAA) are genuinely independent of government control and, consequently, have been harassed by the government. For example, both organizations have had repeated difficulties in having their organizations registered with the Ministry of Justice as NGOs so that they might legally operate.[54] Despite government opposition, however, some of the independent groups have proven quite active. ALA, for example, has various projects including legal education for the general public and legal aid to NGOs and the independent press. Independent lawyers have also joined together to lobby the government on regulatory issues. Thus when the Ministry of Justice "qualified" the Presidential decree on licensing,

51. P. LeGendre, *op. cit.* note 45 and interview with S on 26 April 1999.
52. *Ibid.*
53. See for example, "Lawyer Comments on Council of Europe, Former Premier's Release", *(Baku) Bilik Dunyasi* 19 December 2000.
54. LeGendre, *op. cit.* note 45.

seventy lawyers submitted a joint letter of complaint to the Cabinet of Ministers. It should be pointed out that membership in independent associations is not as widespread as it is in Georgia—in substantive terms there is no equivalent of GYLA (though there is a group called the Azerbaijani Young Lawyers Association, it does not operate on the same scale). Nonetheless, the associations do have a committed core membership.[55] And, as in Georgia, membership in these organizations is some indication for potential clients and colleagues that the lawyer is independent of government authority. In their activities, some of the independent lawyers' groups have received significant financial and technical assistance from international and foreign NGOs keen to promote "civil society" in an authoritarian state. This international support, which includes perks such as foreign travel, has undoubtedly been one of the incentives to join.

Stratification and Professionalization: "Musicians at a Funeral"?

As in Georgia, lawyers in Armenia and Azerbaijan are stratified and legal practice is marked by two different "hemispheres." One of those hemispheres—that centred on the Soviet-style LCBs—is similar in all three states and further description would add little.[56] The more significant differences occur within the hemisphere of business law firms, and are due to the oil wealth which has been generated in Azerbaijan.

While in Georgia there is one firm staffed partly with Western lawyers and in Armenia two or three firms run by diaspora Armenians, Azerbaijan has branches of a number of international firms operating in the oil sector. Some of these firms, which include Baker & McKenzie, Baker & Botts and Ledingham Chalmers, originally had American and European lawyers "commute" to Baku in the early 1990s. Eventually they opened full offices there, staffed by both international and Azerbaijani lawyers. These lawyers are conducting business on a scale not hitherto seen in the region. In addition to "pure" legal activities such as the drafting of contracts, their tasks include complex negotiations with the government—centred at the Presidential Palace—for project approvals. Interestingly, these firms appear to be operating extra-legally since many of them—with the collusion of the government—have simply ignored the licensing requirements.

55. ALA and AAA each have roughly 40 members.
56. For example, the centrally located LCB No. 12 in Baku is comparable to Mtatsminda LCB in Tbilisi, although somewhat more active. The LCB of 23 lawyers, founded in 1958 is smartly signed and clean inside. However, there are few law books, no computers and no possibility of carrying out confidential lawyer-client discussions. The lawyers were mostly elderly and the cases tended to be criminal and small-scale family and property. There were some exceptions however, with a few of the advocates taking on business law cases as well. (Observations and interviews with W and JJ on 3 November 2000.)

The local lawyers hired by these firms are typically the best in the country and many hold LL.M.s from Western universities. A number of them have studied oil and gas law in the US Some independent local law firms have attempted to tap into this market, but have generally been unsuccessful beyond handling litigation files and preparing opinions on Azeri law.[57] The salaries for lawyers—both local and international—working in these firms is without comparison for lawyers working elsewhere in Azerbaijan or the Transcaucasus. However, the phenomenon of law in the Azerbaijani "oil patch" does not detract from place of practice as the primary axis of stratification in that country.[58] The LCB-firm split, which was explored in Chapter 6, remains fundamental to understanding other variants such as management, clients and forms of practice.

Despite the stratification, large numbers of Armenian and Azerbaijani lawyers are professionalizing, albeit unevenly. The rise of legal NGOs in Armenia and Azerbaijan, increased collegiality among reformers, and a slow rise in prestige are all evidence of this fact. As in Georgia, the rise in prestige is closely tied to the fact that lawyers can now *do* something for their clients. An Azerbaijani joke—"lawyers are like musicians at a funeral—you need them for the ceremony but they can't *do* anything for you"—no longer rings as true as it once did.[59] The new role played by lawyers in the oil industry speaks for itself. In addition, both Armenian and Azerbaijani lawyers willing to do civil rights work are increasingly seen by ordinary citizens as the only potential protection against arbitrary state action. Lawyers are also increasingly in demand as Armenia and Azerbaijan attempt to fulfill their legislative obligations under the Council of Europe system and harmonize financial laws with European Union standards.[60] Indeed the Speaker of Azerbaijan's Parliament has publicly bemoaned the lack of lawyers in his institution as an impediment to that body's work.[61]

It should be also be pointed out that there has been an increase in collegiality—and perhaps the beginnings of a common professional identity—*across* Transcaucasian borders. As noted in Chapter 4, academic networks between the three countries are being rekindled in areas such as journal publication, thesis defences and conferences. And students have begun to move between countries in the regions; ethnic Azeri and Armenian students from Georgia have studied

57. Interview with L, *op. cit.* note 19.
58. As in the previous chapter, it should be pointed out that the hemispheres portrayed here exclude some legal occupations such as notaries.
59. This joke is cited in Fitzpatrick, *et al.*, *op. cit.* note 45.
60. The obligation of Armenia to approximate its legislation to that of the European Union is found in the Partnership and Cooperation Agreement signed by Armenia and the European Community (and member states) on 22 April 1996. The Agreement entered into force on 1 July 1999.
61. "Agronomists and historians dominate mostly Azeri Parliament", BBC Worldwide Monitoring—Transcaucasus Unit (6 December 2000), citing the newspaper *Azadlyg*.

in Baku and Yerevan (although this phenomenon is partly due to discrimination faced by ethnic minorities in Georgia) and the American University of Armenia has begun recruiting students in Georgia. There have also been numerous conferences bringing together practicing lawyers and judges in Tbilisi to discuss matters of common concern. Some lawyers' associations in the three countries have also co-operated. Undoubtedly the co-operation has been instigated and financed more by international agencies than Transcaucasian lawyers themselves. For example, having the Open Society Institute as a common funder has put the staff of legal clinics in Tbilisi, Yerevan and Baku in regular contact. They are required to share reports and meet regularly. Nonetheless genuine co-operation is increasing and there is a common sense of purpose among some young reformers on the role of lawyers in the post-Soviet transition. Whether or not these beginnings emerge into a real informal "Transcaucasian Bar" remains to be seen. Certainly much will depend on the ability of Armenia and Azerbaijan to settle differences over Nagorno-Karabakh.

In sum, the Georgian experience with professionalization is largely reflected in Armenia and Azerbaijan. That is, young reformers are professionalizing and successfully pursuing market control and badges of professionalization such as prestige and collegiality. Yet in none of the three countries has monopolization or the state become a focus in the pursuit of market control or collective mobility. A legal pluralist perspective—focussing on reputation and voluntary associations—is key to understanding the new professions throughout the region.

Conclusion: Professionalization and the Rule of Law

This conclusion has two parts. The first summarizes the empirical evidence and considers the implications of these findings for the study of legal professions. These results can be briefly stated. First the break-up of the Soviet Union triggered a rapid de-professionalization for Georgian lawyers. The monopoly of the Collegium was broken, the number of law graduates multiplied, many of the objective conditions for litigation lawyering (including, for a time, functioning courts) were simply absent and most jurists employed by state enterprises lost their jobs. In other words, lawyers found themselves in an unregulated free market with little ability to control the markets or their work. But there has also been a growing movement towards professionalization of lawyers since 1991. Intriguingly, the key to understanding the new professionalism does not lie with the (re)construction of state-mandated monopolies. Rather lawyers have attempted to control their market through voluntary bars and through means—such as enhancing social networks—firmly lodged in culture.

The second section moves beyond an "internalist" view of professionalization and suggests a research agenda for considering the impact of professionalization on the transition itself. Specifically, potential links between professionalization and the rule of law are considered and some suggestions made as to how the findings of this study can be made operational in promoting the rule of law.

Profession on the Rise

Summary of Empirical Findings

This book began by exploring some of the boundaries within which lawyering occurs in Georgia. The boundaries—the first of which is the legacy of history—are inhospitable. Georgia's history is marked by the absence of sustained, centralized law-making and, not surprisingly, a "home-grown" legal profession. In important ways, Georgian lawyers and lawmakers are scrambling to construct a functional bar in the absence of individual or collective memory (real or reconstructed) as to what a legal profession should look like. Another boundary for lawyers is that—as a legal pluralist perspective shows—they are not all that necessary to the way things actually work, at least for large swathes of life.[1] Indeed the persistence of non-state law has structurally meant that Georgian lawyers have grown only slowly in importance as conflict managers, or "architects" of economic or social relationships.[2] Finally, the partly failed state

1. This is of course true for every society to some extent (see L.L. Fuller, "The Law's Precarious Hold on Life", 3 *Georgia Law Review* 1969 No. 1, 530-545). Perhaps, more accurately, I am suggesting that enacted law is less relevant in Georgia than elsewhere, as revealed by the extent of the near-ritualized second economy.
2. See L. Fuller, "The Lawyer as an Architect of Social Structures" in K.I. Winston, ed., *The Principles of Social Order*, Durham, NC 1981, 264.

has produced a host of challenges for lawyers, ranging from corruption in the courts, to decayed courthouses, to lack of access to clients and even occasional threats or beatings from law enforcement agents.

Having established the basic contours within which lawyering occurs, the book then turned to legal education, examining it in three ways. First, it explored teaching methodology and content (static and state-oriented). These aspects are important indicators of how law is perceived by lawyers in the region and influence how law is practiced. Second, the legal education system was examined as a site controlling access to the profession. Despite exponential growth in the number of post-secondary institutions offering law degrees, elite state universities in the capital cities (and exceptionally some private schools), remain distinctly on top. Most students rely on connections or spend large amounts of money—in bribes or on hiring tutors—to get into or through these schools. The brilliant also have a chance to enter. In turn, graduates of these schools can expect what plum jobs exist as foreign ministry officials, lawyers in business law firms and—for those interested in "power careers"—positions as prosecutors. Finally, with respect to the legal education of the public at large, I suggested that increasingly aware clients and potential clients are a force behind lawyers' current upward mobility.

Turning squarely to the issue of professionalization, the book looked at the politics of regulation and self-regulation. Formally at least, Georgia, Armenia and Azerbaijan have different models of lawyer governance. Azerbaijan has essentially restored the monopoly of the Soviet-era Collegium, Armenia has compromised between a mandatory and voluntary bar and Georgia is somewhere in the middle with a "soft" mandatory bar association (the bar is mandatory but the legislation limits its powers over members). The ability of these formal arrangements to govern lawyers' conduct remains to be seen. Certainly the institutions are not immune from the same post-Soviet afflictions touching virtually all state and quasi-state bodies in Georgia and other parts of the Commonwealth of Independent States. In many ways the more important story is found outside state structures.[3]

In fact, fairly shortly after the fall of the Soviet Union the monopoly of the Collegium in Georgia was irreparably eroded and there was no new state structure governing lawyers until 2001. Intriguingly, lawyering was not a "free for all" during this period. The "old guard" remained in the Collegium structure where a governance regime of sorts remained in place. But even for the new lawyers outside of the Collegium, order and some standards of competence and ethics were constructed. Reputation—of individual lawyers and their firms—is the key to understanding this order. Given nascent advertis-

3. Again, Transcaucasia is not unique in this regard; see Arthurs, *op. cit.* chap. 1, note 15, 223-225.

ing by lawyers, and in the absence of official lawyer referral services (or even telephone books of wide distribution), lawyers rely heavily on reputation for business. Word-of-mouth and connections are the ways most lawyers get their clients. This is especially true among the modernized elite lawyers who rely on networks of school friends and ties of kinship and clientelism to negotiate business and legal activities. Ironically then, it is the "young reformers" who are most reliant on traditional mechanisms of social control. A less traditional tool the young reformers use is the foreign import of an NGO. Organizations such as GYLA are in essence voluntary bars, playing a role (however weak) in setting standards and disciplining offenders.

In addition to seeing reputation as the basis for business, most young reformers also see it as an appropriate basis for self-governance (again, I use "self-governance" in the strictest sense of a profession which does not have a state-mandate). For young reformers the best way to improve professional conduct—and to materially gain—remains for lawyers, and their business and voluntary organizations, to compete for prestige on the basis of reputation. Formal governance, they fear, leads to domination by members of the old guard and presents another site for corruption. Thus reformers initially opposed any monopoly for lawyers, or at the very least were ambivalent. While the nature of the current law on the bar in Georgia can best be explained as a compromise between young reformers and old guard, the fact that there is a law on the bar at all is largely the result of European pressure.

This political split between old guard and young reformers is also reflected in work. I suggested that one way to approach the stratification is along the axis of place of work. The "old guard" tends to work in Soviet style LCBs while the reformers tend to work in firms. The former do the vast bulk of criminal defence work while the latter do most of the business work. Management, material conditions of work, lawyers' and clients' backgrounds are all reflected in this split.

Finally, we can look to some of the badges associated with professionalization to gauge movement. While there is little sense of collegiality among lawyers as a whole, collegiality among reformers has grown dramatically, spurred by common membership in NGOs such as GYLA. The prestige of lawyers generally is also growing, as citizens and lawyers start to realize that lawyers' skills can make a difference to the outcome of a trial or business deal. Furthermore, the formal bars and the NGOs are both promulgating codes of ethics (weak as they may be) and promoting a corporate identity. More fundamentally, from a theoretical point of view, lawyers are controlling the numbers of producers and their markets (at least niche but crucial markets such as foreign investment). Although I have questioned its efficacy, the formal bar will also act as a gatekeeper of sorts for access to the profession. Ultimately, despite restrictive boundaries, professionalism is growing. The legal profession is on the way up—albeit unevenly—not out.

Implications for Studies of the Legal Profession

The first decade of Georgian independence presents a rare opportunity to observe the emergence of a new legal profession. I say rare because most studies of legal professions in Europe, North America and elsewhere are, in part at least, necessarily historical.[4] The opportunity to watch the making of the Georgian profession allows for a fresh look at the usefulness of the Weberian perspective as espoused in the "professional project" paradigm of Larson, Abel and others.

Weberian theories of professionalization formed in Western countries have paid close attention to the state. The argument has been put forth succinctly:[5]

> [P]rofessions aim for a monopoly of the provision of services of a particular kind; monopolies can only be granted by the state, and therefore professions have a distinctive relationship with the state.

There are, however, significant differences in professionalization in Western countries, with a particular divide between the Anglo-American and Continental systems.[6] To over-simplify the archetypes, professionalization in the former is thought to have been a bottom-up process while the latter was top-down. But while these different approaches may change the exact nature of the "professional project", they do not necessarily obviate the existence of the "project" itself. As one scholar has suggested, looking at the paradigmatic top-down case of Germany:[7]

> The bureaucratic model [of profession] understates the early traces of a professional identity that later became more clearly defined. Although the rise of the German bar was initiated by the state, attorneys themselves developed a genuine professionalization resembling the English or American practice.

I have attempted to show that a professional project also exists in Georgia, and that the new rise of professionalism is bottom up. This does not mean, however, that: a) professionalization is occurring on the Anglo-American model

4. One of the criticisms Halliday made in *Beyond Monopoly* (*op. cit.* chap. 1, note 12) is that writers on the professions relied too heavily on secondary sources. Halliday's improvement—in the Chicago School tradition of staying close to the subject—involved archival work on the Chicago Bar Association. Since then there have been more studies of this sort and the sociology of the professions has been enriched. Of course, reliance on archives carries with it a whole set of methodological problems as well.
5. M. Macdonald, *The Sociology of the Professions*, London 1995, 66.
6. As well as important distinctions between the English and American models.
7. Siegrist, "Public office or free profession; German attorneys in the nineteenth and early twentieth centuries" in G. Cocks and K.H. Jarauch, eds., *German Professions 1900-1950,* Oxford 1990, 63.

or b) the state is irrelevant. On the contrary, despite some similarities to Western experiences (such as the intriguing parallels with elite New York lawyers outlined in Chapter 5) the new Georgian professionalism has emerged in a peculiar manner, one rooted in a specific historical and cultural context.

Young Georgian lawyers initially opposed state-sanctioned monopoly structures or at the very least were ambivalent towards them.[8] Rather they preferred to attempt market control through means which blended traditional reliance on reputation and networks with voluntary bars adapted from foreign models. In other words, the same mechanisms used to get business and maintain order—reputation/status, connections and voluntary bars—have also been used by lawyers to control markets. In terms of supply, law schools, firms and voluntary bars control the number of producers (or at least successful producers). These elite lawyers also control access to key markets such as work for foreign investors. Finally, this elite creates demand for its services—although this is less obvious than the supply side—most obviously by identifying potential reform projects and then seeking funding from foreign or international aid providers. With respect to the state, the peculiar nature of professionalization can only be understood in the context of the partly-failed state, one largely uninterested in exercising control over lawyers (excepting interference from rogue actors from the power ministries) and one with which young reformers are wary of co-operating to construct a monopoly.

The fact that the new Georgian professionals initially opposed a state-backed lawyers' monopoly suggests that the Weberian fixation on this point is misplaced. Or, at the very least, that it is not universally true. Others have also found the notion of a fixed or universal professional project of monopoly and market control problematic. Looking at the Chicago Bar Association, for example, Terence Halliday argues that the pursuit of monopoly did not consume the energies of the professional association (although, importantly, even that bar association intensely pursued monopoly interests at various times).[9] Another scholar, Wesley Pue, has taken particular aim at the universalist aspects of Abel's version of the professional project:[10]

> The [market control] model itself imports overtones of determinism notwithstanding the best efforts of its promoters to distance themselves from any such unfashionable position. In order to discern any coherent professional "project" whatsoever, great damage is inevitably done to cultural and historical specificity of every sort.

But the demand for greater specificity and context does not necessarily detract from the notion that a version of the professional project exists in all

8. Though when the fact that a law on the bar would be passed became clear, lawyers' opposition was transformed into attempts to shape the legislation.
9. Halliday, *op. cit.* chap. 1, note 12.
10. W. Pue, "'Trajectories of Professionalism?': Legal Professionalism After Abel", 19 *Manitoba L.J.* 1990 No. 3, 384–418.

cases. As one observer puts it, the notion of a professional project is an "ideal type and therefore the extent of the drive for monopoly in any particular case is a matter for empirical investigation".[11] What would be fatal to the "ideal type" itself is if empirical investigation found that attempts at market control were absent altogether in professionalization. I am not aware of any such results. It remains then to suggest a refinement to the notion of the professional project. It is this: while pursuit of monopoly may be a typical course of action for professions, it is not a necessary one. In other words, while would-be professionals may attempt to control markets they do not inevitably do this through a special relationship with the state.[12] The key to understanding market control in Georgia lies in a pluralist perspective which encompasses culture and the peculiarities of post-Soviet transition.

There is one other caveat which needs to be made at this juncture. By its theoretical implications, this book has focused on lawyers and legal associations as self-interested actors. While I do not shy away from this, it is clear that self-interest is not the end of the story. In many cases, the promotion of the rule of law and the self-interest implicit in professionalization happily converge. Aspects of this convergence are considered below. Moreover there are lawyers in Georgia, Armenia and Azerbaijan whose activities in promoting the rule of law—or simply representing particular clients—put them at risk. Motivations of principle, altruism or patriotism certainly play a part here. To recognize this is not to be an apologist for the profession, it simply adds another dimension to the complexity of professionalization in the region.

This book has raised many questions warranting further study. One group of questions involves expanding research within Transcaucasia. Specifically, further work is needed on lawyers in the ethnic minority areas and the areas directly affected by conflict, as well as on other legal occupations (such as prosecutors) which have only been considered here tangentially.[13] Another avenue for further study is comparative. Although some differences with the Russian experience have been noted (it seems Russian lawyers have looked to

11. K.M. Macdonald, *op. cit.* note 5, 33.
12. This finding also has obvious implications for the structural-functionalist view of a bargain between the state and profession for monopoly and self-regulation.
13. Work on lawyers in these areas could also potentially shed light on two preoccupations in Transcaucasia, namely nationalism and conflict. For example, the relationship of minority lawyers to either the state or nationalist systems may be a piece of the puzzle in determining why some minority areas agitate for independence while others do not. So too, examining the particularities of lawyering in Abkhaziia, Ossetia and Nagorno-Karabakh could tell us much about the role of law in post-conflict transition. On the relationship between law and peacebuilding generally, see N.J. Kritz, "The Rule of Law in the Post-Conflict Phase: Building a Stable Peace" in C.A. Crocker, O. Hampson & P. Aall, eds., *Turbulent Peace: the Challenges of Managing International Conflict,* Washington 2001, 801.

the state for patronage more than their Georgian counterparts and the Russian government has sought more control over the profession than its Georgian counterpart), a more complete comparison would be useful. Because Russia and Georgia share a legacy of Soviet law, but have different social and cultural makeups, culture could be isolated as a variable to some extent. On the other hand, different experiences with Soviet law (more corruption in Georgia for example), and Russia's somewhat more successful experiences in state building, its vast scale and the fact that it had an indigenous legal profession in the past, would limit the certainty of any conclusions in this regard. A fascinating comparison could be made with lawyers in the North Caucasian Republics; although they practice law in the Russian Federation, they share cultural traits with Georgian, Armenian and Azerbaijani lawyers.

Implications for the Rule of Law

The aim of this section is to explore some of the potential links between professionalization and the rule of law in Transcaucasia. In fact, links between these two themes are rarely drawn in the literature on legal professions or the literature on the rule of law. While both bodies of scholarship are concerned with the independence of the profession, the interests are fundamentally different. Those who study professions see independence from the state as an aspect of successful professionalization, while those who study the rule of law view lawyers' independence as a bulwark against arbitrary state action.[14] To integrate these two streams of scholarship more fully requires a different perspective from the internalist and market-oriented approach which has largely informed this study (even if lodged firmly in Transcaucasian society, culture and law).[15] Ultimately a comprehensive study of lawyers in Transcaucasia could begin where this study—an account of how lawyers in the region attempt to control their ranks and their markets—leaves off, and examine the impact of lawyers and their professionalization on the rule of law writ large.

Various theoretical definitions of the rule of law have been put forward—spawning vigorous debate.[16] For the purposes of this section, however,

14. An example of the latter is J. Reitz, "Progress in Building Institutions for the Rule of Law" in R.D. Grey, ed., *Democratic Theory and Post-Communist Change*, Upper Saddle River, NJ 1997, 155-159.
15. Halliday called for such a research agenda in 1995: "Market control theory has been a trap from which few scholars have escaped, since it confined lawyers' proactive role to controlling the market for professional services. Shaping markets more globally—their institutions, their norms of operation, their directions of development—has rarely made it onto theoretical or empirical agendas." ("Lawyers as Institutional Contractors: Constructing Markets, States, Civil Society, and Community", *American Bar Foundation Working Paper* No. 9519, 1995, 11.)

I use the pragmatic or working definition put forward by Thomas Carothers writing in *Foreign Affairs*:[17]

> The rule of law can be defined as a system in which the laws are public knowledge, are clear in meaning, and apply equally to everyone. They enshrine and uphold the political and civil liberties that have gained status as universal human rights over the last half-century. In particular, anyone accused of a crime has the right to a fair, prompt hearing and is presumed innocent until proved guilty. The central institutions of the legal system, including courts, prosecutors and police, are reasonably fair, competent and efficient. Judges are impartial and independent, not subject to political influence or manipulation. Perhaps most important, the government is embedded in a comprehensive legal framework, its officials accept that the law will be applied to their own conduct, and their government seeks to be law-abiding.

It is appropriate to use a pragmatic definition such as the one above—which borrows from the theoretical perspective but is grounded in practice—because my concern here is to link the study of a legal profession to the rule of law "on the ground".

Over the last decade, a doctrine of sorts has emerged on promoting the rule of law. This doctrine divides rule of law reform into types or stages, each of which must be fulfilled to produce real change. Carothers suggests three types. The first involves rewriting or modernizing the laws themselves. This is the easiest to understand and implement and, in the early 1990s, was the preferred strategy of reform. An enduring image here is of the law "missionary" getting off the airplane in a post-communist capital, with Western model laws in hand. While modernizing laws is a necessary part of reform it is clearly not sufficient. The second type of reform goes deeper by focussing on institutions. Activities here include retraining judges, prosecutors and police, restructuring the judiciary and improving the infrastructure of courts. Institutional reform also encompasses the legal profession and has the goal of making lawyers independent of government control, improving legal education and establishing codes of ethics and discipline. For Carothers, type three reforms "aim at the deeper goal of increasing government compliance with the law".[18] This of course requires an independent judiciary but also a change in attitude on the part of those in power. Much of the impetus for the latter must come from citizens and "civil society".

16. These definitions generally fall into three categories: formal definitions which focus on law on the books (no retroactive criminal legislation, for example), substantive definitions concerned that a legal system produces justice and functional views tending to measure the extent to which a system restrains state despotism. As R. Grote has noted ("The Rule of Law, Rechtsstaat and Etat de Droit" in C. Starck, ed., *Constitutionalism, Universalism and Democracy—A Comparative Analysis*, Baden-Baden 1999, 271) the rule of law "belongs to the category of open-ended concepts which are subject to permanent debate".
17. T. Carothers, "The Rule of Law Revival", 77 *Foreign Affairs* 1998 No. 2, 95-106, 96.
18. *Ibid.* at 100.

I will now turn to each of the three stages and consider what effect Georgian lawyers have had on them. A preliminary point to be made, however, is that few Georgian jurists oppose the rule of law on a rhetorical level. Indeed, a consistent theme in this book has been that both the archetypal "old guard" and "young reformers" alike have learned to use the language of the rule of law to promote their interests. These uses range from the old guard judge or lawyer opposing exams on the basis of independence to the reformer writing grant proposals to Western donors and using all the right buzzwords.

Type One Reforms—Changing the Laws

Georgian lawyers have made tremendous improvements in this sphere since independence and indeed since I began field-work in Georgia in 1998. As in other ex-Soviet states, legislation in the early 1990s was frequently drafted by non-lawyers.[19] During the mid-1990s lawyers by and large took over the drafting process but did it poorly. By the late 1990s virtually all Georgian legislation was being drafted and vetted by lawyers with a good deal of technical skill. This legislative drafting has not only come from lawyers within government but from lawyers associated with NGOs as well, some of them quite specialized in particular fields through their private practices or through training in Western countries.

Georgian lawyers in government and NGOs have also been inundated with—and sometimes have actively solicited—the advice of Western law reformers. From the late 1990s Georgian lawyers have increasingly grown more critical of simplistic Western transplants, a wariness which is supported by recent empirical studies of the "transplant effect".[20] Nonetheless the transplants are often accepted given the realities of obligations under the Council of Europe system, the goal of membership in the European Union and the ability of donors to set the agenda.

19. This was partly because the expertise that did exist in legal fields of renewed relevance—such as civil law—was concentrated in Moscow and a few other major Russian cities (on the lack of civil law specialists see P.B. Maggs, "The Process of Codification in Russia: Lessons Learned from the Uniform Commercial Code", 44 *McGill Law Journal* 1999 No. 2, 281-300, 283).

20. Using data from 49 countries K. Pistor, D. Berkowitz and J.-F. Richard ("Economic Development, Legality and the Transplant Effect", *European Economic Review* (forthcoming)) challenge the assumption that "*supplying* the right laws on the books will enhance legality". They argue: "the way in which the modern formal legal order that evolved in some Western countries was transplanted into other countries is a much more important determinant of legality and economic development than a supply of a particular legal code." Similarly, in terms of adopting international norms, Oona Hathaway writes in her empirical study that "I find not a single treaty for which ratification seems to be reliably associated with better human rights practices" ("Do Human Rights Treaties Make a Difference?", 111 *Yale Law Journal* 2002 No. 8, 1935-2042, 1940).

Type Two Reforms—Institutions

Many of the old guard are ambivalent towards or actively resist attempts to reform institutions. This is evident with respect to their institution, the Collegium. Structurally, the Collegium and its constituent LCBs have placed little emphasis on ethics or continuing legal education, and this shows in the quality of advocates. (As before, I do not mean simply effectiveness, as there are highly effective old guard lawyers who can "get clients off" through dubious means.) The unwillingness or inability (because of entrenched practices) of Collegium members to bring a "reform spirit" to legal institutions is also apparent with respect to their role in criminal procedure. Putting aside the issue of the *right* to counsel—which is regularly abused in the three Transcaucasian states contrary to domestic and international norms[21]—there is the issue of lawyers themselves, specifically their ethics, competence, availability and affordability. As detailed in previous chapters the old guard often collude with police, investigators or prosecutors for money, or provide less than a vigorous defence out of fear or habit.

Also troubling—and symptomatic of the stratification of the professions in Transcaucasia—is that the young reformers are not, by and large, doing criminal defence work or other "poverty law" cases. The bright, Western-educated lawyers, who claim to adhere to ethical codes and who belong to voluntary professional organizations, work in business firms. Only a small minority of them work for legal clinics financed by external sources or regularly take cases *pro bono*. Accordingly, the bulk of criminal defence work is left to former or present Collegium members. In addition—and despite the proliferation of law schools—there are insufficient numbers of criminal lawyers to meet the demand in many parts of the region. Needless to say, the phenomenon of lawyers preferring commercial over "personal plight" clients has been observed in other contexts and is not all that surprising given financial realities.[22] The difference is that in jurisdictions with stronger state and bar institutions, even the lawyers at the margins of practice are required to show minimum levels

21. The right to counsel is provided for in the constitutions of the Transcaucasian states as well as UN and European conventions which the Transcaucasian States have signed and ratified. The international obligations are provided for in Art. 14(3)(b) and (d) of the International Covenant on Civil and Political Rights (ICCPR), 999 *UNTS* 171 (entered into force 23 March 1976) and Art. 6(3)(c) of the European Convention for the Protection of Human Rights and Fundamental Freedoms (ECHR), Rome, 4.XI.1950. International "soft law" instruments also deal with the question of states' obligations *vis-à-vis* lawyers, including the right to counsel and the independence of the profession (see for example the Preamble to the UN Basic Principles on the Role of Lawyers, adopted by the Eighth United Nations Congress on the Prevention of Crime and the Treatment of Offenders, Havana, 27 August to 7 September 1990).
22. Including Russia, where lawyers appear to be increasingly focussed on commercial work: Solomon and Foglesong, *op. cit.* chap. 4, note 14, 148.

of knowledge (including the contents of ethics codes) and their fees may be paid by a legal aid regime.

An obvious policy implication of this finding is that governments and aid providers should find ways to encourage young reformers to do criminal defence work. Unfortunately there are no easy solutions. Systemic change would help. Many lawyers will "boycott" criminal defence work as long as courts are corrupt and law enforcement agents abusive. For the time being they prefer to carve out what is perceived to be a cleaner "private law world" of structuring business arrangements. But changing the nature of the legal system is a long-term matter, and the pace and nature of change will be distorted if the reform lawyers distance themselves from criminal law work. The current solution seems to be legal clinics, providing heated and clean workplaces and well-paying jobs to attract reformers into this line of work. While the important work being done by clinics should not be denigrated, there are questions about their sustainability (they are almost exclusively foreign-funded) and impact. In my view a partial solution is to be found in providing additional funds for legal aid. The Georgian government, which exclusively shoulders legal aid costs now, cannot immediately afford much of an increase to the legal aid tariff (two Laris per day). A reprioritization on the part of donors, however, would easily allow for an increased rate. An increased rate not only has the potential to lure reformers into criminal defence work but offers the possibility that old guard lawyers will provide better services to their clients. Admittedly, designing effective controls to ensure that aid money blended with government expenditures is not abused is difficult.[23] Also, aid providers would have to overcome their opposition to working with the "old guard" (it is unquestionably easier for them to deal with English speaking, Western-trained young people eager to learn).

Ultimately, however, the specific problem of defence counsel is symptomatic of a larger disengagement of reform lawyers from the state sphere. The best reform-minded young lawyers typically keep themselves at arms length from most ministries and agencies, including the powerful Procuracy.[24] And in their legal practices they avoid litigation and other briefs which would bring them into direct contact with state institutions including courts.

This is not to say young reformers are unconnected to the state however. Legal NGOs are frequent drafters of reform proposals or critics of government policies. But their engagement is at a distance—not in state service *per se*—and is often aligned with the agendas and financing of international organizations and aid providers. This phenomenon of distance has been noticed in some developing countries, and is an area for fruitful investigation in the Transcaucasia.

23. One option would be to turn over the distribution of legal aid funds to the new Bar Association.
24. The Georgian Ministry of Foreign Affairs is the clearest exception to this observation.

In Argentina, for example, a segment of the legal profession has modernized through internationalist strategies such as education in the US and employment with foreign funded NGOs and think tanks. As one study found:[25]

> The best-known of the new generation of notable lawyers outside of the private international law firms remain in the private sphere. They may continue to serve as go-betweens on behalf of business clients and the state, but they also invest very strongly in translating international expertise into private schools and NGOs. They define themselves as public intellectuals...but their platforms are international and private.

At the same time, the study noted, "the public institutions of the state... appear much less modern".[26] The authors of the study suggest that the modernization of this elite in the "gray areas" outside of the "core" of the state has reinforced the weakness of the law and the state itself.[27] Of course, as others have pointed out, principles drawn from studies of the developing South may be of limited relevance to the former communist states of Eurasia, given their very different histories.[28] Nonetheless, the possibility that a modernized, professional elite of lawyers and others can reinforce a weak state is clearly an important issue. Establishing such a link would have implications for the conventional wisdom or means of supporting "civil society", a topic addressed below.

Type Three Reforms—Government Compliance with Law

There is no question that in the late Soviet and early independence era, advocates in the region played a minimal role in the bureaucracy, politics or opposition. Today, however, lawyers are often in the vanguard of reform—including putting pressure on governments to respect the law—through their involvement with civil society.

Along with rule of law reform, "civil society" development is one of the darlings of international aid efforts in the former Soviet Union. Although there are definitional disagreements (on whether, for example, political parties and economic groups are in or out of the definition), civil society is typically understood "as the realm of private voluntary association, from neighbourhood committees to interest groups to philanthropic enterprises of all sorts".[29] More

25. Y. Dezaylay and B. Garth, "Argentina: Law at the Periphery and Law Dependencies: Political and Economic Crisis and the Instrumentalization and Fragmentation of Law", *American Bar Foundation Working Paper* No. 9708, 1998, 103.
26. *Ibid.*, 104.
27. *Ibid.*, 2.
28. See for example, B. Parrot, "Perspectives on post-communist transition" in Dawisha & Parrot, *op. cit.* chap 7, note 13, 1-2. and S. Haggard and R.R. Kaufman, *The Political Economy of Democratic Transitions*, Princeton 1995, 371-377. But, as Adam Przeworski put it (perhaps prematurely) in 1991, "the East has become the South" in terms of "confront[ing] the all too normal problems of the economics, the politics, and the culture of poor capitalism" (*Democracy and the Market*, Cambridge 1991, 191).
29. M.W. Foley & B. Edwards, "The Paradox of Civil Society", 7 *Journal of Democracy* 1996 No. 3, 38-52, 38.

controversial is the link, generally accepted without question in development circles, between civil society and democratization.[30] Michael Foley and Bob Edwards suggest that there are at least two versions of the supposed link and that these versions are contradictory.[31] The first version, posited most famously by Alexis de Tocqueville, "puts special emphasis on the ability of associational life in general and the habits of association in particular to foster patterns of civility in the actions of citizens in a democratic polity".[32] The second version drawing on examples from Eastern Europe and Latin America, "lays special emphasis on civil society as a sphere of action that is independent of the state and that is capable—precisely for this reason—of energizing resistance to a tyrannical regime".[33] While the first version "postulates the positive effects of association for governance... the latter emphasizes the importance of civil association as a counterweight to the state".[34] Foley and Edwards suggest that empirical inquiries need to be made about this link. Such an empirical investigation of lawyers groups in Georgia would likely find that both versions are sometimes true.

Whether one or both versions are correct appears to me to depend on the slice of civil society under examination. Taking GYLA for example, we have a large group with many committed, engaged members. Activities requiring negotiation and organization, within agreed upon rules of procedure, are regularly held (the Board of Directors takes positions on the organization's direction, subject area groups take positions on law reform). These activities build trust, socialize members to understand "generalized reciprocity" and make up "social capital".[35] Does this have an impact on democratic state-building? Yes. GYLA members lobby for legislation, draft legislation, educate the public and sometimes join the civil service or even partisan politics where, by and large, they have a good track record as reformers. But if the first version of civil society has validity in this case, so does the second. GYLA as an organization is non-partisan (though many members have links to the governing party) and does not endorse particular parties or candidates during elections. It criticizes the government on legal reform issues (though less vocally than other activist

30. For a classic discussion of the role "liberal society" plays in the "emergence of a legal order", see R.M. Unger, *Law in Modern Society,* New York 1976.
31. *Ibid.*, 39.
32. *Ibid.* As Tocqueville put it, "civil associations pave the way for political ones" (*Democracy in America*, trans. G. Lawrence, New York 1969, 521).
33. *Ibid.* Václav Havel is one of the proponents of this strand: see V. Havel & V. Klaus, with commentary by P. Pithart, "Rival Visions", 7 *Journal of Democracy* 1996 No. 1, 12-23.
34. *Ibid.*
35. Robert Putnam, who is squarely in the first version of the civil society debate, argues that "social capital, as embodied in horizontal networks of civic engagement, bolsters the performance of the polity and the economy... strong society, strong state": *Making Democracy Work: Civic Traditions in Modern Italy*, Princeton 1993, 173-176.

groups). It also provides legal advice to other NGOs and citizens who may oppose government policy.

In a sense GYLA is too easy a case. If similar questions about civil society—and its relation to the rule of law—are addressed to other organizations such as the Collegium (though perhaps that should be excluded because of its recent quasi-official status) or a neighbourhood group that has lawyers as members, the results may well be different. As Terence Halliday and Lucien Karpik put it, "lawyers cannot be gainsaid either as liberal actors-in-waiting or as perpetual creators of rule of law regimes".[36]

Lawyers and the Demand for Law

While rule of law reform is not a panacea, addressing the three types of law reform set out by Carothers will do much to consolidate democracy, reduce corruption, improve human rights protection and safeguard investment.[37] But an examination of the extent to which progress has been made along these three stages is insufficient to give us a global picture of how law is used in Georgia.

Even if there are good laws (type one reforms), good institutions (type two reforms) and governments which obey the law (type three reforms), citizens and other legal entities may still be uninterested in or unwilling to use laws and courts. Some scholars have examined this question under the rubric of "demand for law". In her pioneering work Kathryn Hendley has considered the demand question in the former Soviet Union.[38] She asks why, for example, Russian companies are so often unwilling to use courts to attempt to satisfy legitimate claims. She concludes that the explanation is to be found in a number of factors: a legacy of distrust of law, the use of informal mechanisms (barter, intermediaries, crime, political connections) and a "top down" reform process which ignores Russian realities. One problem with Hendley's approach, however, is that it pathologizes the Russian experience. As Andras Sajo puts it in a comment on Hendley's findings:[39]

36. T.C. Halliday and L. Karpik, "Politics Matter: A Comparative Theory of Lawyers in the Making of Political Liberalism" in Halliday and Karpik, eds., *Lawyers and the Rise of Western Political Liberalism*, Oxford 1997, 60.
37. Carothers emphasizes the limitations of rule of law reform. Indeed, the failures of the Law and Development projects of the 1960s and 1970s in Latin America and elsewhere are often forgotten. On reconsidering the law and development field, see J.R. Thome, "Heading South But Looking North: Globalization and Law Reform in Latin America", 3 *Wisconsin Law Review* 2000, 691-712.
38. See K. Hendley, "Rewriting the Rules of the Game in Russia: The Neglected Issue of the Demand for Law", 8 *East European Constitutional Review* 1999 No. 4, 89-95. For a further refinement of her concept of "demand"—and a response to critics—see K. Hendley, "'Demand' for Law in Russia—A Mixed Picture", 10 *East European Constitutional Law Review* 2001 No. 4, 72-77.
39. A. Sajo, "The Law of Liposuction", 8 *East European Constitutional Review* 1999 No. 4, 102-104, 103.

Ian Macneil's relational analysis of long-term contractual relationships gives a sophisticated justification for avoiding litigation in such cases from the perspective of economic analysis of law ("Relational Contract: What We Do and Do Not Know," *Wisconsin Law Review* [1985]). Russian businessmen knew from the beginning what Macneil found after many years of research: it is more advantageous to maintain long-term relations with quasi monopolists than to sue them.

Moreover, Hendley's concept seeks to measure the demand for litigation rather than demand for law and lawyers. The demand for litigation can be low while the demand for law high. Individuals or companies may be unwilling to use courts but may be keen on using legal forms in transactions (and this use of legal form can be more than the formalistic, "memorializing" of Soviet era contracts). By seeing demand for litigation as a symptom of an underdeveloped legal system, litigation is implicitly equated with development. By extension (and, to be clear, Hendley does not posit this), the social or other controls which keep people out of courthouses are traditional practices and even impediments to development.

One way to avoid this trap is to consider the question of *engagement with law*. The change in phrase would avoid the demand-supply rubric (if the laws are there, people should be using them) and open up the field for a legal pluralist perspective. How do individuals and other entities use or not use law (widely defined)? And what is the role of lawyers in all of this? While this is a wide avenue for future field-research and analysis, a few suggestions can be made here.

The flip side to the paucity of young lawyers in criminal defence work is that these lawyers are doing other things. As noted above, some have boycotted courts and remain in a private law world, structuring relationships through contract. These contracts provide a measure of order between the parties by facilitating exchange and fostering trust. This exchange in turn is presumably a wealth-creating activity for the economy as a whole.[40] In other words, these lawyers are part of the transition to a market economy, and more specifically a regulated market economy (albeit a privately or quasi-privately regulated one). If this is the case, law schools and aid providers should provide assistance to these lawyers. There are, to the best of my knowledge, no regular university courses on contract drafting and only a few thin published sets of legal forms in the national languages of the region.[41] In law schools in advanced capitalist countries there are also few courses on drafting, but partners in business law firms have expertise to pass down, every firm has an evolving system of

40. For an excellent discussion on the economics of informal contract enforcement see A. Greif, "Contracting, Enforcement, and Efficiency: Economics Beyond the Law" in M. Bruno and B. Pleskovic, eds., *Annual World Bank Conference on Development Economics 1996*, Washington 1996, 239 and accompanying comments by Robert Ellickson and Sally Falk Moore.

41. Though GYLA has offered some contract drafting seminars.

precedents, forms are available on-line and in libraries and lawyers work in a culture familiar with contracts.

Of course it can be argued that contracts are ultimately worthless in the absence of properly functioning courts to enforce them.[42] But as Lon Fuller pointed out, contracts existed before state laws existed and "[t]oday many human relations are effectively organized by contracts that neither party would dream of taking to court..."[43] Looking specifically at Georgia, the fact that so many lawyers are retained to draft contracts—given the poor shape of Georgia's legal system—suggests that clients do not see them as worthless. Perhaps culture, custom, kinship and networks play a different role in enforcing contracts in Transcaucasia than in Russia. Hendley suggests that avoiding paying debts does not bring reputational sanctions in Russia:[44]

> Perhaps a majority of Russian enterprises are living in glass houses on this issue. Sometimes they are the victims and are frustrated by their inability to access their debtors' resources. But they are equally likely to be the perpetrator of a diversionary scheme at some other point. Consequently, the logic of collective action dictates that no one is likely to blow the whistle.

Is the same true in Transcaucasia? The Transcaucasian countries' sizes *vis-à-vis* Russia may play a role here, as trust and repeat contact appear to play a more important role in the small markets of the Transcaucasus.

A related vein of research could explore the extent to which lawyers are channeling disputes into private or quasi-private justice systems. As indicated earlier, natural resources contracts typically involve international arbitration clauses. But are the arbitration courts established by the American and Georgian Chambers of Commerce in Tbilisi (and staffed equally by Georgians and foreigners) also being used? [45] Are there other *fora* of private justice in which lawyers are implicated (international, national, local, sectorally)? Inquiries along these lines should be considered in light of the literature on globalization and the professions. However, it would be a mistake to assume that the "lessons" from this literature, which tend to the view that the professions are being eroded by transnational forces, are applicable to Georgia.[46] In the first instance, Georgia is not fully integrated into the global economy. Secondly, "who and what" Georgian lawyers know is indispensable for any foreign business hoping

42. K. Hendley, "How Russian Enterprises Cope With Payment Problems", 15 *Post-Soviet Affairs* 1999 No. 3, 201-234.
43. L. Fuller, "The Role of Contract in the Ordering Processes of Society Generally" in Winston, *op. cit.* note 2, 174.
44. Hendley, *op. cit.* note 39, 231.
45. On lawyers and arbitration see Y. Dezalay & B.G. Garth, *Dealing in Virtue: International Commercial Arbitration and the Construction of a Transnational Legal Order*, Chicago, London 1996.
46. For such literature, see Arthurs and Kreklewich, *op. cit.* chap. 1, note 15 and Arthurs, *op. cit.*, chap. 1, note 15.

to penetrate the Georgian market. And, finally, the slice of Georgian lawyers most connected with globalization is the most professional by any definition. In other words, any future work in this area will have to pay close attention to the Georgian or Transcaucasian context.

By its theoretical orientations, this book has used Georgia as a site to study the legal profession and to suggest future research on the rule of law. Ultimately, however, I hope that an analysis of these topics has also furthered an understanding of Georgian society and a fascinating, volatile and strategically important region.

Cited Interviewees

(Interview methodology is discussed in the Introduction. Interviewees are cited here by coded initials, with the descriptors of position, gender, age and place of interview.)

A	American law reformer, male, mid-40s (Tbilisi)
B	Head of an LCB, male, 70s (Tbilisi)
C	Law student, IDP from Abkhaziia, male, early 20s (Kutaisi)
D	Advocate, male, early 60s (Tbilisi)
E	Prosecutor, male, mid-40s (Gori)
F	Legal academic, male, mid-50s (Tbilisi)
G	Local politician, male, late 40s (Gori)
H	Founding GYLA member, male, mid-30s (Tbilisi)
I	Human rights activist and Soviet-era dissident, male, late 50s (Tbilisi)
J	Law student, male, late teens (Baku)
K	American law reformer, male, mid 60s (Yerevan)
L	American law reformer, male, late 30s (Baku)
M	Law student, male, late teens (Kutaisi)
N	Legal academic, male, mid-50s (Tbilisi)
O	American-Armenian law reformer, male, mid-30s (Yerevan)
P	Georgian diplomat and jurist, male, late 40s (Pristina)
Q	Judge's assistant, male, early 30s (Tbilisi)
R	Client in civil litigation matter, female, mid-30s (Tbilisi)
S	Law student, female, early 20s (Baku)
T	Lawyer employed by a major Georgian bank, male, early 30s (Tbilisi)
U	Law student, male, late teens (Kutaisi)
V	Law professor, female, late 30s (Tbilisi)
W	Advocate, male, mid-40s (Baku)
X	Advocate and law lecturer, female, late 40s (Tbilisi)
Y	Head of the Collegium of Advocates, male, early 80s (Tbilisi)
Z	Journalist, female, early 20s (Tbilisi)
AA	Head of a Georgian legal NGO, female, mid-30s (Tbilisi)
BB	Georgian lawyer working as an observer for an Intergovernmental Organization, female, early 20s (Tbilisi)

CC	Senior official in the Georgian Ministry of Foreign Affairs, male, early 30s (Galway)
DD	Law professor, female, late 30s (Tbilisi)
EE	Judge, female, mid-30s (Tbilisi)
FF	Law graduate, female, mid-20s (Toronto)
GG	Firm lawyer, male, early 40s (Tbilisi)
HH	Advocate, female, mid-60s (Tbilisi)
II	International human rights observer, female, mid-30s (Tbilisi)
JJ	Head of an LCB, male, late 60s (Baku)
KK	American law reformer, male, early 40s (Tbilisi)
LL	Accident victim, female, late 40s (Tbilisi)
MM	In-house lawyer, male, mid-20s (Tbilisi)
NN	American Law reformer, male, early 30s (Tbilisi)
OO	American lawyer practising in Georgia, male, early 40s (Tbilisi)
PP	Senior Executive of the Georgian Young Lawyers' Association, female, late 20s (Tbilisi)
QQ	Law professor and Armenian Bar Association executive, male, mid-30s (Yerevan)
RR	Legal historian, male, late 60s (Tbilisi)
SS	American law reformer, male, mid 40s (Tbilisi)
TT	Clinical law teacher, female, mid 20s (Yerevan)

Bibliography

Abel, R.L., "American Lawyers" in R.L. Abel, ed., *Lawyers: A Critical Reader*, New York 1997.

____, "Comparative Sociology of Legal Professions" in R.L. Abel & P.S.C. Lewis, eds., *Lawyers in Society: Comparative Theories* (v. 3), Berkeley 1989.

____, "England and Wales" in R.L. Abel & P.S.C. Lewis, eds., *Lawyers in Society: The Common Law World* (v. 1), Berkeley 1988.

____, "United States. Contradictions of Professionalism" in R.L. Abel & P.S.C. Lewis, eds., *Lawyers in Society: The Common Law World* (v. 1), Berkeley 1988.

____, "Lawyers in the Civil Law World" in R.L. Abel and P.S.C. Lewis, eds., *Lawyers in Society: The Civil Law World* (v. 2), Berkeley 1989.

Abel, R.L. & P.S.C. Lewis, "Putting Law Back into the Sociology of Lawyers" in R.L. Abel & P.S.C. Lewis, eds., *Lawyers in Society: Comparative Theories* (v. 3), Berkeley 1989.

Abbott, A., *The System of Professions: An Essay on the Division of Expert Labor,* Chicago 1988.

"Agronomists and historians dominate mostly Azeri Parliament", *(Baku) Azadlyg* 6 December 2000 (cited by BBC Worldwide Monitoring—Transcaucasus Unit).

Ajani, G., "By Chance and Prestige: Legal Transplants in Russia and Eastern Europe", 43 *American Journal of Comparative Law* 1995 No. 1, 93-117.

____. "Legal Education in Russia: Present and Future – An Analysis of the State Educational Standards for Higher Professional Education and a Comparison with the European Legal Reform Experience", 23 *Review of Central and East European Law* 1997 Nos. 3-4, 267-300.

Alexeyeva, L., *Soviet Dissent,* trans. C. Pearce and J. Glad, Middleton, CT 1985.

Aliyev, A., "Students Dream of Hitting Books Abroad", *Baku Sun* 3 November 2000, 2.

Allen, W.E.D., *A History of the Georgian People*, New York 1932, 1971.

Altstadt, A.L., *The Azerbaijani Turks,* Stanford 1992.

____, "Azerbaijan's struggle toward democracy", in K. Dawisha & B. Parrot, eds., *Conflict, cleavage, and change in Central Asia and the Caucasus,* Cambridge, MA 1997.

Altstadt-Mirhadi, A., "The Azerbaijani Bourgeoisie and the Cultural-Enlightenment Movement in Baku: First Steps Toward Nationalism" in R.G. Suny, ed., *Transcaucasia: Nationalism and Social Change*, Ann Arbor 1996.

American Bar Association's Central and East European Law Initiative, "Analysis of the Draft Law on the Bar and the Draft Law on Barrister's Activity" (19 August 1996) (the report is available from the organization's Legal Assessments Department in Washington, DC).

Amnesty International, "Georgia: Summary of Amnesty International's Concerns" (*AI Index* EUR 56/02/98, August 1998).

____,"Georgia – Continuing allegations of torture and ill-treatment" (*AI Index* EUR 56/01/00, February 2000).

Anjaparidze, Z.,"The Impact of Media and Information Exchange on Georgian State-Building" (Tbilisi 1999, *UNDP Discussion Paper* No. 2).

Arthurs, H.W.,"Lawyering in Canada in the 21st Century", 15 *Windsor Yearbook of Access to Justice* 1996, 202-225.

Arthurs, H.W. & R. Kreklewich,"Law, Legal Institutions, and the Legal Profession in the New Economy", 34 *Osgoode Hall Law Journal* 1996 No. 1, 1-60.

Aves, J., *Paths to National Independence in Georgia, 1987-1990,* London 1991.

Avtandil Chachua v. *The Parliament of Georgia* (3 November 1998), Constitutional Court of Georgia.

"Azeri students appeal over expulsion from university due to political leaflet", BBC Worldwide Monitoring—Transcaucasus Unit (27 April 2000), citing newspaper *(Baku) Azadlyg.*

Azrael, J., *Managerial Power and Soviet Politics*, Cambridge, MA 1966.

"The Bar wants not to be examined", *Caucasus Press* 10 May 2001.

Barry, D.D., ed., *Toward the 'Rule of Law' in Russia?*, Armonk, NY 1992.

Barry, D.D. & H.J. Berman, "The Soviet Legal Profession", 82 *Harvard Law Review* 1968 No. 1, 1-41.

Barsoumian, H.,"The Eastern Question and the Tanzimat Era" in R.G. Hovannisian, ed., *The Armenian People From Ancient to Modern Times*, New York 1997.

Basic Principles on the Role of Lawyers, adopted by the Eighth United Nations Congress on the Prevention of Crime and the Treatment of Offenders, Havana, 27 August to 7 September 1990.

Becher, T., *Professional Practice*, New Brunswick, NJ 1999.

Beermann, R.,"Pre-revolutionary Russian Peasant Laws" in W.E. Butler, ed., *Russian Law: Historical and Political Perspectives,* Leyden 1977.

Berenson, S.K.,"Is it Time for Lawyer Profiles?", 70 *Fordham Law Review* 2001 No. 3, 645-690.

Berg, B.L., *Qualitative Research Methods for the Social Sciences,* Boston 1989.

Berman, H., *Justice in the USSR*, New York 1963.

Blua, A., "Azerbaijan: U.S. Lifts Restrictions on Aid", *RFE/RL Feature,* 29 January 2002.

Body of Principles for the Protection of All Persons under Any Form of Detention or Imprisonment (Adopted by UN General Assembly Resolution 43/173 on 9 December 1988).

"Bologna Declaration" (Joint Declaration of the European Ministers of Education Convened in Bologna on 19 June 1999).

Bonnell, V. & G. Breslauer, "Soviet and Post-Soviet Area Studies", April 1998 (working paper available from the Berkeley Programme in Soviet and Post-Soviet Studies, University of California (Berkeley)).

Bremmer, I. & R. Taras, eds., *Nations and Politics in the Soviet Successor States*, Cambridge 1993.

Burney, C. & D.M. Lang, *The Peoples of the Hills: Ancient Ararat and Caucasus*, New York 1972.

Burrage, M., "Mrs. Thatcher Against the 'Little Republics': Ideology, Precedents and Reactions" in T.C. Halliday and L. Karpik, eds., *Lawyers and the Rise of Western Political Liberalism*, Oxford 1997.

____, "Russian Advocates: Before, during, and after Perestroika", 18 *Law and Social Inquiry* 1993 No. 3, 573-592.

Bunce, V., "Should Transitologists Be Grounded?", 54 *Slavic Review* 1995 No. 1, 111-127.

Butler, W.E., *Soviet Law*, London 1988.

Cabinet of Ministers Decision No. 103 (1 May 1998) (Azerbaijan—on licence requirements for providing legal services).

Canadian Bar Association, "Striking a Balance: The Report of the International Practice of Law Committee on Multi-Disciplinary Practices and the Legal Profession" (report summary), Ottawa, 22 August 1999.

Carothers, T., "The Rule of Law Revival", 77 *Foreign Affairs* 1998 No. 2, 95-106.

Chikhladze, G., "Fear Makes Justice Wild", 4 *Georgia/Caucasus Profile* 2000, 22-23.

Cohn, N. & A. Garde, "Mutual Influences of English and French Legal Cultures Through Legal Education", 3 *European Review of Private Law* 1999, 381-387.

"Consent on Bill on Advocacy Reached", *Sarke News Agency* 24 May 2001.

"Constitutional Court of Georgia" (informational pamphlet of the Constitutional Court of Georgia, c. 1997).

Constitution of the Republic of Armenia (5 July 1995).

Constitution of the Republic of Azerbaijan (12 November 1995).

Constitution of the Republic of Georgia (24 August 1995).

Coppieters, B., D. Darchiashvili & N. Akaba, *Federal Practice: Exploring Alternatives for Georgia and Abkhazia*, Brussels 2000.

Council of Europe, P.A. Opinion No. 209 (1999) (recommendation on the accession of Georgia).

Cowe, P., "Medieval Armenian and Literary and Cultural Trends" in R.G. Hovannisian, ed., *The Armenian People From Ancient to Modern Times*, New York 1997.

Dailey, E., "Before It's Too Late: Adopting the Right Law on Azerbaijan's Legal Profession", *Eurasia Insight* 21 August 2001 (online at www.eurasianet.org).

David, R. & J. Brierley, *Major Legal Systems in the World Today*, London 1985.

Dekmejian, R.H., "The Armenian Diaspora" in R.G. Hovannisian, ed., *The Armenian People From Ancient to Modern Times*, New York 1997.

Derber, C., W.A. Schwartz & Y. Magrass, *Power in the Highest Degree,* New York 1990.

de Sousa Santos, B., "Law: A Map of Misreading. Toward a Post-Modern Conception of Law", 14 *Journal of Law and Society* 1987 No. 3, 279-302.

Devdariani, J., "Georgia's new ministers of interior, state security grapple with legacy of mistrust", *Eurasia Insight* 28 November 2001 (online at www.eurasianet.org).

Dezaylay Y. & B. Garth, "Argentina: Law at the Periphery and Law Dependencies: Political and Economic Crisis and the Instrumentalization and Fragmentation of Law", *American Bar Foundation Working Paper* No. 9708, 1998.

____, *Dealing in Virtue: International Commercial Arbitration and the Construction of a Transnational Legal Order*, Chicago, London 1996.

Dobson, R.B., "Georgia and the Georgians" in Z. Katz, ed., *Handbook of Major Soviet Nationalities*, New York 1975.

"Draft Law of Georgia on the Bar" (1996) (put forward by the State Committee for Reform of Juridical and Legal Organization of the Ministry of Justice).

"Draft Law of Georgia on Barristers' Activity" (9 June 1996) (put forward by Parliament's Legal Affairs Committee).

Dragadze, T., *Rural Families in Soviet Georgia*, London 1988.

Dudwick, N., "Political Transformations in Postcommunist Armenia: Images and Realities" in K. Dawisha & B. Parrot, eds., *Conflict, Cleavage, and Change in Central Asia and the Caucasus*, Cambridge 1997.

Durkheim, E., *Professional Ethics and Civic Morals*, trans. C. Brookfield, Westport, CT 1983.

European Convention for the Prevention of Torture and Inhuman or Degrading Treatment or Punishment, *ETS* No. 126, 26 November 1987.

European Convention for the Protection of Human Rights and Fundamental Freedoms, *ETS* No. 5, 11 November 1950.

Falcão, J., "Lawyers in Brazil" in R.L. Abel and P.S.C. Lewis, eds., *Lawyers in Society: The Civil Law World* (v. 2), Berkeley 1989.

"Fate of Russia's Akhalkalaki Base Still Unclear", *RFE/RL Caucasus Report,* Vol. 3(45), 16 November 2000.

Fitzpatrick, C.A., *et al.*, *Restrictions on the Independent Legal Profession in Azerbaijan*, International League for Human Rights, 1999 (online at www.ilhr.org).

Feldbrugge, F.J.M., "The New Constitution of Georgia", 22 *Review of Central and East European Law* 1996 No. 1, 9-17.

____, *The Constitutions of the USSR and the Union Republics: Analysis Texts and Reports*, Alphen aan den Rijn, NL 1979.

____, ed., *Encyclopedia of Soviet Law,* Dobbs Ferry, NY 1973.
____, "A History of Georgian Law", 3 *Georgica* 1998, 2-5.
____, "Law of the Republic of Georgia", 18 *Review of Central and East European Law* 1992 No. 4, 367-375.
"Female Lawyers", 16 *Soviet Law and Government* 1977 No. 2, 87-95.
Fesenko, A. & V. Shneyer, "Azerbaijan Now Licenses the Practice of Law", 9 *Russia and Commonwealth Business Law Report* 1998.
Foley, M.W. & B. Edwards, "The Paradox of Civil Society", 7 *Journal of Democracy* 1996 No. 3, 38-52.
Freedom for Russia and Emerging Eurasian Democracies and Open Markets Support Act of 1992 (Freedom Support Act). Public Law 511, 102nd cong., 2nd sess. 24 October 1992.
Friedman, L.M., "Lawyers in Cross-Cultural Perspective" in R.L. Abel & P.S.C. Lewis, eds., *Lawyers in Society: Comparative Theories* (v. 3), Berkeley 1989.
Friedrich, C.J., ed., *Totalitarianism*, Cambridge, MA 1954.
Friedrich, C.J. & Z.K. Brzezinski, *Totalitarian Dictatorship and Autocracy*, Cambridge, MA 1956.
Friedson, E., *The Profession of Medicine,* New York 1970.
____, "The Theory of Professions: State of the Art" in R. Dingwall & P. Lewis, eds., *The Sociology of the Professions*, New York 1983.
Frye, T., "The Two Faces of Russian Courts: Evidence from a Survey of Company Managers", 11 *East European Constitutional Law Review* 2002 Nos. 1-2, 125-129.
Fuller, L., "Georgia Appears to Backtrack on Abkhaz Accords", *RFE/RL Caucasus Report*, Vol. 4(5), 2 February 2001.
____, "Embattled Georgian Prosecutor-General Resigns", *RFE/RL Caucasus Report*, Vol. 4(6), 8 February 2001.
____, "South Ossetian President Strengthens His Position", *RFE/RL Caucasus Report*, Vol. 4(14), 10 April 2001.
____, "Papering over the Cracks in Georgia", *RFE/RL Caucasus Report*, Vol. 4(16), 26 April 2001.
____, "How Unified Is the New Armenian Opposition Alignment?", *RFE/RL Caucasus Report*, Vol. 4(32), 24 September 2001.
____, "Georgia's Robin Hood Stakes His Political Future", *RFE/RL Caucasus Report*, Vol. 4(33), 8 October 2001.
Fuller, L.L., "The Law's Precarious Hold on Life", 3 *Georgia Law Review* 1969 No. 1, 530-545.
____, "The Lawyer as an Architect of Social Structures" in K.I. Winston, ed., *The Principles of Social Order*, Durham, NC 1981.
____, "The Role of Contract in the Ordering Processes of Society Generally" in K.I. Winston, ed., *The Principles of Social Order*, Durham, NC 1981.

Gadzhiev, A., "Azerbaijan: Imminent Passage of Law on the Legal Profession Cause for Alarm", *Eurasia Insight* 1 February 2000 (online at www.eurasianet.org).

Galanter, M., "Justice in Many Rooms: Courts, Private Ordering, and Indigenous Law", 19 *Journal of Legal Pluralism* 1981 No. 1, 1-47.

____, "Lawyers in the Mist: The Golden Age of Legal Nostalgia", 100 *Dickinson Law Review* 1996 No. 3, 549-562.

"General Procurator's Office Is Taking Over the Case", *Svobodnaia Gruziia* 14 July 1999.

Georgia Consulting Group, "History, Clients and Practice Areas" (undated brochure).

____, "GCG Georgian Law Update" (February 1999).

____, "GCG Georgian Law Update" (March 1999).

____, "GCG Georgian Law Update" (April 1999).

Georgia Legal Reform Baseline Study, Focus Group Report, April 1998. (A study commissioned by the Georgian government and the World Bank and carried out by the Georgian Opinion Research Business International, Tbilisi.)

"Georgian Majority Parliamentary Faction Renews Criticism of Interior Minister", *RFE/RL Caucasus Report*, Vol. 3(43), 3 November 2000.

Georgian Opinion Research Business International (GORBI), "Judicial Reform in Georgia: A Study of Public Opinion" (final report prepared for the World Bank, Spring 2000).

Georgian Presidential Order No. 726 of 30 December 1998 (on judges' salaries).

Giragosian, R., "The War on Terrorism: Implications for the Caucasus", *Eurasia Insight* 29 September 2001 (online at www.eurasianet.org).

Glonti, G., "Problems Associated with Organized Crime in Georgia" (undated, Institute of Legal Reforms, online at www.geo.net.ge/reform/eng/publication).

Goldenberg, S., *Pride of Small Nations: The Caucasus and Post-Soviet Disorder,* London 1994.

Grant, N., *Soviet Education,* Middlesex 1964.

Greif, A., "Contracting, Enforcement, and Efficiency: Economics Beyond the Law" in M. Bruno and B. Pleskovic, eds., *Annual World Bank Conference on Development Economics 1996*, Washington 1996, 239.

Griffith, E., "Law and Lawyers in the USSR", 61 *New York State Bar Journal* 1989, 18-23.

Griffiths, J., "What Is Legal Pluralism?", 24 *Journal of Legal Pluralism* 1986, 1-56.

Grigolia, A., *Custom and Justice in the Caucasus: The Georgian Highlanders* (Ph.D. Dissertation, University of Pennsylvania, 1939).

Grossman, G. ,"The 'Second Economy' of the USSR", 26 *Problems of Communism* 1977 No. 5, 24-40, 35.

Grote, R., "The Rule of Law, Rechtsstaat and Etat de Droit" in C. Starck, ed., *Constitutionalism, Universalism and Democracy—A Comparative Analysis*, Baden Baden 1999.

Hagan, J. and F. Kay, *Gender in Practice: A Study of Lawyers' Lives*, New York 1995.

Haggard, S. & R.R. Kaufman, *The Political Economy of Democratic Transitions*, Princeton 1995.

Haimson, L.,"The Problem of Social Stability in Urban Russia, 1905–1917", 23 *Slavic Review* (Part I) 1964 No. 4, 619-642 and 24 *Slavic Review* (Part II) 1965 No. 4, 1-22.

Halliday, T.C., *Beyond Monopoly*, London 1987.

____, "Lawyers as Institutional Contractors: Constructing Markets, States, Civil Society, and Community", *American Bar Foundation Working Paper* No. 9519, 1995.

Halliday, T.C. & L. Karpik,"Politics Matter: A Comparative Theory of Lawyers in the Making of Political Liberalism" in Halliday and Karpik, eds., *Lawyers and the Rise of Western Political Liberalism*, Oxford 1997.

Hathaway, O.,"Do Human Rights Treaties Make a Difference?", 111 *Yale Law Journal* 2002 No. 8, 1935-2042.

Havel, V.,"The Power of the Powerless" in J. Vladislav, ed., *Václav Havel or Living in Truth*, London 1986.

Havel, V. & V. Klaus, with commentary by P. Pithart, "Rival Visions", 7 *Journal of Democracy* 1996 No. 1, 12-23.

Hazard, J.N., "Furniture Arrangement as a Symbol of Judicial Roles" in A.D. Renteln & A Dundes, *Folk Law. Essays in the Theory and Practice of Lex Non Scripta*, Madison 1994.

____, *Settling Disputes in Soviet Society: The Formative Years of Soviet Legal Institutions*, New York 1960.

Heinz, J.P. & E.O. Laumann, *Chicago Lawyers: The Social Structure of the Bar*, New York 1982.

Heinz, J.P., R.L. Nelson, E.O. Laumann and E. Michelson, "The Changing Character of Lawyers' Work: Chicago in 1975 and 1995", 32 *Law and Society Review* 1998 No. 4, 751-775.

Hendley, K.,"'Demand' for Law in Russia—A Mixed Picture", 10 *East European Constitutional Law Review* 2001 No. 4, 72-77.

____, *Trying to Make Law Matter*, Ann Arbor 1996.

____,"How Russian Enterprises Cope With Payment Problems", 15 *Post-Soviet Affairs* 1999 No. 3, 201-234.

____, "Rewriting the Rules of the Game in Russia: The Neglected Issue of the Demand for Law", 8 *East European Constitutional Review* 1999 No. 4, 89-95.

"Higher Education on Trial", 9 *East European Constitutional Review* 2000, No.3.

Hovannissian, R.G., *The Republic of Armenia* (v. 3), Berkeley 1996.

____, ed., *The Armenian People From Ancient to Modern Times*, New York 1997.

Human Rights Watch, "Georgia—Backtracking on Reform: Amendments Undermine Access to Justice", Tbilisi, October 2000.

____, "Council of Europe Cautioned on Early Admission for Armenia, Azerbaijan", 26 January 2001 (online at www.hrw.org/press/1999/jan/aze0125.htm).

Huskey, E., "The Limits to Institutional Autonomy in the Soviet Union: The Case of the *Advokatura*", 34 *Soviet Studies* 1982 No. 2, 200-227.

____, *Russian Lawyers and the Soviet State*, Princeton, NJ 1986.

____, "Specialists in the Soviet Communist Party Apparatus: Legal Professionals as Party Functionaries", 40 *Soviet Studies* 1988 No. 4, 538-555.

____, "Between Citizen and State: The Soviet Bar (Advokatura) Under Gorbachev", 28 *Columbia Journal of Transnational Law* 1990 No. 1, 95-116.

Inghels, A. "Une Répbublique Sociale à l'Oeuvre" in *L'Internationale Socialiste et la Géorgie*, Paris 1921.

"Inter-Clan War in Akhalkalaki: The Only Idea They Share Is That of Autonomy" (cited in *CIPDD Monitor*, 21 September 1998).

International Committee of the Red Cross, *ICRC in Georgia/Abkhazia: Information Sheet*, Tbilisi 1998.

International Covenant on Civil and Political Rights (ICCPR), 999 *UNTS* 171 (entered into force 23 March 1976).

"Is Russia Seeking to Impose an Economic Stranglehold on Georgia?", *RFE/RL Caucasus Report*, Vol. 3(46), 30 November 2000.

Janda, R., "Something Wicked That Way Went: Law and the Habit of Communism", 41 *McGill Law Journal* 1995 No. 1, 253-267.

Javakhashvili, I., *Kartuli Samartlis Istoria*, Tbilisi (reprinted) 1984 ("The History of Georgian Law").

Jershild, A., *Orientalism and Empire: North Caucasus Mountain Peoples and the Georgian Frontier 1845-1917*, Montreal 2002.

Johnson, K., "Explaining the Nikitin Acquittal", 9 *East European Constitutional Review* 2000 No. 4, 91.

Johnstone, Q., "Bar Associations: Policies and Performances", 15 *Yale Law & Policy Review* 1996 No. 1, 193-243.

Jonas, T., "Georgia's New Investment Law", 25 *CIS Law Notes* 1997.

Jones, S.F., *Georgian Social Democracy 1892–1921: In Opposition and Power* (unpublished Ph.D. dissertation, University of London, 1984).

____,"Russian Imperial Administration and the Georgian Nobility: The Georgian Conspiracy of 1832", 65 *Slavonic and East European Review* 1987 No. 1, 53-76.

____,"Populism in Georgia: The Gamsaxurdia Phenomenon" in D.V. Schwartz & R. Panossian, eds., *Nationalism and History: The Politics of Nation Building in Post-Soviet Armenia, Azerbaijan and Georgia*, Toronto 1994.

____, "Georgia: A Failed Democratic Transition" in I. Bremmer & R. Taras, eds., *Nations and Politics in the Soviet Successor States*, Cambridge 1993.

Jordan, P., "Russian Advocates in a Post-Soviet World: The Struggle for Professional Identity and Efforts to Redefine Legal Services" (unpublished Ph.D. dissertation, University of Toronto, 1997).

____, "The Russian *Advokatura* (Bar) and the State in the 1990s", 50 *Europe-Asia Studies* 1998 No. 5, 765-791.

Kaminskaya, D., *Final Judgment: My Life as a Soviet Defence Attorney*, New York 1982.

Kapanadze, G., "Zhvania and Saakashvili May be Arrested", *(Tbilisi) Resonance* 31 March 1999, 1 (cited in *CIPDD Monitor*, 31 March 1999).

Karst, J., *Littérature géorgienne chrétienne*, Paris 1934.

"Kartlos Garibashvili Urges to Discuss the Draft of the Bill on Legal Profession", *Caucasus Press* 10 May 2001.

"Kartlos Is Saved by Friendship", *Svobodnaia Gruziia* 2 July 1999, 1.

Kasirer, N., "Apostolat Juridique: Teaching Everyday Law in the Life of Marie Lacoste Gérin-Lajoie (1867-1945)", 30 *Osgoode Hall Law Journal* 1992 No. 2, 427-470.

Kassow, S.D., *Students, Professors, and the State in Tsarist Russia*, Berkeley 1989.

Kekelia, M. Sasamartlo, *Organizatsia da procesi sakarveloshi Rusettan sheertebis cin*, Tbilisi 1970 ("Court Organization and Process in Georgia before joining Russia").

Khachatrian, H., "Parliament Shooting Trial Poses Challenge for Armenian Political Institutions", *Eurasia Insight* 13 June 2001 (online at www.eurasianet.org).

"Constitutional Amendments in Armenia: A Necessary but Difficult Task", *Eurasia Insight* 21 August 2001 (online at www.eurasianet.org).

Khachatryan, H.M., *The First Constitution of the Republic of Armenia*, Yerevan 1998.

Khetsuriani, J., "Death Penalty in Georgian Law", 1 *Georgian Law Review* 1999, 3-9.

Kinzer, S., "The 'Man of the Year', Just 29 and Via Manhattan", *New York Times* 4 June 1998, A4.

____,"Georgia, Judging That Most Judges Shouldn't, Readies Replacements", *New York Times* 12 July 1999, A4.

Kleinhans, M.-M. & R.A. Macdonald, "What Is a *Critical* Legal Pluralism?", 12 *Canadian Journal of Law and Society* 1997 No. 2, 25-46.

Komaxidze, M., *Sabchota Advokaturis Ormotsdaati Tseli*, Tbilisi 1974 ("Fifty Years of Soviet Advocacy").

Korkelia, K., "Treaty Law and Practice in Georgia", 25 *Review of Central and East European Law* 1999 No. 3, 445-457.

Kotkin, M.J., "The Law School Clinic: A Training Ground for Public Interest Lawyers" in J. Cooper and L.G. Trubek, eds., *Educating for Justice: Social Values and Legal Education*, Aldershot 1997.

Kovacic W.E. & B. Slay, "Perilous Beginnings: The Establishment of Antimonopoly and Consumer Protection Programs in the Republic of Georgia", XLIII *Antitrust Bulletin* 1998 No. 1, 15-43.

Kritz, N.J., "The Rule of Law in the Post-Conflict Phase: Building a Stable Peace" in C.A. Crocker, O. Hampson & P. Aall, eds., *Turbulent Peace: the challenges of managing international conflict,* Washington 2001.

Kritzer, H., "The Professions are Dead, Long Live the Professions: Legal Practice in a Post-Professional World", 33 *Law & Society Review* 1999 No. 3, 713-759.

Krygier, M., "Traps for Young Players in Times of Transition", 8 *East European Constitutional Review* 1999 No. 4, 63-67.

Kucherov, S., *Courts, Lawyers and Trials Under the Three Last Tsars*, New York 1953.

____, "Legal Education" in F.J.M. Feldbrugge, G.P. van den Berg and W.B. Simons, eds., *Encyclopedia of Soviet Law*, No. 28 *Law in Eastern Europe*, (F.J.M. Feldbrugge, ed.), Dordrecht 1985.

"La Géorgie saignée par les trafics et la contrebande", *Le Monde* 9-10 April 2000, 3.

Lang, D.M., *A Modern History of Georgia*, London 1962.

____, *The Georgians*, London 1966.

____, *Last Years of the Georgian Monarchy, 1658–1832*, New York 1957.

Larson, M.S., *The Rise of Professionalism*, Berkeley 1977.

Law on Advocates and Advocate Activity, 27 January 2000 (Azerbaijan).

Law on the Constitution of Georgia, 31 January 1996.

Law of Georgia on the Bar, 20 June 2001.

Law of Georgia on the Notariat, 3 May 1996.

Law on Procedure in the Constitutional Court, 22 March 1996 (Georgia).

Law of the Republic of Armenia on Advocate Activity, 18 June 1998.

"Lawyer Comments on Council of Europe, Former Premier's Release", *(Baku) Bilik Dunyasi* 19 December 2000.

LeGendre, P., *Legislative Regulation of the Legal Profession in Azerbaijan*, International League for Human Rights, 2001 (available online at www.ilhr.org/ilhr/reports/legal/leg_reg.html).

Leuprecht, P., "Innovations in the European System of Human Rights Protection: Is Enlargement Compatible with Reinforcement?", 8 *Transnational Law & Contemporary Problems* 1998 No. 2, 313-336.

LeVine, S., "A Lesson in the Caucasus: Even War Has Rules", *New York Times* 14 February 1999, 15.

Levin-Stankevitch, B.L., "Transfer of Legal Technology and Culture: Law Professionals in Tsarist Russia" in H.D. Balzer, ed., *Russia's Missing Middle Class, The Professions in History*, Armonk, NY 1966.

"Life of a Lawyer under Threat in Court", *Human Rights in Georgia Monthly Bulletin* (Nos. 22-23/2000, 27 November 2000).

Lijphart, A., "The Comparable-Cases Strategy in Comparative Research", 8 *Comparative Political Studies* 1975 No. 2, 158-177.

Lomonosov, A.M. & R.W. Makepeace, "Legal Education in Russia—Present Challenges and Past Influences", 31 *Law Teacher* 1997 No. 3, 333-347.

Macdonald, K.M., *The Sociology of the Professions*, London 1995.

MacDonald, R., "La Répubique Géorgienne socialiste" in *L'Internationale Socialiste et la Géorgie*, Paris 1921.

Macdonald, R.A., *Lessons of Everyday Law/Le droit du quotidien,* Montreal 2002.

Maggs, P.B., "The Process of Codification in Russia: Lessons Learned from the Uniform Commercial Code", 44 *McGill Law Journal* 1999 No. 2, 281-300.

Makashvili V.& D. Purtsiladze, *Iuridicheskaia nauka v Akademii nauk Gruzinskoi SSR*, Tbilisi 1983 ("Legal Science at the Georgian SSR Academy of Sciences").

Manvelichvili, A., *Histoire de Géorgie*, Paris 1951.

Marmaros, D. & B. Sacerdote, "Peer and Social Networks in Job Search", 46 *European Economic Review* 2002 Nos. 4-5, 870-879.

Mars, G. & Y. Altman, "The Cultural Basis of Soviet Georgia's Second Economy", 35 *Soviet Studies* 1983 No. 4, 546-560.

Matossian, M.K., *The Impact of Soviet Policies in Armenia*, Leiden 1962.

McCahery, J. & S. Picciotto, "Creative Lawyering and the Dynamics of Business Regulation" in Y. Dezalay & D. Sugarman, eds., *Professional Competition and Professional Power,* London 1995.

Merry, S.E., "Legal Pluralism", 22 *Law and Society Review* 1988 No. 5, 869-896.

Merryman, J.H., *The Civil Law Tradition*, Stanford 1969.

Mikatadze, Z. Z., "I'll Seat You and Your Lawyer on a Broken Bottle", *Resonance* 28 January 1998.

Millar, J.R., "The Little Deal: Brezhnev's Contribution to Acquisitive Socialism" in T.L. Thompson & R. Sheldon, eds., *Soviet Society and Culture*, Boulder 1988.

Morgan, D., "The Customs of the Ossetes and the Light They Throw on the Evolution of Law", 20 *Journal of the Royal Asiatic Society* 1888, 364-412.

"MPs Have Different Opinions of Bill on Advocacy", *Sarke News Agency* 22 May 2001.

Nodia, G., ed., *Political System in Georgia*, Tbilisi 1998.

North, D.C., *Transaction Costs, Institutions and Economic Performance*, San Francisco 1992.

O'Dair, R., *Legal Ethics: Text and Materials*, London 2001.

Örücü, E., "Mixed and Mixing Systems" in E. Örücü *et al.*, eds., *Studies in Legal Systems: Mixed and Mixing*, The Hague 1996.

Osakwe, C., Book Review of *Russian Lawyers and the Soviet State: The Origins and Development of the Soviet Bar, 1917–1939* by E. Huskey, 19 *New York University Journal of International. Law & Politics* 1987 No. 3, 739-750.

Owen, T.C., *The Corporation Under Russian Law, 1899–1917*, New York 1991.

Papuashvili, G., "Presidential Systems in Post-Soviet Countries: The Example of Georgia", *Georgian Law Review* 1999 No. 3, 3-23.

Parrot, B., "Perspectives on Post-Communist Transition" in K. Dawisha & B. Parrot, eds., *Conflict, Cleavage, and Change in Central Asia and the Caucasus*, Cambridge 1997.

Parsons, T., "A Sociologist Looks at the Legal Profession", *Essays in Sociological Theory*, Glencoe 1954.

Partnership and Cooperation Agreement Between the European Communities and their Member States of the One Part and Armenia, of the Other Part, 22 April 1996 (entered into force on 1 July 1999).

Partnership and Cooperation Agreement Between the European Communities and Their Member States, of the One Part and Georgia, of the Other Part, 22 April 1996 (entered into force on 1 July 1999).

Pataria, A., "Personal Thesis Regarding the Draft Law on Legal Practice" (undated, distributed at a GYLA meeting on 22 September 1998).

Paterson, A., "The Legal Profession in Scotland—An Endangered Species or a Problem Case for Market Theory" in R.L. Abel & P.S.C. Lewis, eds., *Lawyers in Society: The Common Law World* (v. 1), Berkeley 1988.

Perri 6, Book Review of *Émile Durkheim: Law in a Moral Domain* by R. Cotterrell, 27 *Journal of Law and Society* 2000 No. 3, 481-485.

Peter, J., *Freedom's Ordeal: The Struggle for Human Rights and Democracy in Post-Soviet States*, Philadelphia 1998.

Picker, J.M. & S. Picker, "Educating Russia's Future Lawyers—Any Role for the United States?", 33 *Vanderbilt Journal of Transnational Law* 2000 No. 1, 17-77.

Pistor, K., D. Berkowitz & J.-F. Richard, "Economic Development, Legality and the Transplant Effect" (forthcoming, *European Economic Review*).

Podgorecki, A. & V. Olgiatti, *Totalitarian and Post-Totalitarian Law,* Aldershot 1996.

Pol, J.L.V., "Stable Instability of Displaced People in Western Georgia: A Food-security and Gender Survey after Five Years", 12 *Journal of Refugee Studies* 1999 No. 4, 349-366.

Potier, T., *Conflict in Nagorno-Karabakh, Abkhazia and South Ossetia: A Legal Appraisal,* The Hague 2000.

Powell, M.J., *From Patrician to Professional Elite,* New York 1988.

Przeworski, A., *Democracy and the Market,* Cambridge 1991.

Public Defender of Georgia, *Annual Report,* Tbilisi 1999.

Pue, W., "'Trajectories of Professionalism?': Legal Professionalism After Abel", 19 *Manitoba Law Journal* 1990 No. 3, 384-418.

____, "In Pursuit of a Better Myth: Lawyers' Histories and the Histories of Lawyers", 32 *Manitoba Law Review* 1995 No. 4, 730-767.

Purtseladze, D., ed., *Zakony Vakhtanga VI,* Tbilisi 1980 ("The Laws of Vakhatang VI").

Putnam, R.D., *Making Democracy Work: Civic Traditions in Modern Italy,* Princeton, NJ 1993.

Qaukhchisshvili, S., ed., *The Georgian Chronicle,* trans. K. Vivian, Amsterdam 1991.

Quigley, J., "The Romanist Character of Soviet Law" in F.J.M. Feldbrugge, *The Emancipation of Soviet Law,* Dordrecht 1992.

Ramasastry, A., S. Slavova & L. Vandenhoeck, "EBRD Legal Indicator Survey: Assessing Insolvency Laws after Ten Years of Transition", *Law in Transition,* Spring 2000, 34-42.

Rand, R., *Comrade Lawyer,* Boulder 1991.

Rayfield, D., *The Literature of Georgia,* Oxford 1994.

Reich, N. & W. Stoffel, "Legal Education in a Unifying Europe", 1 *European Law Faculties Newsletter* 2000, 16-20.

Reitz, J., "Progress in Building Institutions for the Rule of Law" in R.D. Grey, ed., *Democratic Theory and Post-Communist Change,* Upper Saddle River, NJ 1997.

Report of the UN Special Rapporteur on Torture, 2001 (UN Doc. E/CN.4/2001/66/Add. 1).

"Revised Draft Law on the Bar", 1 March 2000 (the "Gudauri Draft").

Rhinelander, L.H., "Russia's Imperial Policy—The Administration of the Caucasus in the First Half of the Nineteenth Century", 17 *Canadian Slavonic Papers* 1975, 218-235.

____, *Prince Michael Vorontsov,* Montreal 1990.

____, "Viceroy Vorontsov's Administration of the Caucasus" in R.G. Suny, ed., *Transcaucasia: Nationalism and Social Change,* Ann Arbor 1996.

Rogers, L., "Law Practice in Central and Eastern Europe" 6 *Journal of East European Law* 1999 No. 9, 91-95.

Rueschemeyer, D., "Comparing Legal Professions: A State-Centred Approach" in R.L. Abel & P.S.C. Lewis, eds., *Lawyers in Society: Comparative Theories* (v. 3), Berkeley 1989.

Ryan, S.M., "Out from Under Soviet Rule: With the Help of C.E.E.L.I., Former Satellites Rebuild a Legal System", 11 *Criminal Justice* 1996, 11-19.

Sabloff, P.L.W. ed., *Higher Education in the Post-Communist World. Case Studies of Eight Universities*, New York 1999.

Said, K., *Ali and Nino*, New York 2000.

Sajo, A., "The Law of Liposuction", 8 *East European Constitutional Review* 1999 No. 4, 102-104.

Scheetz, E., "Criticsm of the Administrative Organs in Georgia", *Radio Liberty* 60/77, 14 March 1977.

Schevardnadze, E., Address to the Second Summit of Heads of State and Government, Council of Europe, Strasbourg 11 October 1997 (text of speech online at www.coe.fr/cm/sessions/97summit/georgia.htm).

Schmitter, P.C. and T.L. Karl, "The Conceptual Travails of Transitologists and Consolidologists: How Far to the East Should They Attempt to Go?", 53 *Slavic Review* 1994 No. 1, 173-185.

Schultz, L., "Legal History, Georgia" in F.J.M. Feldbrugge, G.P. van den Berg & W.B. Simons, eds., *Encyclopedia of Soviet Law*, No. 28 *Law in Eastern Europe*, (F.J.M. Feldbrugge, ed.), Dordrecht 1985.

Schwartz, D.V. & R. Panossian, eds., *Nationalism and History: The Politics of Nation Building in Post-Soviet Armenia, Azerbaijan and Georgia*, Toronto 1994.

Seron, C., *The Business of Practicing Law: The Work Lives of Solo and Small-Firm Attorneys,* Philadelphia 1996.

Shelley, L., *Lawyers in Soviet Work Life*, New Brunswick, NJ 1984.

____, "Lawyers in the Soviet Union" in A. Jones, ed., *Professions and the State: Expertise and Autonomy in the Soviet Union and Eastern Europe,* Philadelphia 1991.

Siegrist, H., "Public Office or Free Profession; German Attorneys in the Nineteenth and Early Twentieth Centuries" in G. Cocks and K.H. Jarauch, eds., *German Professions 1900–1950,* Oxford 1990.

Simmis, K., *USSR, The Corrupt Society: The Secret World of Soviet Capitalism,* New York 1982.

Simons, W.B., "The Commonwealth of Independent States and Legal Reform: The Harmonisation of Private Law", *Law in Transition* Spring 2000, 14-24.

Smith, G., V. Law, A. Wilson, A. Bohr & E. Allworth, *Nation Building in the Post-Soviet Borderlands: The Politics of National Identities,* Cambridge, UK 1999.

Solomon, P.H., Jr., "The Case of the Vanishing Acquittal: Informal Norms and the Practice of Soviet Criminal Justice", 39 *Soviet Studies* 1987 No. 4, 531-555.

____, "Putin's Judicial Reform: Making Judges Accountable as well as Independent", 11 *East European Constitutional Review* 2002 Nos. 1-2, 117-124.

____, "The Role of Defence Counsel in the USSR: The Politics of Judicial Reform Under Gorbachev", 31 *Criminal Law Quarterly* 1989 No. 2, 76-93.

Solomon, P.H., Jr. & T.S. Foglesong, *Courts and Transition in Russia: The Challenge of Judicial Reform*, Boulder, CO 2000.

Spaho, E., "Dire Straights: Albanian Legal Education", 9 *East European Constitutional Review* 2000 No. 3, 90-93.

Stefes, C.H., "Debilitating Georgian Corruption", *Transitions Online* 2 October 2000 (online at www.tol.cz).

____, "The Incompatibilities of Institutionalized Corruption and Democracy in the Former Soviet Union: The Case of Georgia" (unpublished Ph.D. dissertation, University of Denver, 2002).

Stephan, P.B., III, "Institutions and Elites: Property, Contract, the State, and Rights in Information in the Global Economy", *University of Virginia Law & Economics Research Paper* No. 01-9, 2001.

Stetar, J. and A. Pohribny, "Towards a New Definition of Quality: Taras Shevchenko National University (Kyiv University), Ukraine" in P.L.W. Sabloff, ed., *Higher Education in the Post-Communist World. Case Studies of Eight Universities*, New York 1999.

Stier, K. "Proposed Law Amendments Threaten to Stall Judicial Reform Efforts in Georgia", *Eurasia Insight* 12 June 2002 (online at www.eurasianet.org).

Stover, R.V., *Making It and Breaking It: The Fate of Public Interest Commitment During Law School*, Evanston 1989.

"Students of Tbilisi State University Against the Increase of the Education Fee", *Sarke Information Agency* 1 October 1999 (online at www.sarke.com).

Suny, R.G., ed., *Transcaucasia. Nationalism and Social Change*, Ann Arbor 1983.

____, *The Making of the Georgian Nation*, Bloomington 1994.

"Supreme Court Demanded to Release Tengiz Asanidze Immediately", *Sarke Information Agency* 29 December 1999 (online at www.sarke.com).

Swietochowski, T., "National Consciousness and Political Orientations in Azerbaijan, 1905–1920" in R.G. Suny, ed., *Transcaucasia. Nationalism and Social Change*, Ann Arbor 1983.

____, *Russia and Azerbaijan: A Borderland in Transition*, New York 1995.

Tamanaha, B.Z., "The Folly of the 'Social Scientific' Concept of Legal Pluralism", 20 *Journal of Law & Society* 1993 No. 2, 192-218.

____, "A Non-Essentialist Version of Legal Pluralism", 27 *Journal of Law and Society* 2000 No. 2, 296-321.

Tarkashvili, Z., "Lawyers Will Have to Learn", *Resonance* 19 January 2000 (cited in *South Caucasian Human Rights Monitor*, January 2000).

"Tbilisi Criticizes Armenian Visit to Abkhazia", *RFE/RL Caucasus Report*, Vol. 3(45), 16 November 2000.

"Tbilisi State University" (information pamphlet prepared by the university c. 1997).

"The Bar Wants Not to Be Examined", *Caucasus Press* 10 May 2001.

Teubner, G., "The Two Faces of Janus: Rethinking Legal Pluralism", 13 *Cardozo Law Review* 1992 No. 5, 1443-1462.

____, "'Global Bukowina': Legal Pluralism in a World Society" in G. Teubner, ed., *Global Law Without a State*, Aldershot, UK 1997.

Thome, J.R., "Heading South But Looking North: Globalization and Law Reform in Latin America", 3 *Wisconsin Law Review* 2000, 691-712.

Thomson, R.W., trans., *The Lawcode (Datastanagirk) of Mxit'ar Goš*, Amsterdam 2000.

Thürer, D., "The 'Failed State' and International Law", 836 *International Review of the Red Cross* 1999, 731-761.

"The Time for Applications Expired", *Svobodnaia Gruziia* 20 August 1999, 7 Icited in *CIPDD Press Digest*, 20 August 1999).

de Tocqueville, A., *Democracy in America*, trans. G. Lawrence, New York 1969.

"Today's Session of the Parliament Has Actually Been Interrupted", *Sarke News Agency* 6 June 2001 (online at www.sarke.com).

Toumanoff, C., *Studies in Christian Caucasian History*, Washington 1963.

Tskitishvili, A., "Elite Judges Punished for Their Offences Against Citizens", *Resonance* 2 November 1998 (cited in *CIPDD Monitor*, 2 November 1998).

Tucker, A., "Introduction: Higher Education on Trial", 9 *East European Constitutional Review* 2000 No. 3, 88-89,

Unger, R.M., *Law in Modern Society*, New York 1976.

United Nations Development Programme, *Human Development Report: Georgia, 1996*, Tbilisi.

____, *Human Development Report: Georgia 1997*, Tbilisi.

____, *Human Development Report: Georgia 1998*, Tbilisi.

____, *Human Development Report: Georgia 1999*, Tbilisi.

____, *Human Development Report: Georgia 2000* (online at www.undp.org.ge).

Universal Declaration of Human Rights (Adopted and Proclaimed by UN General Assembly Resolution 217 A(III) of 10 December 1948).

van den Berg, G.P., *The Soviet System of Justice: Figures and Policy*, Dordrecht 1985.

Villa, S.H. & M.K. Matossian, *Armenian Village Life Before 1914*, Detroit 1982.

Walker, E.W., "Sovietology and Perestroika: A Post-Mortem" in S. Solomon, ed., *Beyond Sovietology: Essays in Politics and History*, Armonk, NY 1993.

Wall, T., "Bush Administration Uses Economic Levers to Encourage Anti-terrorism Co-operation", *Eurasia Insight*, 22 October 2001 (online at www.eurasianet.org).

Waters, C., "Georgian Lawyers Get in Line", *Eurasia Insight*, 23 August 2001 (online at www.eurasianet.org).

____, "Georgian *Realpolitik*", 28 *Peacekeeping and International Relations* 1999 No. 4, 2.

Welt, C., "Georgia Annual Report 1999: 'A Return to Eurasia'", *Transitions Online* (online at www.tol.cz).

Wendel, W.B., "Nonlegal Regulation of the Legal Profession: Social Norms in Professional Communities", 54 *Vanderbilt Law Review* 2001, 1955-2053.

Whitman, J.Q., *The Legacy of Roman Law in the German Romantic Era*, Princeton, NJ 1990.

Wilkins, D.B., "Who Should Regulate Lawyers?", 105 *Harvard Law Review* 1992 No. 4, 799-887.

Williamson, A., "Building a Professional Legal Corps for Georgia: The Georgian Young Lawyers' Association Raises the Bar for Legal Services" (promotional literature from the Tbilisi Office of the Eurasia Foundation, January 2001).

Wilton, C., *Beyond the Law: Lawyers and Business in Canada, 1830–1930*, Toronto 1990.

World Bank, "Georgia Judicial Assessment", *Report* No. 17356-GE, 10 April 1998.

____, "Coordinating Reforms in the Public Sector: Improving Performance and Combatting Corruption" (Briefing notes for the workshop held on 21–23 June 1998 in Tbilisi).

____, "World Bank Approves US$ 114.9 Million for Georgia", *News release* No. 99/2288/ECA, 29 June 1999.

Wright, E.O., *Class, Crisis & the State*, London 1978.

Zaslavsky, V., "Success and Collapse: The Traditional Soviet Nationality Policy" in I. Bremmer and R. Taras, eds., *Nations and Politics in the Soviet Successor States*, Cambridge UK 1993.

Zile, Z., *Ideas and Forces in Soviet Legal History*, New York 1992.

Zoidze, B., "The System of the Civil Code of Georgia", *Georgian Law Review* 1998 No. 1, 3-14.

____, "The Influence of Anglo-American Common Law on the Georgian Civil Code", *Georgian Law Review* 1999 Nos. 1-2, 10-19.

Index

G

H

I

J

K

L

About the Author

Christopher Waters is a Lecturer in Law at the University of Reading in the United Kingdom. He teaches international law, a subject which he has also taught at universities and peacekeeping training centres in Canada, Georgia, Armenia and Kosovo. Dr. Waters holds degrees from the University of Toronto, Queen's University and McGill University and is a member of the Bar of Ontario. He has worked on several human rights and rule of law initiatives in Eastern Europe and the former Soviet Union. He is also the Deputy Director of the Centre for Euro-Asian Studies at the University of Reading.

MIX
Papier aus verantwortungsvollen Quellen
Paper from responsible sources
FSC® C105338

If you have any concerns about our products,
you can contact us on
ProductSafety@springernature.com

In case Publisher is established outside the EU,
the EU authorized representative is:
Springer Nature Customer Service Center GmbH
Europaplatz 3, 69115 Heidelberg, Germany

Printed by Libri Plureos GmbH
in Hamburg, Germany